Managing a management development
institution

Management Development Series No. 18

Managing a management development institution

Edited by Milan Kubr

Roger Talpaert
Samuel Paul
Jean-Claude Mouret
Milan Kubr
Ivor Kenny
Chris Higgins

Henry Gómez
Enrico de Gennaro
Max Daetwyler
Daniel Bas
Robert Abramson

Prepared within the INTERMAN project
with the financial support of
the UNDP Interregional Programme

International Labour Office   Geneva

ISBN 92-2-102955-7

First published 1982
Third impression 1987

Printed by the International Labour Office, Geneva, Switzerland

CONTENTS

PART II

APPENDICES

INTRODUCTION

This book is about key issues in managing management development institutions. The authors, all of whom have years of experience in institutional management, decided to write it because many institutions tend to overlook the fact that what the institution is capable of achieving depends critically on how it is managed.

To begin with, the quality of the institution's management has a direct influence on its technical credibility and image. A management school or centre does not operate as a black box, of which the external world would merely see the products without knowing anything about its internal processes. On the contrary, whatever the mandate and work methods of a particular institution are, the external world has innumerable opportunities to observe how it thinks, lives and works. The pitfalls and somersaults of institutional management are hidden neither to course participants nor to existing or potential client organisations. Unfortunately, in quite a few cases, these cannot but conclude that the old popular saying "the cobbler's sons go ill-shod" (which has its equivalent in all cultures) applies only too well to the world of management education and training.

Several factors over which management institutions have little control have affected their management adversely. Some of them have suffered from the laisser-faire approach predominant at the univeristy, in the social sciences in particular. Others have not escaped the influence of the out-dated rules and practices of the bureaucracies that are their parent bodies. In general, however, the managerial rationality that engendered the industrial revolution and has become essential to the production of tangible goods, has been largely missing in service sectors whose products are intangible.[1] This includes education and training establishments, consulting, accounting and engineering firms, lawyers, architects, maintenance operations and many other services in both the private and the public sector. But management development institutions are in a more delicate position than others aforenamed, since management development and improvement is their very product and raison d'être.

This by itself would justify a special effort to improve the management of management institutions. They have to be seen to practise what they preach. However, some much deeper reasons make this effort even more necessary.

If asked about their role and mission, most management development institutions in both industrialised and developing countries invariably reply that they view themselves as agents of change. Their aspirations reach far beyond showing that the number of their participants and their annual budgets keep growing. They want to play an active role in increasing the professional competence of the management population and in assisting business and governments alike to manage their affairs more effectively. Some institutions even quote broad development goals such as helping to create new employment opportunities, increase the responsibility of business towards society, develop underprivileged rural areas or reduce their country's material and technical dependence on foreign capital and expertise.

This poses a number of questions for institutional management. More specific objectives have to be derived from global institutional purposes and goals. Certain fundamental choices have to be made concerning the management concepts to be promoted, the sectors and clients to be served, the selection of methods of action, the links to be forged with business and governments, the priorities in assigning resources, the make-up of the teaching staff, the professional competence to be built up, the organisational structure to adopt and so on. Coherence and synergy have to be sought in order to maximise results with limited resources.

Such strategic decisions are not easy to make and translate into specific programmes and actions. There are no universal models that guarantee success in all circumstances. A programme that is highly successful in a European country may be a complete failure in Western

---

[1] Cf. T. Levitt: "Marketing intangible products and product intangibles", in Harvard Business Review, May-June 1981, pp. 94-102.

Africa. Objectives easy to achieve in one environment
may appear unattainable in another. It is the primary
task of the institution itself, and of those who sponsor
it and want to see it prosper, to find imaginative
approaches suitable to particular environments.

This being said, one must be careful not to fall
into the other extreme: overemphasising the uniqueness of
every situation instead of trying to see what has or has
not worked in other cases and what factors may have contributed to success or failure. Indeed, re-inventing the
wheel is the last thing management institutions can
afford to do, irrespective of their sophistication and
location. Strategic management is not a privileged dom-
ain of the most advanced institutions nor is a set of
rigid rules: it is a concept, a state of mind, which can
be applied in any environment and at any stage of development if the institution is prepared to tackle fundamental questions concerning its purpose, objectives, orientation, resources, competence, performance and effectiveness. If there is determination to address these crucial
issues, a convenient opportunity and way can always be
found even in young and less-experienced institutions.

Aware of this, many management institutions have
shown keen interest in learning from others and sharing
experience. The ILO Management Development Programme,
the European Foundation for Management Development, the
International Association of Schools and Institutes of
Administration, the Asian Productivity Organisation, the
American Assembly of Collegiate Schools of Business and
other bodies have already served as platforms for exchanging experience of institutional management through directors' meetings, workshops, comparative studies, study
tours, exchange of data and materials among institutions
and the like. This publication is an attempt to make
further progress in this endeavour.

Clientèle

The book is intended for institutions which define
themselves as being in the "management education and development business". There are many labourers in the vine-
yard: management schools, faculties and departments,
graduate schools of business administration, management
development centres and institutes, training centres of
management associations, in-company management centres
and training departments, administrative staff colleges,
schools and institutes of public administration, productivity centres, small enterprise development centres and so
on.

The primary focus is on institutions providing
training, consulting, advisory and research services to

managers and helping to improve management in practice, in both the public and private sectors. Simultaneously, considerable attention is paid to management problems of schools providing undergraduate and graduate studies of management and business administration within or outside university.

Schools and institutes of public administration have many common features and points of interest with management institutions. Management training of public administrators is one of their main functions. In addition, quite a few of them are currently undergoing very significant changes as traditional approaches to teaching and training administrators give way to newer concepts and approaches known under such names as development management, development administration, public management, public programme management and the like. Undoubtedly, public administration institutions will be able to use many ideas and experiences described in this book.

Additionally, our publication may interest parent bodies and other stakeholders who are directly linked with management institutions by providing resources, orienting programmes and assessing performance. Some of them may even be in the process of planning and designing a new institution: it is at this stage that the experience of other institutions might be particularly valuable and, in a sense, more easily applicable.

Acknowledgements

This guide grew from an international project entitled "Co-operation among management development institutions", implemented with the support of the United Nations Development Programme. In surveys and individual discussions on fields in which institutions would like to share experience the management of the institution itself was over and again assigned highest priority. Many institutions agreed to supply information, including internal materials showing practices applied and qualitative assessments of performance and results. Four institutions provided detailed descriptions of their strategic choices and management experience, which are reproduced in Part II.

The European Foundation for Management Development was particularly helpful in making its studies of the subject available. Its refreshing report "L'arroseur arrosé", published in 1978, has to be mentioned by name. Every professional interested in the concepts, value systems and strategies of management institutions will enjoy reading it.

It is impossible to list all the institutions in the industrialised and developing regions, ILO experts in the field and at Headquarters and many other persons whose support and expertise made it possible to complete this project and to whom the ILO Management Development Branch extends its sincere thanks.

The international team of authors included:

Roger Talpaert, Secretary General of the European Institute for Advanced Studies in Management in Brussels, formerly Secretary General of the Belgian Fondation Industrie-Université and Managing Director of the Office Belge pour l'Accroissement de la Productivité;

Samuel Paul, former Director of the Indian Institute of Management in Ahmedabad (IIMA) and ILO Chief Technical Advisor attached to the Centre for Management Development in Lagos;

Jean-Claude Mouret, until recently Director General of the Centre d'Enseignement Supérieur des Affaires (CESA) in Jouy-en-Josas;

Milan Kubr, Head of Research and Programme Development in the ILO Management Development Branch, formerly Chairman of the Department of Industrial Economics and Management at the Prague School of Economics and Honorary Secretary of the Czechoslovak Committee of Scientific Management;

Ivor Kenny, Director General of the Irish Management Institute (IMI) in Dublin;

Chris Higgins, Director of the University of Bradford Management Centre;

Henry Gómez, Director of Research at the Instituto de Estudios Superiores de Administración (IESA) in Caracas;

Enrico de Gennaro, former Director of the Instituto Post-Universitario per lo Studio dell'Organizzazione Aziendale (IPSOA) in Turin and ILO Chief Technical Advisor in Argentina and Nigeria;

Max Daetwyler, Deputy Director of the Centre d'Etudes Industrielles (CEI) in Geneva;

Daniel Bas, former Director of the Institut Supérieur des Sciences Economiques et Commerciales (ISSEC) in Cergy-Pontoise, Director of International Co-operation at the Ecole Supérieure de Commerce in Lyons and ILO Chief Technical Advisor attached to the Centro de Informação,

Formação e Aperfeiçoamento em Gestão (CIFAG) in Lisbon; and

Robert Abramson, Professor at the Graduate School of Public and International Affairs of the University of Pittsburgh and former ILO Chief Technical Advisor in Zambia and Tanzania.

Milan Kubr co-ordinated the project and edited this publication.

PART I

THE INSTITUTION'S PROFILE: BASIC STRATEGIC CHOICES

1

A management development institution keen to improve
its own management and performance needs a solid foundation, a clear criterion, to which it can refer in examining issues such as the relevance of its staff structure
and work methods, or the appropriateness of its internal
organisation and operational planning and control systems.
For, as Peter Drucker put it, it is more important for
any organisation to do the right things than to do things
right.

Therefore, our rather comprehensive review of issues
involved in managing a management development institution
and of opportunities for upgrading the quality of institutional management has to start by looking at the fundamental choices faced by professional management development institutions in both industrialised and developing
countries. Sections 1.1 and 1.2 will deal with these
institutions' nature and purpose, as well as with questions such as what effectiveness and social utility mean
when applied to an institution in this particular field.
Section 1.3 will review a range of basic alternatives
concerning the nature and destination of the institution's
services. Choices concerning resources have to be consistent with choices concerning services: this will be
the thrust of section 1.4. Finally section 1.5 will look
at the management institution from a different angle:
that of the external environment, which in any case will
have its own image of what the institution is and what it
may be able to achieve.

1.1 Effectiveness and strategy

Raison d'être

The very existence of a management development institution relies on certain basic assumptions. They constitute its raison d'être. At the risk of stating the

9

self-evident, we feel that these assumptions should be briefly recalled before discussing institutional purpose and strategy.

The first assumption concerns the professional nature of management. Following the establishment of graduate business schools at the Dartmouth College in 1900 and at Harvard University in 1908, L.D. Brandeis described business as a profession as far back as 1912. Although there are many definitions of a profession, there seems to be growing consensus on some essential common characteristics: (1) high degree of generalised and systematically organised knowledge, (2) competent application of this knowledge to a class of practical problems of considerable complexity, (3) orientation primarily to community rather than to individual interest, (4) high degree of self-control through internalised codes and voluntary organisations, and (5) community sanctions and system of rewards viewed as symbols of work achievement.[1]

Management in private business and public organisations as well as management theory may still lack some of the attributes of a profession, but what is essential is that they are systematically evolving towards professionalism. An important feature of this evolution is the advancement of professional management education, training and consulting. It is, of course, absolutely true that even the best management education cannot replace experience and that competent managers will never be produced in schools. But this applies to all professions. Neither surgeons nor international lawyers expect to reach high levels of excellence without years of meaningful and diversified experience. However, good education and training acquaints the future professional with generalised collective experience, spares him innumerable errors and equips him with methodology for learning from experience, solving new sorts of problems and contributing to the advancement of the profession. Also it helps to protect society from dilettanti, who can hardly do more harm to the community in any other field than in the management of business and government affairs.

According to the second assumption, professional management education and development should be viewed as a

---

[1] Cf. K.R. Andrews: "Towards professionalism in business management", in Harvard Business Review, Mar.-Apr. 1969: and G. Kanawaty: "Turning the management occupation into a profession", in International Labour Review, May-June 1977.

life-long process.[1] This is so for several reasons. The practice of management is developing very rapidly and management theory is striving to keep pace with this evolution. Both practical experience and theoretical thought pass across geographical, cultural and political borders with ever greater ease. Practising managers need to be updated from time to time even if they remain in the same post; organisations keen to improve their performance need to benefit from useful management experience of others. However, practising managers do move within and between organisations. Hence the need to help them in their movement upwards by broadening their knowledge and horizons, or by further specialised training if they are to face new situations and deal with new problems while continuing the work in the same speciality or functional area.

The third assumption is the crucial one. According to it, management development schools and centres constitute an appropriate institutional base for teaching management and helping to improve it in practice. They are viewed as bodies able to generalise experience, develop new theory, transmit generalised experience to both would-be and practising managers and help increase the learning and problem-solving capacity of organisations. The worldwide acceptance of this third assumption and, indeed, of the two previous ones, has been demonstrated by the unprecedented growth of management development institutions over the last 20 years in both industrialised and developing countries, irrespective of ideologies and political régimes.

This third assumption implies that management institutions have a major social function to fulfil. But it by no means implies that management institutions are the only instrument for developing managers and promoting professional management. In enterprises and other organisations, management development tends to be viewed as a process in which formal training and retraining play an important role, but which also includes many other essential ingredients such as managerial career planning, challenging practical assignments in which a manager can acquire and practice new skills, on-the-job coaching, job rotation, self-development, appropriate use of external or internal consultants, improvements in communication within the organisation and so on. A management development institution can co-operate with client organisations in several of these areas in addition to providing formal

---

[1] Cf. Management Education in the Second Development Decade (Geneva, ILO Management Development Branch, mimeographed, 1972) and G. Wills: Continuing studies for managers (Bradford, MCB Publications, 1981).

education and training. However, it can never assume all
the management development responsibilities of an organisation and, in particular, of the individual manager
himself. Perhaps too much has been written about the
"need to develop managers" and not enough about the "managers' need to develop themselves".

Effectiveness and efficiency

To be effective and to be seen to be effective by
their environment is a fundamental aspiration of professional institutions. But what is an effective institution? Can we define common objective criteria that would
help any institution to assess its effectiveness despite
the great variety of environmental situations and requirements, programmes, curricula, intervention methods, and
so on?

The five above-mentioned characteristics of a profession may help us to arrive at a broad understanding of
how to apply the effectiveness criterion to management
development institutions. In principle, an institution
that wants to be effective is guided by these characteristics and applies them in its work. It aims at developing good theory from generalised experience, puts high
emphasis on applying in practice what is taught in the
classroom, seeks the definition of its purpose and
achievement in the external world, i.e. in the community
it serves, exercises self-discipline in its own behaviour
and endeavours to promote management as a profession
whose constructive contribution to the development of
society is duly recognised.

The third of these five characteristics is perhaps
the crucial one. Institutional effectiveness is above
all relevance to society and service to national development. This tallies with the concept of effectiveness as
applied to other non-profit organisations, programmes,
projects, etc., which are normally considered to be
effective if they are achieving the basic purpose for
which they were established,[1] measured in terms of the
social progress they have helped to bring about.

Thus, if this concept is adopted, the numbers of
participants or consulting assignments and the volume of
training carried out may be good indicators of the institution's growing reputation and demand for its services,
but do not permit conclusions to be drawn concerning its
actual effectiveness. This being said, we have to point

---

[1] Cf. R.N. Anthony and R.E. Herzlinger: Management
control in non-profit organisations (Homewood, Illinois,
Irwin, 1980), p. 5.

12

out that in practice we are still far from being able to measure institutional effectiveness by the means of meaningful and reliable quantitative indicators. As a rule, a qualitative assessment has to be made, supported wherever possible by relevant quantitative data. The objective value of such qualitative assessments can be enhanced by evaluating the impact of the institution from several angles and by obtaining feedback from those who most accurately represent the institution's target population.

Efficiency is normally defined as the ability to maximise outputs while minimising inputs. To achieve the same effects (improved management practices, increased performance of client enterprises and government agencies, etc.) institution A may need to expend a much smaller volume of staff time and finance than institution B; it will therefore be more efficient than institution B, which may also be achieving its purpose but at a far greater price! At the other extreme, an institution may attach a great deal of importance to efficiency without really understanding what effectiveness means. It may be simply in the business of selling courses and its staff may be able to carry a high teaching load. Its financial results may be more than satisfactory. Yet sooner or later the relevance of its programmes to community needs and priorities is bound to be challenged and the period of its financial prosperity will be over.

In truly professional institutions, there may be some conflict between effectiveness and efficiency, but it tends to be confined to single cases and to periods of transition. As effectiveness and efficiency are interlaced and influence each other, in the long run a management institution has to aim at being both effective and efficient.

Three archetypes

To ease the transition from broad concepts of social utility and effectiveness to more specific questions of institutional strategy and management, it may help to visualise some basic archetypes or models. They are obviously gross oversimplifications and seldom exist in a pure state. Nevertheless, they fairly truly reflect typical institutional behaviour observed in a great number of cases.

The first archetype includes institutions that are predominantly production-oriented. Their endeavour is directed to delivering good-quality products (courses, graduates, research reports), which are somehow regarded as given, because they have been fixed as goals by higher authority, or stem from tradition or reflect the institution's conviction that it is doing the right things. The ultimate social utility of these products is taken for granted; the focus is on improving the product on the basis of the institution's own intellectual effort, values and experience. Somehow the institution follows its own internal logic. Convinced that it must know the clients' needs better than they do, it prefers to offer fully developed products than to interact with clients in the process of product development. Parenthetically, such behaviour is not dissimilar to that of some traditional manufacturers of industrial equipment who obstinately keep offering the same good-quality but rather obsolete product irrespective of dropping demand.

The second archetype is market-oriented. "Market" should be taken here in the broad sense of target group and users, not in the strictly commercial sense of a group of potential buyers. The institution actively seeks to know what its markets - individuals or organisations - want or think they need, and then sets out to design and supply a product responding to this need. In a somewhat broader interpretation, one can also call this a "stakeholder approach". The institution tries to give the best possible returns to all groups having a stake in its activities as measured against their own expectations. Here again ultimate social utility is not the issue. The institution cares about usefulness as perceived by the stakeholders only. For example, it will easily get involved in various passing fads to please its clients.

The third archetype is society-oriented. Institutions in this group try to understand and define the ultimate purpose they can serve in society and undertake to achieve this purpose as best they can. This ultimate purpose is related to economic development and social betterment: the institution has a developed sense of civic co-responsibility for achieving global national goals and defines its objectives, markets and services in this spirit. In doing this, it does not hesitate to raise issues of which its constituents and other stakeholders may be unaware and to swim against the stream if this serves a significant social purpose.

We call such an institution a "pro-active" one. It behaves simultaneously as a strategist and as an entrepreneur, although its motivation is not profit or power, but social utility. It is a sort of "social entrepreneur" and the risk involved is not primarily financial - it can be - but concerns professional reputation, career, a sense of self-achievement and even a good conscience.

The reader himself has certainly established the relation between the three archetypes and the concept of effectiveness as discussed above. Indeed, these archetypes can be viewed as three steps to institutional

14

effectiveness. Many institutions have passed through these three stages in their search for higher relevance and social utility.

The difficulty of being a pro-active institution is not negligible. Understandably so. It is easier to visualise conscious collective action in response to existing situations, needs and problems than to a non-existing desired state of affairs, in which the expectations and goals of the institution and of various groups in its environment may be disparate, if not contradictory. Achievements are also so much harder to demonstrate and evaluate. What is more, institutions tend to drift from being pro-active to reactive and from reactive to passive. Many have their origin in some kind of grand design and are to some extent entrepreneurial at the start. Few remain so for very long. When the initial motivations have weakened, they tend towards some kind of steady state, responding more or less effectively to perceived demands. They bureaucratise to such an extent that their social function is not much more than an excuse to keep up a convenient protection from the outside world. As Crozier has shown, it may take a crisis to reverse this trend, to question the very existence of the institution or at least the utility of its product, when the pressure of new ideas, or new representations of what should be achieved, somehow becomes too strong.

Strategy

Strategic management of an institution is the process of defining, redefining and implementing its basic choices concerning purpose, goals and objectives, target sectors and populations, means of action, resource allocation and organisation, and patterns of institutional behaviour in interacting with the environment. Strategy can be defined as the institution's response to environmental opportunities, challenges and threats, consistent with its competence and resources.[1]

Elements of strategic management can be observed in any institution. But only an institution that chooses to be pro-active can fully appreciate the vital importance of strategy. It realises soon that without a genuine strategic approach it will inevitably drown its enthusiasm and resources in improvisations and campaigns producing no more than passing effects. For it is possible to be active but ineffective, committed but unproductive.

Some management institutions may doubt the necessity of a strategic approach for various reasons, such as

---

[1] Cf. K.R. Andrews: The concept of corporate strategy (Homewood, Illinois, Irwin, 1980).

the absence of a competitive environment, their monopolistic position, a precisely predetermined clientèle or full centralisation of important decisions in the parent body. However, even if the total spectrum of strategic choices is somehow restricted for any reason, there is no country and no economic system where a pro-active management institution could hope to follow one straightforward, fully predetermined and preplanned path without facing any alternative options in pursuing its purpose and aim. Also, the issue of strategic choice should be seen from a wider perspective than that of a single institution: a particular decision involving choice may not be within the institution's competence, but it has to be made somewhere.

All in all, "nonprofit institutions need strategy far more than profit-making organisations. Their goals are more complex, their sources of support are more complex, and the interaction between their support and performance is more complex. Consequently, the problem of identifying optimal policies and potential strategies must be inherently more complex. In fact, most institutions would find their planning and policy formulation much easier if they were profit-making organisations. Then at least they would have a common denominator for their objectives and strategies."[1]

1.2 Defining purpose

The definition of the institution's purpose[2] is the most fundamental choice, one which provides the orientation and framework for all other basic choices. Therefore it enjoys a prominent place in strategic management.

Below the surface: ultimate purpose

As already mentioned, the concept of an effective institution assumes that purpose is defined in relationship to the environment, in terms of socially desirable changes to be ultimately achieved. The mere description of activities, target groups or operational objectives to be found, for example, in brochures and performance reports is not sufficient to appreciate what a given institution finally achieves, what its contribution to society

---

[1] Strategy for institutions (Boston, Boston Consulting Group, 1970).

[2] Several alternative terms are used to indicate the institution's purpose: ultimate purpose, aim, broad aim, goal, ultimate goal, mission, ultimate objective, development objective or general objective.

16

ultimately is. Apparently identical activities may in
fact serve different and diversified purposes, or at
least have different consequences. If an existing institution is reviewed, it is necessary to seek this real
ultimate purpose behind whatever statements of purpose
are officially used; if a new one is planned, a clear
conception and definition of the ultimate purpose pursued
is one of the main things to be discussed and agreed upon
by the various stakeholders.

The matter is not simple at all if taken seriously,
i.e. if the definition of purpose is not meant to be used
merely as a publicity statement for attracting clients
and funds. What is sought is neither an intermediate or
penultimate purpose, nor a superultimate one. This may
look self-evident, but in practice it is not.

For example, many institutions are happy to state
that their purpose is to provide training, consulting and
other services for increasing managerial competence.
Training, research, etc., is clearly only an intermediate
product, the numbers of persons trained or the research
reports produced cannot indicate whether any ultimate purpose is being achieved. However, even increased managerial competence may be another intermediate, higher-level,
product, or penultimate purpose. For increased competence
has to be reflected in more substantive changes, such as
improved organisational performance, or in broader sectoral objectives, such as increased production of goods
satisfying basic needs, or the creation of new employment
opportunities.

We could thus continue our search for higher-level
and socially more meaningful purposes. But where to stop?
Some institutions have been unable to avoid another extreme: their statements of purpose are too remote from
what an institution can actually embrace and tackle. For
example "to increase the standards of living" or "to
accelerate economic development" are universal development goals but not appropriate purpose definitions for a
management development institution. If they are adopted,
this creates a vacuum between the very global definition
of purpose and work objectives and programmes, which cannot be in any way related to such vague statements.

The prevailing tendency is therefore to use definitions that relate the institution's roles to requisite
environmental change, but are kept realistic enough to
provide a practical basis and starting point for strategic
planning, programming and evaluation. Qualitative terms
are used in practice rather than quantitative ones and
precise time limits are seldom fixed, or the definition
refers to a relatively distant time horizon. However, it
appears that there is considerable scope for increasing

the use of quantitative indicators even for defining the basic purpose and some institutions are making serious efforts in this direction.

In many situations, institutions may be reluctant to refer to more than increased competence of managers in defining their purpose. To change managerial behaviour, enhance organisational performance and achieve selected sectoral goals (increased production of food, better distribution of consumer goods or drinking water to rural areas) may be a formidable task to which an institution can contribute through management training combined with practical interventions, but which cannot be achieved by any institution alone. For example, a distorted wage or price system may annihilate all training efforts. The institution may be able to suggest a different policy but somebody else will have to support and apply it.

This underlines a salient feature of management institutions' social role and inputs in development: in certain respects an institution can play its role effectively on the condition that other partners in the development process also play their respective roles effectively. In particular, should there be conflict between the definition of purpose used by the institution and explicit or hidden purposes pursued by its constituents and clients and other important groups in the environment, the institution's purpose may have to be redefined if no other solution can be found.

The institution's philosophy or doctrine

The terms used in definitions of institutional purposes are broad and general. Terms such as "management improvement", "higher standards of management", "economic and social performance", or "socially desirable change" lend themselves to different interpretations even if an effort is made to assort them with some more detailed indications about when and how this is to be achieved. If the existence of a particular problem is acknowledged by all concerned, this does not mean that there is any consensus on the best way of solving it. Institutions are often established because there is a general belief that management education, training and consulting will have a positive impact on practice, but when the institution starts making specific action proposals or turning out its first products sponsors frequently discover that they had something else in mind or just gave too little thought to the issue.

There is nothing surprising about that. After all, management practice is a combination of science and art, a matter of both rationality and individual and group interests, an area where decisions can be based on exact calculations as well as on feelings and emotions. Compromise is the only way out of many crisis situations for business and government practice.

Once more, it is necessary to go under the surface to find out about the values, beliefs and different approaches concerning the existing practice of management, the interests motivating managerial decisions, the changes that can and must be made, the methods used to generate and implement change and the contribution that is really expected from a management institution by various groups in the environment.

Two examples chosen at random should suffice to illustrate what we have in mind.

In many countries, participative management, including workers' participation in decision-making in undertakings, is one of the topical issues in which government, employers, trade unions and individual persons are very interested, but their views on it may differ. A management institution will have to teach about participation and it may be asked to deal with its various aspects in the course of in-plant interventions. In theory, the institution can be neutral and eclectic and explain the advantages and shortcomings of various concepts of participative management. In practice, it is impossible to avoid value judgements and if an institution is to contribute towards practical improvements, it has got to support one of the possible approaches - in the belief that it is the right one in the given situation.

The second example concerns the institution's attitude to various burning, but, for some reason, delicate and hidden issues of management. These could be problems touching on the interests and competence of individuals or groups in power, issues in which people in organisations have a strong emotional involvement, practices governed by deeply rooted traditions viewed as unchangeable, and so on. Some institutions have resorted to an escape solution: they teach about models, systems and scenarios, although everybody knows that in the daily life of organisations managers and supervisors struggle with such concrete problems as absenteeism, power cuts, and the lack of reliable production records.

Thus, when referring to improving management in the definition of its ultimate purpose, and when reflecting this definition in the design of curricula, selection of participants, advice to clients, choice of research topics or the selection of information to be disseminated, the pro-active institution is bound to clarify its own values and beliefs. They may concern management in society in general, the benefits to be drawn from better management and their distribution, the potential of current management to attain higher performance standards, the level of standards to be attained, the changes that are necessary, the social groups from which managers should be recruited, the personal attributes of potentially good managers, the chances and priorities of social development, and many similar questions.

It is fully legitimate to call this sum of values and beliefs institutional philosophy, or doctrine.[1] Answers to questions which are in the realm of this institutional philosophy or doctrine are not provided by general management theory. The institution has to find its own answers based on its own role perception, experience, and contacts with the environment. Only then will it be conceptually prepared to engage in the wide range of strategic choices discussed in the following sections.

1.3 Strategic choices: services

The definition of ultimate purpose discussed above constitutes the fundamental choice in institutional strategy. Further strategic choices to be made concern the nature and destination of the institution's services, as well as the provenance and the structure of its main resources. They are, of course, closely interlaced with the definition of purpose by making it more specific (e.g. suggesting in what sector this purpose should be achieved) and indicating basic conditions for its achievement (e.g. profile of faculty or sources of finance consistent with the purpose). The totality of strategic choices determines the institution's over-all profile and position on the national or international management development scene.

A salient feature of strategic choices is that they are made for a relatively long time, either because they react to a long-term need and opportunity or because it is just impossible to change them frequently without considerable loss. They may not be irrevocable, but they cannot be revoked rapidly and at short notice (as operational decisions can be). Hence the importance of solid strategic analysis preceding such choices. However, it has to be acknowledged that many strategic choices are made in partial ignorance and it would be unrealistic to require that they must not be changed, even if the conditions change. For example, financial resources on which the institution counted may be unavailable in the event, another institution may launch the same programme and do

---

[1] For doctrine in institution-building, see J.W. Eaton (ed.): Institution building and development: From concepts to application (Beverly Hills, Sage Publications, 1972).

it better, etc. In such cases even a substantial strategic choice may have to be reconsidered.

Speaking about choices implies that there are at least two alternatives. These may be mutually exclusive, but frequently they are not. Many institutions make the mistake of selecting A or B when the optimum choice is A and B. For example in many cases, instead of working only for the private or the public sector, more and more institutions in developing countries prefer to serve both and transfer experience between them. Other instances of dichotomy which proved to be very harmful to management institutions will be discussed below.

On the other hand, A and B must not be incoherent and disperse resources instead of concentrating them on priorities and augmenting synergy. There is no synergy if course participants come from certain organisations but all consulting assignments are done in other organisations. There is synergy if a research project requested and financed by a group of business firms also produces material that can be converted into teaching stuff for use in management courses.

Finally, strategic choices may be made independently by an institution that is free to determine its own product, market, educational objectives and so on. However, in many situations, certain strategic choices are likely to be made for a network of institutions belonging to a more or less structured national or sectoral system. This may reduce uncertainty and enhance policy orientation and co-ordination, as will be discussed in chapter 3. On the other hand, certain alternatives may be unavailable or the institution may be asked to accept an alternative that would not normally be its first choice.

This section will provide a brief review of the principal choices concerning the institution's clientèle and services. Section 1.4 will look at choices concerning resources.

Roles in lifelong management development

Section 1.1 has referred to management development as a lifelong process. In designing an institution, one of the first choices concerns its particular role in this process. Historically, two basic alternative roles have evolved in most countries:

(1) educating would-be managers; or

(2) updating and upgrading practising managers.

In an ideal generalised model of lifelong professional education, these roles and their complementarity would be more or less precisely defined and it should not be difficult for an institution to determine, in agreement with other professional institutions if possible, at what point its contribution should be situated. In management development, a number of different models exist. This is very much influenced by the over-all philosophy of educational systems in various countries, but, in addition, individual management institutions tend to perceive their roles quite differently. Describing a wide range of national models in detail is beyond the scope of this publication. We will rather confine ourselves to commenting on the choices typical of a variety of concrete situations.

The first typical choice is full concentration on educating would-be managers. Institutions within this role are located at university in many cases; management education may be organised as a separate faculty or as a special department within a faculty of economics, social sciences, engineering and so on. Management schools have been established outside the traditional univeristy in several countries. University-based management education may be organised as first-degree, undergraduate education, as graduate studies of administration or management, or as a combination of both. Doctoral studies constitute a special case since their primary focus is on educating teachers, researchers and consultants rather than management practitioners.

The second typical choice is full concentration on updating and upgrading practising managers. It has been adopted by a wide range of management institutes and centres in all countries. Effective service to the practitioner and immediate applicability is the main objective. Such service is provided at various points of the management career (middle-management programmes, top management and executive programmes) and in various functional and technical areas in addition to general management.

In many cases, choosing one of these two basic alternatives has led to a profound dichotomisation of theory and practice, of education and training.

To certain university-level establishments, academic standards are the only criterion of interest; practical application, mentioned as a second characteristic of a profession in section 1.1 above, not only does not seem to worry them, but is even considered as something that could jeopardise academic standards if emphasised in curricula. This is reflected in their lack of interest in engaging in post-experience management training or in consulting. On the other hand, some of the practically oriented training centres emphasise, with considerable pride, that they are not interested in any theory and have nothing in common with the management academics.

This dichotomy has seriously hampered the advancement of professional management development in many cases. However, there seems to be a growing understanding of the already-mentioned fact that it is not A or B, but A coupled with B, that is bound to be the effective approach in professional management development. A number of management schools have expanded their offerings of programmes for practitioners and strengthened their links with industry through tailor-made in-plant programmes and consulting. Quite a few centres that started with short training programmes in general and functional management have gradually prepared themselves for introducing MBA or similar programmes of management studies.[1] This does not mean that specialisation would have to disappear and that to be effective every management institution would need to develop a complete range of programmes from first pre-employment education to top management and very special refresher programmes. It is the double dichotomy between education and training and between theory and practice that needs to be overcome.

Target groups

Under this title, several choices will be mentioned whereby the institution defines its client base (including organisations and individuals) and, consequently, its specialisation consistent with the profile of this base. The following will be discussed:

(1) sectoral focus;

(2) service to the open market or reserved programmes;

(3) levels of management;

(4) service to generalists or specialists;

(5) service to special categories of clients;

(6) geographic focus.

---

[1] Several concrete examples are in the case studies in chapters 7-10. For a detailed description of experience of the Cranfield School of Management, see G. Wills: Continuing studies for managers (Bradford, MCB Publications, 1981). Examples from public administration institutes are in Inayatullah (ed.): Management training for development: The Asian experience (Kuala Lumpur, Asian Centre for Development Administration, 1975).

(1) Choosing whether to be an intersectoral centre or
institute or to specialise in a particular sector is a
very critical decision, one which predetermines many
other choices. Such decisions may have been made beforehand by a sectoral body (ministry, sectoral organisation
of employers) if it chooses to establish and support its
own institution. In most cases, however, institutions
have some possibility of choice and they may have to revise this choice at various points of their existence.

In principle, a distinct sectoral focus is desirable
if a better impact can be obtained by sectorally specialised staff and interventions. For example sectoral management programmes tend to be preferred in the construction sector due to the relationship between management
and technology, particular atmospheric and climatic factors and also certain traditional practices used throughout the construction and building trades. Sectoral institutions for small enterprises are often established because many problems of small businesses and feasible solutions differ from what is found in large organisations;
the package of assistance offered and the intervention
methods used are also different.

In developing countries, a pronounced sectoral focus,
with all its consequences, may be desirable if considerable impact is to be made in a sector that should receive
priority treatment in development. For example, despite
repeated emphasis on rural development and on the management of major social development programmes, most developing countries lack an adequate institutional base for
improving management in these sectors. This reflects the
fact that in most cases their management schools and
centres focus almost entirely on the modern segments of
the economy and are unprepared for dealing with the very
different problems inherent in rural and social development.

In mixed economies, particularly in the developing
countries, many management institutions serve both public
and private sector organisations. The institutional set-
up should permit the institution to pay equal attention
to both sectors and their respective roles in national
development. A major advantage is the interaction between
public and private managers, which can be instrumental in
improving mutual understanding and economic and technological co-operation between the two sectors.

Many institutions originally established for one
sector have become increasingly interested in working
with both sectors. For example a recent review of the
Kenya Institute of Administration (KIA) recommended that
the Institute should "also serve as the national centre
where managers from the two sectors can converge to

24

discuss current national issues as well as share operational skills."[1] It even suggested that private-sector executives should be appointed to the KIA's board. However, a different view can be heard occasionally, according to which the two sectors should educate their managers separately because of certain differences in the goals, policy and institutional set-up of the public and private sector.

An intersectoral focus is preferred by many institutions (serving higher echelons of management in particular) because it facilitates the exchange of experience and prevents the inbreeding from which some of the older traditional sectors, e.g. in manufacturing, have suffered. Also, sectoral specialisation is seldom feasible in small sectors and countries. A compromise is sometimes found in the creation of sectoral units within intersectoral institutions or in joint programmes of intersectoral management institutions with sectoral ministries or institutes of engineering.

(2) A major question faced by management institutions concerns the proportion between scheduled open programmes and those tailored to the needs of one or a small group of client organisations and reserved for their personnel. Over the last ten years, the proportion of such reserved programmes has grown in many institutions, attaining 30-40% of the total volume of their training activity in some cases.

The volume of training required and the benefits obtained from company-specific training materials and from coupling training with consulting and action research in the same organisation are the key criteria used by institutions and their clients when deciding whether to choose this approach. To the institution this provides a better opportunity for learning about the clients' needs. On the other hand, the institution also has to consider seriously the risk involved in becoming excessively dependent on a limited number of clients. For example changes in the clients' training policies or cuts in their training budgets may hit the institution very hard.

(3) In respect of levels in the management hierarchy, the main criteria affecting choice are the need for a comprehensive approach embracing several levels and the compatibility of training and other services provided to clients at different levels.

----

[1] Report of the Committee of Review into the Kenya Institute of Administration 1978-79 (Nairobi, Government Printer, 1979), p. 60. See also section 2.5.

Many management centres find it very useful to engage simultaneously in programmes for middle, higher and top managers, to obtain an increased effect from "passing the same message" to cadres who view and can handle a certain class of problem from different angles. To associate several levels of management in tailor-made in-plant programmes (training, organisation development and other interventions) is more and more considered to be an essential condition of successful in-plant interventions. At the Centre Européen d'Education Permanente (CEDEP) in Fontainebleau, for example, established by a consortium of important European companies in 1971, mixing managers from different member companies, hierarchical levels, functions and nationalities in one programme has been adopted as a basic policy.[1]

But it is often felt that for both technical and social reasons, very different levels of management should not be trained at the same institution. For example, in public administration training, different institutions tend to be used for high level administrators and for junior administrative personnel. In industry, supervisory training is rarely organised at the same institution as higher and top management training.

(4) Concerning general or specialist management education and training, different considerations apply in the pre-employment and post-experience phase.

Initial management education provides the student of management with the whole spectrum of basic knowledge of facts and methods he may need whatever his individual career path will be. However, as he will rarely start in general management immediately, an effort is often made to provide him with more specialised knowledge in one functional area, such as finance and accounting or international marketing. Or, management is combined with engineering in educational establishments preparing primarily for production and plant management.

In post-experience education and training, institutions normally decide whether they should cover general management, specialist management functions and areas, or both. General management programmes are in most cases designed to respond to the needs of a particular management level as discussed above; emphasis tends to be on de-specialisation, on relations between various management functions and on environmental aspects.

---

[1] A detailed description and evaluation of the CEDEP is given in R.M. Hogarth: Assessing managerial education: A summary of the CEDEP project (Bradford, MCB Publications, 1978).

Many institutions choose to offer programmes for specialists in parallel to general programmes. In principle, specialist programmes are for those whose career is within one special field, such as marketing, personnel or finance. They tend to combine elements of general management with a deeper treatment and updating in the given speciality.[1] Synergy is achieved if the institution uses its capabilities for developing both specialist programmes and the corresponding aspects in its general management programmes, and if it uses multifunctional teams in practical in-plant interventions.

(5) Focus on selected special categories of professionals may be desirable on a temporary or rather long-term basis.

For example in France and some other European countries several institutions have recently started offering special programmes, subsidised by government, for redundant middle-aged managers. Programmes for woman managers have developed at several institutions, in the United States in particular. Another example is general management programmes designed for engineers with experience in production.

Some institutions have chosen, or have been asked to assume, certain functions of support to other institutions. This may include programmes in training management teachers, trainers, consultants and researchers, training directors, small enterprise advisors and extension officers and so on.

(6) As regards the geographic focus, the choice may range from institutions serving a limited region or area within a country through nationwide institutions to international institutions working at regional or inter-regional level.

As a rule a rather limited geographical area would be assigned to an institution established to provide management and technical services to smaller local businesses (urban or rural) or training junior and middle-level personnel for local organisations (supervisory management, accounting, production control, etc.). In large countries this may also concern some of the higher-level management development, in particular in areas of high industrial concentration and local demand for institutional services. Most existing management institutions are authorised or requested to provide services to the whole country. In large countries the advantages of concentrating resources and directly exchanging management experience between its regions have to be weighed against increased transport expenses and other disadvantages of centralisation. Unfortunately, records of management institutions provide ample evidence of the fact that organisations located close to

---

[1] Several examples can be found in the case studies in chapters 7-10.

the institution tend to get more help than those in remote
locations, irrespective of the urgency of their needs.
This may be sometimes alleviated, although with considerable difficulty, by creating regional branches or sub-
centres of central institutions.

In a relatively small number of cases, management
development institutions have been directly given an international orientation in their mandate.

In principle, they belong to one of two basic types.
First, independent (as a rule private) institutions, which
have decided to work for the international management development market, i.e. seek clients in a number of countries
in all regions.[1] As they have to respond to common needs,
their programmes (with the exception of specially tailored
programmes, which they also organise in some cases) cannot
be designed for specific countries. They tend to focus,
therefore, on developments in management that are of universal interest, on international business operations, and
on problems of multinational firms. Their services cannot
be cheap, therefore they have to attain a considerable
level of competence to attract clients from many countries
and be very imaginative and flexible in adapting their programmes to new trends and challenges in international business and development.

The second type are international institutions established by joint decision of, and sponsored by, a group of
governments. Examples of such institutions can be found
both at regional and inter-regional level. In most cases
management development is one of their functions: other
functions may include sectoral research, training and information services in public administration and the like.
For example, to improve management of public enterprises
is one of the main objectives of the Ljubljana-based
International Centre for Public Enterprises in Developing
Countries (ICPE).

This second type can be viable if the need for an
international institution is clearly established and if
the constituent governments make and respect adequate financial commitments. This is necessary especially during
the formative stage, when the opportunities to generate
income from services are limited.

Other problems met by this type of institution may
include the interference of international politics in
matters of staffing, programme planning and, in fact, all
decisions of strategic dimension. This may slow down the
building of professional competence. Political change in
the international arena may have a very strong impact on
the institution.

[1] See also chapter 7.

Some of the difficulties of institutions established directly as international are overcome by running international activities (management courses, training of trainers, research projects, clearing-houses of training materials) through well-established national institutions. This can be very useful in technical areas where an existing institution has already demonstrated considerable competence and opening its doors to clients from other countries or establishing a new special service for them may be the quickest, cheapest and technically most interesting way of making this experience accessible internationally.

Programme content

It is fair to start our comments on programme content, i.e., on the substance and orientation of curricula and related teaching and training materials,[1] by making it clear that in this highly responsible area management institutions can count on very little guidance and help. Some co-ordination and control may be exercised by parent bodies, e.g. by a university senate, a ministry of education or the institution's own governing body. But it may be a rather defensive one: a university senate may resent new course types considered as non-academic, a ministry of education may be more interested in preventing frequent changes in curricula than in the actual content. A ministry of industry may express a few general requirements on what managers should know but rarely more than that. Attempts have been made to suggest a common body of knowledge for the management professionals and define general grounds for curricula design in certain areas.[2]

In some countries, associations of management and of professional schools of management and administration have started organising exchange of experience on curricula and stimulating general studies to help orient curricula. All in all, these have been only very first steps, whose real impact on making curricula more relevant to practice has been limited.

---

[1] Comments concerning the content of curricula also relate, by implication, to the content of practical advice provided to clients through consulting and similar interventions, and of any other institutional services.

[2] See, e.g., Training systems and curriculum development for public enterprise management: Recommendations for national policies and programmes (London, Commonwealth Secretariat, 1979) or Guidelines and standards for curricular development for public administration/public management (Brussels, International Association of Schools and Institutes of Administration; mimeographed paper).

Under the circumstances, the curricula adopted by a particular institution reflect its own professional profile and perception of the environment above all. A proactive institution would consult clients extensively and try to be as objective as possible in identifying present problems and assessing future trends and changing needs, but the final choice in the content of curricula will have to be its own. Thus, while every institution's ambition is to have a curriculum of maximum relevance, there are many interpretations of what relevance means. This has been clearly established by a recent survey by the International Academy of Management.[1] Different choices are made by institutions on every aspect of curricula: the selection of disciplines and subjects taught, their absolute and relative weight and their sequencing, the function and share of electives, the pace of change in curricula and so on. This is not unrelated to the state of management theory, currently divided into varying schools or approaches, affecting both curricula and advice to practising managers.[2]

Essentially, in deciding what to teach, "management schools have four alternatives: to teach management as it is, as it should be, as it will be, or as a combination of two or three of these alternatives".[3]

There is a clear tendency in most professional management institutions to combine the first three alternatives. But institutions tend to differ in their interpretation of what the current status of management affairs is, how to change it in the short run, and how to prepare managers for the future. This, of course, has many implications not only for the choice of topics to be covered, but also for teaching techniques and other work methods used by the institution as well as for its links with the client base.

More specifically, the following comments on choices concerning curricula can be made.

---

[1] Management education: A world view of experience and needs (Report of the Committee of the International Academy of Management on Guidelines for Curricula in Schools of Business and Management, under the chairmanship of C.R. Wynne-Roberts, former chief of the ILO Management Development Branch).

[2] Cf. H. Koontz: "The management theory jungle revisited", in Academy of Management Review, 1980, No. 2.

[3] H.L. Hansen: "Business schools and management education", in Pakistan Management Review, Second quarter 1980, p. 17.

(1) On meeting future needs:

Both pre-employment and post-experience management programmes tend to be designed with some regard to future needs. This question is so important that we will return to it in discussing the strategic management process (chapter 2) and links with the environment (chapter 3) in more detail. However, it is necessary to recognise that even the most rigorous study of future trends cannot establish a faithful picture of the environment and of plausible management patterns in, say, 10 or 20 years - when current students of management will be assuming more general and higher-level management responsibilities and participants in post-experience programmes will still be in charge of their organisations or departments. The best that can be recommended is that instead of overloading the participant with facts that may soon become irrelevant, the focus should be on methods and attitudes likely to help the manager perceive and analyse future problems, devise new solutions, communicate with people and learn from every new situation.

(2) On reacting to new challenges:

Relevance implies timely adaptation to new needs and challenges. While some stability in curricula is desirable,institutions should not hesitate to reform them if the realities of the external world require it. The need for a reform may be the result of current change, or of a better perception of what changes are likely to occur in the future. Post-experience management programmes tend to be more flexible in this respect. It takes a long time for some business schools to start seriously dealing with topics such as labour-management relations, environmental management, management under galloping inflation, effective choice of technology, management of social services and development programmes, and so on.

(3) On preferring a particular school of management thought:

In the absence of a universal theory of management, individual teachers and consultants and whole institutions tend to design programmes and recommend solutions reflecting their preference for or adherence to one of the current schools of management thought. This is not a basically unfair approach; however, an impression should never be created that the approach taken is the only feasible and scientifically correct one if others exist; wherever possible, the existence of alternative approaches should be acknowledged, giving the participant an opportunity to exercise judgement and make his own choice.

(4) On harmonising education and training:

On the surface, there is no problem, but in many management schools, especially in developing countries, there is a serious one. Using the need to maintain academic standards as a pretext, they are reluctant to admit that management education is first and foremost preparation for practical functions and responsibilities, and that some training in practical management skills would make the young graduates much more useful to their countries than purely academic education. This pitfall has been avoided by most post-experience management centres, whose programmes tend to view educational and training aspects as complementary and mutually reinforcing. Nevertheless, in certain cases, the emphasis on training for narrowly-defined functions and tasks may have been overdone and the educational function of management development programmes underestimated.

(5) On combining disciplinary and interdisciplinary approaches:

While management practice is always interdisciplinary, the prevailing approach is to construct the first phase of management studies on disciplines such as economics, mathematics, information science, statistics, sociology and psychology. This is not challenged, but it should be noted that some management schools remain prisoners of this disciplinary approach in their total teaching, research and advisory activity, instead of helping students and managers to look at complex problems through the eyes of various disciplines and arrive at solutions meeting interdisciplinary criteria.[1]

(6) On using foreign models:

It is relatively easy to criticise a foreign model, but difficult to replace it by a valid national one. Using a foreign management or training technology may be the only alternative available in a particular case, e.g. when professional management education and training starts being introduced in a country as a completely new field. Not only developing countries, but also most industrialised ones, have had some recourse to models based on foreign management experience and thinking. Also, the first generation of management teachers and trainers in developing countries studied in most cases at business schools and management centres in the United States or in Europe; they brought foreign models with them when returning home.

In a truly professional institution, there are limits to this. Close contacts with local management practice

---

[1] Cf., e.g. H.A. Simon: "The business school: A problem in organisational design", in Journal of Management Studies, Feb. 1967.

and intensive 'research should inspire it to eliminate clearly nonfunctional models, retaining some, adapting others and ultimately developing local models for those aspects of management that are unique and are not found in other environments.

The problem in many developing countries is that management and educational models reflecting conditions of technologically advanced and highly structured industries continue to be taught for years and their re-examination is being delayed. For example operations research models are taught instead of courses on how to manage under conditions of imperfection and support deficiency, and history of economic thought instead of efficient organisation of workshops and offices. Or, in some African countries, the education and training of accountants is geared to British standards, and local institutes of professional accountants even resent attempts to devise national standards and remodel education accordingly.

Intervention means

To a management institution that aims at being effective and socially useful as discussed in section 1.1 above, the question of how to operate is no less crucial than that of defining objectives, target groups and programme content. Experience has given ample evidence of situations where an important, if not the principal, determinant of success or failure was the choice of the intervention means used.

Under "intervention means", often called "means of action", "intervention methods", "functions" or "activities" in institutional practice, the following are normally understood:

(1) basic intervention means including teaching and training, consulting and research;

(2) complementary intervention means such as information and documentation, computing and various other services to the management public (to individuals and organisations).

Given a free choice (some limiting factors will be discussed below), an institution would, as a rule, consider the results to be achieved as the first basic criterion for choosing its intervention means.

Thus if an institution pursues purely intellectual objectives, i.e. imparting generalised knowledge and sharpening general analytical capabilities and intellectual judgement, it may see no need for any in-plant consulting or action research. On the other hand, if immediate practical application of a single management technique is sought, not only consultancy in general, but consultancy in which the whole job is done without any participation of the client and without any training, may be seen as an appropriate method.

Nowadays, these two situations would be regarded by most institutions as extremes that tend to disappear from the management development scene. Though they have not faded away totally, as already mentioned most institutions pursue deeper and more complex objectives. They tend to embrace, in varying degrees and proportions, the development of knowledge, skills, values and attitudes of the manager, and also contribute to an effective practical utilisation of everything he has learned. It is therefore recognised that while some learning can take place in the classroom or through individual study, an essential part of learning (in particular that related to judgement needed in practical situations and in dealing with people) cannot be easily separated from action.

In applied disciplines such as management, theory is generalised experience: if an institution does not want to be totally dependent on research undertaken and published by others, it has got to study concrete management experience itself and aim at identifying general trends and patterns behind individual actions and situations. Hence the need for research based on field study and fact-finding.

This brings us to the second basic criterion for selecting intervention methods: learning from practical experience for the benefit of which the institution exists, including learning about the real impact achieved in practice. Clearly, only a pro-active institution would consider this second criterion as valid as the first one, or even more valid, since even the second archetype, the market-oriented, or reactive, institution may be satisfied by the feedback communicated by the client instead of trying itself to discover more about the ultimate impact of its activities. This second criterion is, in fact, only the reverse of the same coin, since it is difficult to make any judgement about actual practical impact without learning about it through first-hand experience.

Today most writers about management education, training and development therefore consider teaching and training, consulting, and research to be necessary and mutually supportive components of the institution's portfolio of intervention means, and elements of a single learning-intervening process, which must be carried out in close collaboration with the client system.

The qualification "mutually supportive" should not be overlooked since, in many cases, institutions are

Figure 1   Characteristics of an effective learning-intervening process

---

The research is problem-centred, emphasises the decision-maker's perspective, and gives substantial attention to the organisational processes through which actual outcomes are shaped.

The design of seminars and teaching materials is one of the most important foci of research activity.

An important product of the research is a set of simple conceptual frameworks useful to development managers in thinking through the particular types of problems they face.

The research process includes direct work with the client system.

The consulting activities aim to increase the problem-solving capabilities of the client system itself rather than to solve problems for the client.

Attention is given in both consulting and training activities to improving organisational structures and management systems.

The executive seminars are designed to bring together key personnel from either a single organisation or a single programme system in order to instil an organisational sense and to build individual skills.

The opportunity to interact with experienced executives in a seminar context is viewed as a major opportunity for testing the validity and utility of tentative research conclusions and for identifying additional issues to be studied.

The training seminars are designed to produce specific behaviour changes identified as important during the diagnostic study of the client system.

---

active in all three areas, but in each of them deal with different topics and clients, assign the work to different faculty members and fail to ensure transfer and cross-fertilisation between research and training, consulting and research, and so on. Figure 1 is a description of an effective learning-intervening process based on experience of several institutions in Asia and Latin America.[1]

---

[1] Reproduced from D. Korten (ed.): Population and social development: A challenge for management schools (Caracas, Instituto de Estudios Superiores de Administración, 1979), pp. 109-110.

A diagram showing how research can be used to improve training and consulting services with a view to increasing their practical impact is reproduced in Figure 2. While such a model simplifies the reality considerably, it clearly indicates some key relationships within the portfolio of intervention means.[1]

Within each basic means of intervention, there are further significant choices to be made to ensure effectiveness and coherence. This concerns the whole spectrum of teaching and training methods from lecturing and self-study to action learning, the broad range of consulting approaches from those taken by traditional resource consultants to pure process consulting, as well as the variety of research methods from desk-study to action research geared to developing new management systems and approaches. An in-depth analysis of criteria for choosing among these methods would be beyond the scope of this publication.

In practice, the choice of intervention means depends, too, on the institution's capabilities and some other factors. As a rule only mature and technically well-equipped institutions can apply a complete and integrated portfolio. New and young institutions normally put more weight on training, trying to increase the share and role of consulting thanks to the client contacts established through training. Only well-established institutions that have provided evidence of their expertise and commitment can hope to be consulted on policy issues by government and by business firms. Research can seldom be an extensive activity at this initial stage; topics for problem-oriented research tend to be identified through both training and consulting and, besides, it takes time to develop research capabilities. This emphasises the need to view the basic intervention means and their mutual relations in a time perspective and to foresee changes in the combination of them in the institution's strategic plan.

Some other factors may be adverse to consulting and action-related research: an excessively high teaching-load imposed on faculty, outdated and inadequate subsistence-allowance rates discouraging travelling to client organisations, legislation preventing the charging of fees for consulting interventions, or high premiums put on research that meets academic criteria rather than those

---

[1] Adapted from R. Zaki: Management training, consulting and research: Are they separate? (Arusha, East African Community Management Institute, technical paper, 1976).

Figure 2 Model for integrating management research with training and consulting

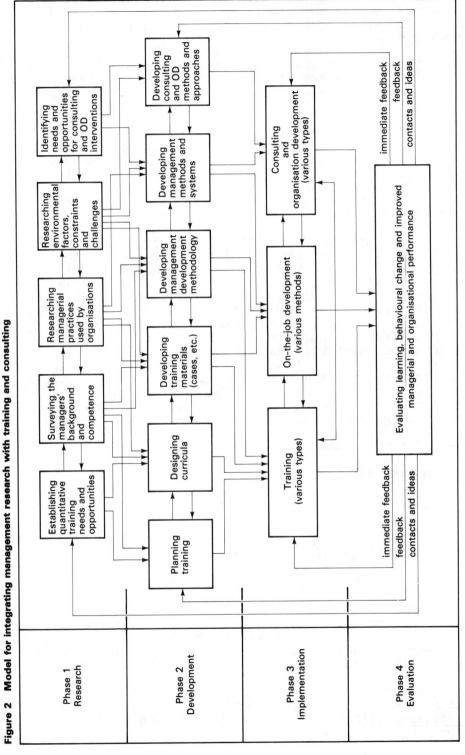

37

of practical usefulness. Also, it may be difficult to harmonise consulting with teaching if it is viewed as useful but within the private province of individual faculty members.[1]

Providing for exchange of experience among clients is a distinct feature of the range of means of intervention discussed above. It is all the more prominent in an institution set up as an association with corporate and/or individual members, who join it in order to gain access to experience of others. In addition, various other means of action can be used for this purpose. For example the Dansk Management Centre has organised several "clubs" in which Danish enterprises, public authorities and social organisations get together to work on issues of strategic management and exchange experience with various approaches to strategic planning.

Complementary intervention means have to be briefly mentioned, too. Collection and dissemination of information is one of those means whose role and potential is much underrated in many institutions. It is also an example of an area where a single institution can seldom make an impact given the magnitude and complexity of the information scene in the management field and where several institutions should usually get together before deciding on objectives and work method.

Further intervention means include various services to management established and operated at the institution instead of being run separately in individual public or private organisations. Examples are

- accounting and computing services;

- management assessment and recruitment;

- product design and testing;

- market surveys;

- feasibility studies and project design;

- negotiating and guaranteeing credits.

---

[1] "Never was a strategy more unfortunately wrong than the early encouragement of consultancy as a "right" of business school staffs as a way privately to supplement their income. Whilst it enriches the classroom anecdotes, it impoverishes the development of generalised knowledge resources, which are at the heart of the business school's contribution." G. Wills: Today's revolution in management education (Bradford, MCB Publications, 1981), p.3.

Some of these services, such as product testing or providing guarantees for credits, are no longer within the management development field. However, to include them in one institution together with training and consulting may be a sound strategic step in planning a small business development institution. In other cases, groups of public enterprises or their supervisory bodies may opt for a common service organised by a management institution for economy reasons or because of staff shortages, or to achieve standard quality.

Distinctive roles in development programmes

A special case of a complex strategic choice, one which combines several of the choices mentioned above, concerns a management institution's roles in particular development programmes. This choice may be faced in any country, but it is typical of developing countries.

There is no development programme or project without considerable management problems and needs. These may include designing and introducing management systems in newly-established organisations, identifying problems and devising remedial measures in existing programmes and projects, improving the management of systems delivering social services to the population, efforts for rationalising work and raising productivity in rural areas, and so on. Training tends to be a major component in any case. However, the sort of management and training that is needed in various programmes, hence the demands on institutional capability and intervention means, may vary considerably from case to case. In particular, as long as the institution stays in the sphere of modern sector of the economy, into which urban programmes and projects tend to fall, it may apply its conventional portfolio of intervention means with a good chance of success. When it moves to the unstructured and largely unexplored grounds of social and rural development, its total value system, technical capabilities and work methods may have to be reconsidered on the basis of experience acquired in close contacts with the client base that is served.[1] Clearly, the change required may be so profound that the institution may have to depart from some of its previous choices.

---

[1] For a detailed discussion of this important issue see D.C. Korten (ed.): Population and social development management: A challenge for management schools (Caracas, Instituto de Estudios Superiores de Administración, 1979), and D.C. Korten and F.B. Alfonso: Bureaucracy and the poor: Closing the gap (Singapore, McGraw-Hill, 1981). See also S. Paul: Strategic management of development programmes (Geneva, International Labour Office, forthcoming).

Notwithstanding the difficulties involved, management institutions in developing countries should aim at being closely associated with major development programmes, both in the modern sector and in the social and rural development. This is justified by the magnitude of the challenge and of the resources at stake, as well as by the fact that in many cases there may be no other suitable institutional base for such a task. A similar conclusion has also been drawn in the public administration sector of a number of countries, which have viewed the involvement of national public administration institutes in comprehensive programmes of administrative reform as an essential aspect of their effectiveness.[1]

The question of institutional responsibility has to be considered in this connection. Should the institution accept responsibility for specific training inputs, for delivering defined components of management systems for the programme, or for the quality of management and for progress actually made by the programme? One trap is to be avoided: even if its involvement in improving programme management is very deep, a management institute cannot normally accept the operational responsibility incumbent on a ministry or other public or private agency within whose competence the programme lies.

1.4 Strategic choices: resources

Following the review of selected fundamental choices concerning the scope and orientation of the institution's services, we must now consider another group of choices: alternative approaches to acquiring, creating, allocating and organising the institution's resources. After all, sound choices concerning purpose and services may be totally nullified by inappropriate decisions on resources.

Ideally, institutional resources should be determined and organised after the purpose and the portfolio of services have been defined. The need for consistence and coherence cannot be overemphasised. In practice, however, some resources tend to constitute a constraint that may eliminate or partially limit certain choices concerning purpose and services. The process has to be reversed: the question is then: what strategies are accessible to us taking account of the resource constraints that we are unable to remove? The implications of this fact for the processes of strategic management will be discussed in greater detail in chapter 2.

---

[1] Cf. Inayatullah (ed.): Management training for development: The Asian experience (Kuala Lumpur, Asian Centre for Development Administration, 1975).

Institutional resources are not only human, material or financial. For example appropriate and effective links with constituents and clients can be regarded as a major resource (of expertise, inspiration, power, demand for services, access to finance, etc.). Therefore, the brief review of essential choices concerning resources given in this section will not exhaust the subject. Chapter 3 will examine the whole network of links with the environment, chapter 4 will deal with the management of human resources in more detail, chapter 5 will focus on organising resources consistently with the strategic choices made, and, last but not least, chapter 6 will look at operational aspects of resource allocation and utilisation.

Organisational affiliation and independence

Generally speaking, management development institutions are aware of the strategic bearing of this choice. Nevertheless, its impact on the institution's ability to achieve its purpose is often underestimated, especially in the case of new institutions in developing countries. The main and frequent error is that, while taking a progressive decision to sponsor a management institution, a constituent organisation (as a rule a ministry) is not prepared to consider any alternative other than keeping the institution within its own jurisdiction and retaining the authority to make all important decisions about it.

Appropriate organisational affiliation is crucial, because it predetermines to a large degree several other choices and essential features of the institution, such as its potential for action and innovation, credibility, clients' confidence, staff structure and motivation, and sources of finance.

If the main objective is to improve management in private business, the sponsor should aim at modelling the institution as closely as possible on a well organised and dynamic private enterprise: emphasising entrepreneurship, innovation and achievement. The institution must not be paralysed by centralised controls and numerous regulations. The clients must have full confidence in its ability to grasp and treat business problems as practising managers would handle them, and there should be no mistrust.

Independent institutions whose reputation is based on performance are best placed to meet these criteria. In western industrialised countries and exceptionally in developing countries some of these institutions are totally autonomous, private organisations. In many cases, however, they are attached to managers' associations, entrepreneurs' organisations or chambers of commerce. If there is to be government involvement (which in any case requires good relations and an atmosphere of mutual confidence between government and business) an arrangement should be sought that de-emphasises governmental control and stresses the features mentioned above. For example organising the institution as a private (limited) company, an association or a foundation, and refraining from administrative and political interference in its daily operation.

If the purpose is to improve management in public enterprises, it is normal to attach the institution to a body with major responsibility for developing the sector and increasing its performance (ministry of industry or another sectoral ministry, a holding corporation, a public enterprise board, etc.). The degree of independence of the enterprises and the sort of entrepreneurial and managerial behaviour that the government wants to stimulate have to be reflected in the design of institutions serving the sector. The fact that the institution is to observe and teach public policy does not necessarily imply that it cannot be given a degree of independence commensurate with that of the enterprises themselves.

If both public and private enterprises are to be served, which is very frequently the case in mixed economies, the affiliation and autonomy of the institution must be acceptable to both sectors. As a rule, an alternative similar to that used by private sector institutions would be chosen.[1]

Institutions serving the public administration sector are normally regarded as part of it. However, even in this sector institutions tend increasingly to postulate greater technical independence and administrative and financial autonomy to be able to organise themselves and operate as truly professional bodies and

---

[1] "The institutions that have grown strongest over the years are government-sponsored but not government-managed, and autonomous". K. Chowdry: "Strategies for institutionalising public management", in L.D. Stifel, J.E. Black and J.E. Coleman (eds.): Education and training for public sector management in developing countries (New York, Rockefeller Foundation, 1977), p.107. In 1976 a joint mission by the director of the Bangladesh Management Development Centre and his ILO adviser to a number of Asian institutions concluded that "whilst most of the institutions were initially established under a department of government, the rate of their development increased when they became established as autonomous organisations under their own governing body."

not just as other ministerial units to which any project can be assigned and directive given by the bureaucracy.[1] However, to determine an optimum degree of independence is not an easy task. For to be pro-active and effective, for example in contributing to substantive reforms of the administrative machinery, the institution must not stand aside from the main stream of government action and be perceived as an alien body, where officials can be sent for courses, but which would not be allowed to take part in the process of national policy formulation.

If the main purpose is to prepare future managers through management studies (undergraduate and graduate), the basic choice is whether or not to attach the institution to a university.

University-based management institutions (faculties, schools, departments, centres, institutes) are very common. Their advantages are in the links with supporting disciplines and in the access to university facilities, such as teaching rooms or libraries; they exercise a positive influence on the traditional university by bringing it closer to the world of practice. But in some universities there also are considerable disadvantages. The university may impose academic standards of its own, overrating research and academic degrees and underrating experience and practical training. Certain university senates are reluctant to admit management as an applied academic discipline. Administrative regulations and procedures may be cumbersome and recruitment of staff with business experience difficult.

In many cases, therefore, new management education institutions have been set up independent of the university, both in industrialised and in developing countries.[2] In certain cases they have been established even outside

---

[1] Public administration institutes "may be under considerable government control even when they have corporate status. This creates a disposition towards conformity with ministerial directions and toward the avoidance of risking their necks by advocating the cause of institutional autonomy ... Institutions too narrowly tied to the existing power structure may not become sources of innovation in changing this structure". Inayatullah (ed.): Management training for development: The Asian experience (Kuala Lumpur, Asian Centre for Development Administration, 1975), pp.52-55 and 77.

[2] See also chapters 7-10.

the purview of the **ministry of education** so as to make
sure that the needs of management practice are met and
that industry and commerce have a greater say in shaping
the institution and view it as their own establishment.

Human resources and leadership

Human resources constitute the principal asset of
any professional institution: institutions develop,
flourish, stagnate and decay with arrivals, growth and
departures of professional staff.[1] Institutional memory
is in the brains of its professionals above all; in
social sciences and social development only a relatively
minor part of expertise can be recorded and stored in
training materials, and in consultancy or research reports.

Building a strong professional staff[2] is therefore
the only possible strategy open to institutions that do
not want to stay on the periphery of the management
development scene. The question is what profile of staff.
Detailed decisions on the mix of staff categories to be
employed will depend on choices related to roles in lifelong education, sectoral focus, means of intervention
used, etc. But there are some desirable common characteristics, such as strong practical bias, interdisciplinary
orientation and commitment to improving management
practices.[3]

An important choice concerns full-time or part-time
faculty. Many institutions started operating with a
very small full-time faculty; in certain cases there
used to be only a director and one or two programme

----

[1] "In a professional organisation, the professional
quality of the people is of primary importance and other
considerations are secondary. Therefore, managers of
professionals spend much of their time recruiting good
people and then seeing to it that they are kept happy."
R.N. Anthony and R.E. Herzlinger: Management control in
non-profit organisations (Homewood, Illinois, Irwin,
1980), p.45.

[2] We use the terms "professional staff" and "faculty"
interchangeably. It is pertinent to point out that the
term "faculty" is more popularly used in universities and
management institutions which are mainly concerned with
teaching.

[3] See section 4.1.

44

co-ordinators, while all teaching was done by external collaborators. Eventually, this was generally agreed to be an acceptable initial solution, but a dead-end path if followed in the long run. Strategies currently pursued by pro-active institutions combine full-time and part-time faculty, a leading role being played and a substantial portion of the teaching and most of the research being done by full-time staff. However, in some leading management schools the proportion of part-time faculty is deliberately kept quite high in order to maintain close links with the world of practice.[1]

Another strategic issue is professional team-building. Given a faculty of the same initial background and technical profile, two institutions can evolve in totally opposite directions. In the first, the individual employed fulfils his contract by delivering an agreed number of hours of teaching in accordance with an agreed over-all curriculum. The institution is no more than "a collection of scholars housed under one roof".[2] In the other case, the choices made concerning the portfolio of mutually supportive means of intervention, the roles in lifelong education, the links with the client base and the ultimate purpose to be achieved impose team-building, team-work and an "esprit de corps" in all aspects of institutional management and activity. This appears to be the only choice available to institutions aspiring to play a pro-active role.

Within the institution's human resources, leadership is generally recognised as the most precious asset, in particular in the formative stage of a new institution. "Leadership is considered to be the single most critical element in institution building, because deliberately induced change processes require intensive, skillful, and highly committed management both of internal and of environmental relationships. Leadership is considered primarily as a group process in which various roles such as representation, decision-making, and operational control can be distributed in a variety of patterns among the leadership group. The leadership group comprises both

---

[1] For example in 1980-81 the Ecole Supérieure de Commerce in Lyons had a faculty of 36, which is relatively small for such an institution, but used nearly 200 part-time teachers, who shouldered 52% of the total teaching load.

[2] H.L. Hansen: "Business schools and management education", in Pakistan Management Review, Second quarter 1980, p.18.

the holders of formally designated leadership positions and others who exercise important continuing influence over the institution's activities."[1]

Ideally, leadership is both internal and external. Internal leadership provides a unifying and driving force thanks to which a group of professionals with diverse backgrounds and personal value systems will be brought to think in terms of common strategy, adhere to it and aim at implementing it. This implies that internal leadership requires considerable technical competence in addition to administrative skills and personal qualities.[2] Successful leaders are deeply rooted in their institution; if they were chosen from the outside they have been able quickly to develop an intimate relationship with the institution and a deep understanding of the capabilities, values and aspirations of its staff.

External leadership concerns relations with the institution's constituents and clients in particular. The external world must see that the institution has a capable leader, one who deals personally, with determination and perspective, with matters that are critical to the institution's future. Building and strengthening links with the environment is the main goal of external leadership.

Institutions that begin to operate without leadership are inevitably headed for trouble. However, in practice it may be necessary to choose among managers who are stronger in one or another aspect of leadership. In addition, the development stage of the institution is a key variable. In the formative stage external leadership may require most of the director's attention and time, and he may share the internal leadership role with the faculty chairman or director of studies. In periods of consolidation, when the institution becomes large and complex and has to look for new internal sources of innovation and improvement, providing internal leadership may be the director's crucial function.

---

[1] Eaton J.W. (ed.): <u>Institution building and development: From concepts to application</u> (Beverly Hills, Sage Publications, 1972), p.22.

[2] Cf. sections 4.4, 5.1 and 5.4.

Physical facilities and their location

A management institution needs convenient physical facilities, adapted to the sort of programmes it runs and the size of its staff. The local climatic and other factors, such as heat, humidity or the occurence of dust-carrying winds, and even the learning and socialising habits of local people, ought to be given due consideration if new facilities are planned. Prestige facilities may attract participants in one case and repel in another. For example there have been instances of small enterprise development and training centres where participants cannot feel at ease since everything is so different from what they meet in their normal business activity.

A convenient location for a management institution is in a quiet area with good ambiance for educational and research activities, but relatively close to the organisations most participants come from and where most practical interventions will be made. The frequency of other contacts (with ministries, universities, libraries, etc.) should be kept in mind. Good transportation, communications and accommodation are also necessary.

The organisational affiliation of the institution is a significant but not necessarily determining factor of its physical location. The availability of buildings often plays a major role in decisions, but in some cases has been the cause of an inconvenient location. The same applies to locations chosen for political or prestige reasons while ignoring more essential criteria.

Size and rate of growth

The various choices discussed hitherto will very much predetermine the size of the institution, which is best expressed by the quantitative strength of its main operating resource - its professional staff. However, services for the same clients and the same range of activities can in many cases be grouped, institutionalised and physically located in one or more organisations, which brings some further criteria and choices into the picture.

There is the criterion of rationality and efficiency. One larger institution may often be more efficient than two or more small institutions provided it does not embrace incompatible activities and does not move too far away from the clients. A larger institution will be able to afford information, documentation, computing, printing, administrative, catering, accommodation and other support facilities unthinkable in a small centre.

The criterion of "critical mass" is fundamental. Institutions that are too small do not employ enough professionals to cover the essential areas of management and also the main supporting disciplines. They cannot constitute interdisciplinary and multifunctional teams and they are too dependent on a few individuals. The probability of having in their centre some individuals of exceptional talent and productivity is reduced.

An empirical figure of 30 to 50 competent and operational professionals has often been mentioned as one defining the critical mass for a management school or centre that has to establish departments for various functions and areas of management, combine the use of various means of action and operate at several levels of the lifelong management development process. If some staff members are not fully operational (staff in training, junior staff requiring a great deal of guidance and supervision), the figure may have to be increased. Nevertheless, a smaller management institution may be viable if it develops some special competence and does not try to spread its efforts too thinly over many areas, if it uses external collaborators effectively, or if it ties itself through a twinning arrangement with another institution (local or foreign) from which it can enlist professional support.

As a rule an institution with 10 to 20 full-time faculty members would be considered small, with 30 to 50 members medium, and with 60 or more members large. In addition, the number of part-time faculty members and the volume of work borne by them have to be taken into consideration.

Numbers of participants are indicative of size to some extent in the case of institutions with full-time long-term programmes; however, the additional volume of post-experience training, consulting and other activities can be considerable and must not be ignored in assessing size.

How big should a given management institution be at a given point in time? Or, in other words, what size should it be initially and how fast should it grow? The foundation of the institution in the first instance will clearly embrace consideration of initial size even if growth paths are not always discussed. If there is a very explicit and limited set of objectives, e.g. to train 600 middle managers a year from a sector dependent on a particular ministry in a restricted range of topics, then the evaluation of size is relatively simple. On the other hand, if the institution is to serve the open market at a range of post-experience levels over a wide spectrum of subject areas, appraisal of size is much more difficult;

growth in such a case will clearly depend on performance in identifying and satisfying the market.

However, experience indicates that a very fast rate of growth tends to jeopardise performance and disrupt the institution. Reaching an optimum cruising size and attaining the desired level of institutional competence may take anything from 5 to 10 years, or more if the institution has to start with relatively inexperienced junior staff.

There are some other factors that often limit growth. For example a business school designed for an annual in-take of 100 divided in two parallel classes may find it impossible to increase the number of participants by 20%, but could consider a third parallel class, and expand facilities and faculty accordingly. The number of rooms in the residence may be another limiting factor. To some institutions, the main limiting criterion is their desire to maintain an integrated professional team sharing common values, which is difficult to achieve if the institution is too big.

For these and similar reasons some institutions do not strive to grow even if demand and acquired capability would permit them to do so.[1]

Finance

There are various alternative sources of finance and ways of channelling financial resources to management institutions; choosing among them and achieving a balanced portfolio of financial resources is the object of financial strategy. The impact on institutional behaviour cannot be over-emphasised. In a sense, the sources of finance and the conditions on which the institution will receive it may have an even stronger influence on what the institution will actually do than some conceptual considerations concerning purpose and technically desirable orientations. After all, he who pays the piper calls the tune!

There are arrangements ensuring full financial security. For example the institution may receive the whole of its resources from one constituent (public or private) and

---

[1] For example the Cranfield School of Management does not plan to grow beyond its present size, defined by a faculty of 53, an annual in-take of 150 graduate students, and about 70 short-term post-experience programmes per year of an average length of 2.1 weeks per programme.

its financial security will be guaranteed as long as the financial situation of the constituent itself remains healthy. Such total financial dependence tends to carry with it limited decision-making and operational autonomy. But there are cases in which constituents are prepared and even prefer to provide resources without interfering in the operation of the institution. Or acceptable rules are agreed upon for exercising no more than general surveillance over the use of the resources.

A variant of this first alternative is one where total finance is provided by two or more constituents according to an agreed scheme. For example, a management centre can be sponsored jointly by an employers' federation, a chamber of commerce and a government ministry.

In a growing number of cases, public and private sponsors tend to grant resources for precisely defined activity areas or projects submitted by institutions (research projects, preparatory work for new sectoral courses, staff development programmes, etc.). This can be an efficient way of orienting the institution towards areas in which the constituents or clients are particularly interested. Problems arise if in a desperate search for resources an institution accepts commitments that are not congruent with its basic strategic choices.

Total self-financing is the other extreme on the scale of choices. It means, in its purest form, that the institution's total income is generated by selling services. The services have to correspond to demand; the institution has to be strongly market-oriented. Its total independence is emphasised. However, this may compel the institution to respond only to short-term demands perceived by the clients and to neglect various developmental and more difficult activities and social objectives - unless it can afford to charge fees including provision for such activities.

The most frequently chosen financial strategy is one combining the above-mentioned alternatives in various ways and proportions. There is the view that even within the public sector a part of the institution's income can be generated by selling services to other public organisations. On the other hand, even very independent private institutions may find it difficult to cover all their financial needs by selling services. They look for additional resources for research and programme development work, for training intended for organisations and individuals who cannot pay high fees, and similar purposes.

As already mentioned, a balanced portfolio of financial resources is the target: indeed, many institutions prefer to give up a seemingly comfortable situation in which their total resources are provided by the government or another major sponsor, in order to enhance their independence and give the clients more opportunity to show for what "products" they are prepared to pay.

The following examples illustrate different approaches to financial strategy (without revealing identity):

- an Indian institution wants to keep grants from Government below 50% of its annual budget to avoid constraints that would intervene if this figure were exceeded;

- a private international institution views the following portfolio as balanced: 70% from fees, 20% from business associates and 10% from other sources;

- a British institution (totally self-financing) does not earn more than 3% from fees paid by any single client organisation and feels that this helps to maintain independence;

- an African institution earns 90% of its self-generated income from training, but feels that a healthier proportion would be 55% from training, 35% from consulting and 10% from research;

- two British management schools, both university-based, have very different financial portfolios: the first one obtains 75% of its annual funds from the Government via the parent university and 25% from post-experience training and research income, while in the other one the figures are 40% and 60% respectively.

Pricing policy is an important element and feature of financial strategy. Prices influence the clients' decisions on whether to call for the institution's services and occasionally may be one of the factors determining a client's decision to turn to another institution. Pricing policy is a particularly delicate issue at autonomous institutions that have to generate the totality or a major part of their finance by selling services in a competitive setting.

The actual cost of professional services is the normal starting point for pricing. However, varying strategic considerations will together determine the final price. For example:

- some client groups may pay lower prices or get free service (new small enterprises, clients from rural and underprivileged areas, certain government agencies, members of the institution);

- certain grants may be tied to maintaining a defined
price level or providing free service (in the United
Kingdom, management institutions receive a grant for
every MBA student within limits agreed to with the
University Grants Commission, but no grant for short
programmes offered to managers from private and public
enterprises; in France and other countries grants can be
obtained for retraining redundant managers and so on);

- different prices may be charged for scheduled educational and training programmes and for in-plant interventions (consulting, tailor-made courses);

- considerably higher prices are as a rule charged for
shorter programmes for senior management than for longer
programmes for would-be and junior managers and in many
centres the latter are heavily subsidised by the former
(the fee charged by the CEI in Geneva for a one-week top
management programme is in the order of 6,000 Swiss francs,
while the fee for one week of their 35-week MBA programme
is 600 francs).

An institution would not normally cost and price each
programme in isolation, but rather its programme portfolio as a whole. There may also be special promotional
considerations, such as the desire to offer a balanced
programme to major clients even if some courses cannot be
charged for at real cost, in the hope that the clients
will make use of both the less and the more profitable
programmes.[1]

1.5 The institution's image

Organisations and individuals constituting the institution's clientèle, or potential clientèle, have their
own, subjective perception of its purpose, values and
capabilities. This perception is often called the institution's "image". If the clients are free to decide
whether to use its services or not, this image will
strongly impinge on their decision. Not only has the
institution to make the right strategic choices and implement them effectively: this fact must be correctly perceived by its clients and its environment in general.
In summary, the institution must be "acceptable" to particular clients in a particular environment. It must not
be viewed as a strange body, which does not speak the
same language as its clients.

Two examples can demonstrate this. In the first
case a former minister who became an opponent to the

---

[1] For operational aspects of costing and pricing see
section 6.3.

government in power in a developing country, published a book in which he referred, among other things, to his ideas and plans concerning the existing management centre. The government's image of the institution was so adversely influenced by this that it abolished the institution.

In another case a management school in a European country, known for high academic standards, tried to further enhance its image by a publicity campaign in which it called itself "a new war-college for winning economic battles". Neither the message, nor the medium used (a respectable daily paper) were congruent with the institution's real image and the new label had to be rapidly dropped.

Our readers will certainly be able to recall cases of institutions which have suffered a great deal from labels such as "this institution is too theoretical", "it is built on foreign models", "it does not understand the needs of public managers", "it cannot do more than middle-management training", and so on. There may be a grain of truth in these statements. But even if they are largely incorrect, it may be very difficult to prove that the opposite is closer to the truth and make the institution acceptable.

Every institution's image is a rather complex matter. In fact, there is not just one image, but a number of them. Professional image or credibility (competence and ability to tackle technical problems of concern to the clients) is not the same thing as socio-political image (values, aspirations, behaviour, ties with particular groups in the environment). Even more important, in any society different organisations and individuals are most unlikely to have an identical image of a particular management institution. Experience has shown that differences can be considerable and it is not unusual for completely divergent images to co-exist. It is also known that it requires years of efforts to build a good image and reputation, while a single rash act can easily destroy it.

Appropriate strategic choices, competence demonstrated in action, and participation in the life of the community are, obviously, the main factors affecting image. There are other factors, too, which are not under the institution's full control. For example competitors or institutions following a different doctrine may spread rumours about the relevance, credibility, practicality, commitment, etc., of the institution in question. This should not happen among professional institutions, but occasionally it does. Public opinion is also influenced by the press. In France, for example, every summer a leading daily paper publishes its rating of management schools (French and foreign) based on a questionnaire

survey. Selected value judgements made by the respond-
ents are also divulged.[1] While such publication reflects
the existing image, it strongly influences image, too.

If the institution's image is so important, it is
highly desirable to control it. It is essential to know
what the image is in various quarters. This may require
some effort since the image is seldom explicitly stated,
and direct questions may lead to evasive answers. But,
if it really wants to, any institution can discover how
it is perceived by others. The findings may be surprising. They often reveal that the institution has a totally
different opinion of itself than do other organisations
and groups.

The various images identified have to be analysed.
The questions to be asked are: Is our image different
from what we would like it to be? If so, why? Should we
change our strategy? Why do we have a different image in
different circles or organisations? How does our image
influence the support we are getting, the clients'
interest in our services and so on? Are there external
forces that try to tarnish our image? If so, why? If
the image needs to be rectified in one way or another,
this cannot be left to chance. It will be wiser to define
a plan of action for improving the institution's image,
using the various contacts and means linking the institution with its environment.

_____

[1] Cf. Le Monde de l'éducation, July-Aug. 1981,
pp. 25-28.

THE PROCESS OF STRATEGIC MANAGEMENT

2

Manuals and guides can describe alternative approaches and point out instances of good strategic choices thanks to which institutions have been successful. But they cannot provide ready-made strategies for the whole range of developmental situations in which particular institutions operate. Strategic management is an activity that every institution has to undertake with a full knowledge of its complexity and of the various difficulties to be overcome, and making full use of the institution's environmental contacts and information. The effort of the institution's management and professional staff will be of crucial importance to success, whatever external inputs into strategy may be forthcoming from constituents, clients or other sources.

The appropriate methodology and organisation of strategic management are important not only because they save time and effort, but because they increase the probability of arriving at an optimal strategy and enlisting support for it both inside and outside the institution. This chapter will therefore review the main elements of the strategic management process in some detail. This will include a discussion of strategic planning as applied by management development institutions.

2.1 Strategic analysis

It would be hazardous to make strategic choices shaping the institution's profile, and committing considerable resources, without appropriate analysis. Even if uncertainty cannot be completely avoided and the institution may have to take some risk, it wants to be sure that it has done everything possible to be well informed and documented, to be aware of accessible alternatives and to make use of any experience and innovative thinking that can be tapped and mobilised within the institution and in its environment.

If there is no time for a thorough analysis or if the institution has doubts about its present ability to analyse strategy, it might be better to postpone the basic choices or at least some of them. For example an institution may have to postpone for some time a decision concerning its more pronounced and restrictive sectoral focuses as long as it is not sure about the specific needs, future development prospects and demand for management training in certain sectors. Thus, the main steps in strategic analysis may be implemented in the sequence described below. However, the strategic management cycle can be adapted to specific conditions in each case and carried out as an exercise of gradual approximation.[1]

Environmental analysis

Environmental analysis (or appraisal) provides the institution with information on relevant environmental factors seen in a time perspective, bearing in mind the trends and pace of change in various components of the environment. Because of the multiplicity and complexity of factors that affect management and institutions serving management, environmental analysis endeavours to get a sufficiently deep insight into a wide spectrum of factors constituting the economic, geographic, physical, technological, political, legal, socio-cultural and educational environment in the given case.

Factors influencing management or constituting a challenge to managers and to management institutions will be distilled from neutral factors; particular attention will also be paid to existing or potential impeding forces. A global assessment of management systems and practices and of managerial competence in sectors or organisations representing potential clients is an important part of environmental analysis.

In environmental analysis, there is a problem of both excess and shortage of information. A vast amount of information on various aspects of the total environment is available to every institution, but not all that information is relevant to its strategic management. The scope of the analysis will have to be limited and irrelevant environmental aspects, or aspects too remote and too general in a particular case, omitted. For example a management centre working exclusively for local management within one country will pay less attention to inter-

---

[1] Appendix 1, "Guidelines for a strategic audit of a management development institution", gives an over-all outline and a list of questions that can be used in preparing strategic analysis.

national political and economic relations than an international management institute. If, on the other hand,
there is a shortage of information on essential environmental factors, a special effort may be necessary to fill
the gaps before trying to make any decisions of a strategic nature.[1]

Establishing needs and demand

An important part of environmental analysis concerns
the clients' needs and expressed or potential demand in
the areas where the institution intends to offer and develop services.

In this connection the subtle difference between
needs and demand is worth stressing. Generally speaking,
management development needs can be viewed as the gap
between the existing and desired level of management competence, a gap that can be bridged by training combined
with other actions and measures likely to improve the
quality of management in practice. Needs can be determined more or less objectively once the present level of
competence has been identified and the desired level
determined. On the other hand, to be converted into
demand, needs have to be perceived by the individuals and
organisations concerned and various other factors have to
be considered, such as motivation for training and self-
development, or the availability of funds to pay course
fees. As a rule management institutions can help stimulate demand for their services; indeed, this is part of
their strategy, and, among its other effects, strategic
analysis should help to identify measures that have this
stimulating effect.

Also, demand for the services of a particular institution will be influenced by the situation on the market.
It is necessary to consider whether there are competing
programmes, and whether other institutions are likely to
enter the same field. Even internal programmes in important client organisations cannot be ignored: under
certain circumstances such organisations may prefer to
initiate programmes which are normally offered by management institutions.

The establishment of most management institutions
has been preceded by some survey of needs in organisations representing potential clients. However, in many
cases these surveys have been of little use to strategy

---

[1] For a more detailed discussion of an institution's
environment and of environmental information, including
checklists of relevant factors, see chapter 3, "Links
with the environment".

owing to their scope and the methods used. As a rule strategic and operational issues are mixed, a short-term perspective prevails, an excess of detailed data is collected but not synthesised and macro-factors important for establishing future needs and trends are ignored. For example for strategic decisions concerning programmes in marketing management it is not necessary to collect individual views on the application of a particular market-survey or promotional technique. It is more important to find out about sectoral changes with major implications for the distribution and marketing of goods and services, changes occurring in the traditional market structures and channels, the influence of international trade on domestic marketing and so on.

In practice every institution engaged in strategic management is directly interested in the qualitative side of needs and demand, as this has a direct bearing on programme development and innovation. The relevance of management research cannot be overemphasised in this connection. Quite a few institutions have suffered from the lack of development perspective in their main areas of action since they have used all resources for direct client services, without making provision for conceptual work needed for future programme reorientation and development.

The importance of establishing quantitative demand differs from case to case.

Forecasting demand will be important for a newly-established, independent institution and for centres with a substantial post-experience activity. Forecasting will also be essential for institutions embarking on under-graduate and postgraduate managerial education in highly competitive conditions. For the well-established and successful institution, on the other hand, demand is often constrained by availability of places, e.g. there can be a ratio of as much as 30:1 between applications and places on some of the better undergraduate schools programmes in Great Britain, so quantitative forecasting is of less significance. However, if a wider approach is taken in a particular country in order to plan the development of a whole network of institutions, it is important to forecast the global demand before considering which institutions should be encouraged to grow and to what size.

Where forecasting is carried out, it is common for it to be a mixture of quantitative extrapolation and subjective judgement. Once a time series for a given type of programme has been built up, a projection may be made which is tempered by the views of the faculty responsible. The concept of the product life cycle may also be useful

in this context. For undergraduate and postgraduate
studies, government departments may be able to provide
valuable inputs - demographic trends, national statistics
for the relevant educational sectors, etc. - which constitute essential components of the data base from which
market shares may be calculated, historically and as
future projections.

Identifying opportunities

"Opportunities" refers to areas in which the institution might concentrate its future action in order to
make a notable contribution to the improvement of management practice. It is not necessarily confined to spectacular technical innovations: any area or action where an
institution may be able to make an effective contribution
and fill an existing gap may be viewed as an opportunity.

Independent institutions, in particular those
engaged in post-experience management training and consulting, are fairly free to define what an opportunity is.
At the beginning a great number and wide range of opportunities might be identified; further analysis will have
the effect of eliminating those that are not within the
institution's competence or are deliberately abandoned
for other reasons.

In the 1970s management centres in several European
countries saw a new opportunity in the growing need to
help managers to understand and handle problems of labour
relations, collective bargaining, workers' participation,
communication with young workers and so on, arising as a
result of recent developments on the European social and
educational scene. Some institutions have become very
active in this area, while others have decided not to
take such an opportunity.

Less independent institutions, whose profiles and
programmes are determined by government or other constituents, may feel that their opportunities are more limited.
However, their basic attitude should be the same, even if
certain opportunities may require negotiations with the
parent body or may eventually have to be dropped as unrealistic in the given context.

The time dimension of opportunities will also have
to be considered. Current opportunities may have an
uncertain future (is management under inflation a lasting
opportunity?). The main purpose of the exercise is to
identify future opportunities and make a preliminary
assessment of their magnitude.

Such an approach will also show in many cases that
an opportunity is "conditioned", i.e. the institution

might enter a new area and make an impact if business owners, government or other institutions also decide to intervene in the same area and harmonise their respective interventions.

Strengths and weaknesses

To be able to decide what opportunities to take and what to reject, the institution needs to develop an objective, unbiased understanding of its real role in the total process of enhancing the competence, practices and effectiveness of management in a particular environment, and of those of its strengths and weaknesses that can already be identified or are expected to develop in the future.

Vague assessments, such as "we are able to make a major impact" or "60% of our professionals have a PhD", are to be avoided. The institution wants to know what its teams and individuals are actually able to achieve in teaching and research, what practical problems they can tackle and what their sectoral background and experience, theoretical level, flexibility, adaptability to new situations and commitment is. The institution's links with business and government, its ability to raise finance for new action, and other such questions must also be considered.[1]

There are no absolute strengths and weaknesses. An apparent strength may be no strength at all if it relates to an area in which there is no demand for action; an apparent weakness may be no weakness if it does not jeopardise the institution's capacity to achieve its objectives. Strengths and weaknesses have therefore to be examined in the light of current and future opportunities. A comparison with other institutions can be enlightening.

Preselecting potential alternatives

As a next step in strategic analysis the institution will try to narrow down the list of opportunities by comparing them with its strengths and weaknesses. Each alternative will be subject to a sort of feasibility study, comparing it to the institution's purpose, defining its resource and cost requirements, new linkages to be created, benefits, disadvantages and risks involved. Wherever possible, the results to be achieved if a particular alternative is chosen will be expressed in the form of objectives; when choosing between strategic alternatives the institution will thus also choose between

---

[1] For more detail, see appendix 1.

alternative objectives, or between different dimensions
of the same objectives.

This will help establish a short list of strategies
and strategic objectives. It may also generate suggestions for redefining the institution's purpose if the
existing definition does not provide a proper framework
for an important strategic choice that the institution
wishes to make.

Coherence and synergy analysis

Strategy does not involve isolated individual
choices, but sets of inter-related choices whose range
and complexity differ from case to case. Strategic
analysis has therefore to explore such sets of choices in
their totality, trying to determine what benefits will be
gained and what problems created by combining several
strategies. The objective is to develop coherent sets of
strategies with a view to avoiding the undesirable internal competition for resources, conflicts of interests and
excessive strain on institutional management that would
result if incompatible and inconsistent strategies had to
be co-ordinated. An overriding objective is synergy,
which can be achieved by combining strategies that are
mutually supportive, complement each other, and achieve
higher effectiveness with the use of the same amount of
resources. Examples of synergy have already been given
in chapter 1.

2.2 Strategic decisions

Let us assume that strategic analysis has produced
information on what the alternative courses of action
could be, including the external and internal implications
of different strategies. This is the moment when management will make its choices, aware of the fact that the
institution may have to live with good or bad choices for
many years.

Seemingly, to take these decisions should be easy if
strategic analysis has been carried out correctly. Some
alternatives may even look so obviously effective and
promising that anybody would choose them. Nevertheless,
there are realities which make strategic choices difficult and demanding on managerial experience, judgement
and even intuition.

Problems of choice

First, we have already mentioned that certain strategic choices may look very attractive, but the institution may be unable to remove constraints that make them
unrealistic. At the same time the institution may for

various reasons be forced to make choices it would normally prefer to avoid.

Secondly, even the most thorough strategic analysis cannot be absolutely complete and convincing. As mentioned, in many cases there will be a shortage of quantitative data and even if some quantitative implications of an alternative choice are shown, often these will be no more than an estimate. Statements of what is "important", "promising", "priority", "crucial" and the like, may be biased due to the analyst's personal experience and preferences. Such bias will be reduced if alternatives are reviewed collectively and discussed with clients, but it is difficult to eliminate it completely.

Thirdly, in most cases there will be the problem of matching limited resources with virtually unlimited needs and considerable opportunities. This is common in prosperous business firms and also in successful institutions. If resources limit the scope of choice, to what strategies should we allocate them as a matter of priority? Should we ignore opportunities that are real but are beyond our resources? Should we pass them on to another institution or should we earmark at least modest resources for them in order to prepare ourselves for the future? All this is difficult to decide. Under the circumstances many institutions commit the same error: they spread their resources too thin for fear of leaving an interesting opportunity to somebody else and losing it for ever.

Fourthly, the more interesting choices and opportunities often involve more risk and more managerial and staff effort. The institution must consider whether it is able and willing to take such risks and to generate the requisite effort. This may involve overcoming resistance and withstanding pressure from staff and even within the institution's management itself. If the choice is very demanding on staff, will all staff members support it?

Purpose and objectives

In certain cases, i.e. if a new institution is being planned or if strategic analysis shows that the institution's very purpose ought to be redefined, strategic decisions will concern this purpose or ultimate goal.

However, in most instances the strategic choices will lead to establishing new objectives, or redefining existing objectives within the given purpose to reflect changes occurring in the environment and in the institution itself.

62

As mentioned in chapter 1, the definition of purpose tends to indicate the over-all effect to be achieved in relatively broad terms and without specifying time limits, or within a relatively distant time-horizon. Qualitative terms will be used rather than quantitative ones. Within this broad directive the institution's objectives indicate what specifically has to be done in order to achieve the purpose, using the resources that can be mobilised. Objectives will express specific results to be achieved, i.e. they should not be a mere description of activities. If possible, objectives should be:

- stated in a way understandable to all units and individuals concerned;

- related to a specific period of time;

- measurable and controllable;

- challenging but not unrealistic.

If an objective cannot be quantified, it is desirable to state it with sufficient clarity so that there is some way of judging whether or not it has been achieved.[1]

The number and scope of objectives to be adopted will differ from case to case. For example for the period 1980-84 the National Institute of Business Management in Colombo has developed 54 specific objectives grouped under 13 wider objectives. Each wider group refers to a major activity area (consulting, training, research, computer services), or to aspects such as growth rate, internal efficiency and healthy financial situation and improvements in staff competence and utilisation. Each objective is supported by one or more quantitative performance indicators.[2]

In a good number of cases the quantification of objectives reflecting strategic choices does not present any difficulty. For example a sectoral reorientation of programmes can be measured by numbers of programmes, numbers of participants, numbers of participant-days or fees earned from various sectors (if the same price policy is applied to all of them). It is easy to measure growth, the allocation of professional staff time to

[1] Cf. R.N. Anthony and R.E. Herzlinger: Management control in non-profit organisations (Homewood, Illinois, Irwin, 1980), p. 230.

[2] See National Institute of Business Management corporate plan, 1980-84 (Colombo, NIBM, 1979).

priority areas, or the rate of programme innovation, not to speak of financial objectives.[1]

Even qualitative objectives should lend themselves to assessment of achievement. A strategic objective such as "to become a leading organisation in the country (region) in the area of post-experience management training" is qualitative and its assessment will be influenced by subjective views of individual persons. However, if the institution claims to be a leading body, this is likely to be reflected in the number of course applicants, in requests from industry for advice and consulting, in successful publications, in the clients' interest in the institution's business associates scheme[2] and so on. An objective such as "to be attractive as an institution in which to work", used by one institution, is qualitative, but it is possible to measure and evaluate staff turnover, the number and quality of job applications received by the centre or the intellectual output of professional staff; even attitude surveys can be organised to measure achievement of this objective.

The hierarchy and denomination of objectives in a particular case may be stipulated by a planning or project design methodology used by the institution or applied throughout the sector to which the institution belongs.[3] Irrespective of the terms used in various methodologies, the tendency appears to be the following:

(1) long-term (7-10 years) and medium-term (3-5 years) objectives specify major results to be achieved in implementing strategy;

(2) short-term and operational objectives (1-2 years or less) are management tools used in planning and control to indicate progress to be made towards the realisation of longer-term and higher-level objectives.

---

[1] See also appendix 2.

[2] See chapter 3, section 3.2.

[3] "Structures of objectives are almost as diffuse as structures of purpose and philosophies." G.A. Steiner: Top management planning (London, Macmillan, 1969), p. 150. For example various technical co-operation agencies have different guidelines for project design and evaluation; institutions to which such projects are attached are sometimes influenced by those methodologies in adopting their own hierarchy of objectives.

Objectives and resources

Making the right decisions concerning resources is as important as determining the right objectives for outputs and action. However, this has been overlooked by some institutions, which consistently focus their strategic analysis on opportunities for action but do not realise that they are moving on thin ice if they do not examine and develop their resources accordingly. The fact that parallel strategies have competed for limited internal resources, or that apparently very sound strategic choices have been based on superficial or unrealistic assumptions concerning resources, has caused the failure of strategic plans in many cases.

Certain objectives should therefore define institutional capability and determine the results to be achieved in developing resources, i.e. in ensuring the institution's growth, improving staff competence, reallocating staff to major action areas, building information banks, making the institution better known, expanding facilities or achieving a healthy financial situation. The great advantage of strategic management is that it prevents these predominantly inward-looking objectives from becoming an aim in themselves by consistently relating them to the institution's purpose and subordinating them to objectives that are outward-looking.

Policies

Some strategic choices lead to defining policies, i.e. guidelines for action, or rules governing the institution's behaviour in matters of importance. For example "to recruit staff with at least 5-7 years of managerial experience" is a statement of policy whose application will help the institution to implement a strategic choice concerning the profile and competence of its faculty. Under certain circumstances the same strategy can be expressed as a quantified objective, i.e. "within 7 years, 70% of the faculty members should have 5-7 years of managerial experience". Clearly, the latter is a very precise target with many implications for recruitment and staff development (including, for instance, detachment to industry of some faculty members who have less than the required experience).

Announcing strategic decisions

Strategic decisions can be formulated and announced in various ways. A strategic plan is a tool used by many institutions; therefore the following section will discuss it in some detail. Other tools include institutional statutes, action programme declarations, reports to boards and parent bodies, directors' messages to staff, policy guidelines concerning various activity areas and so on.

In choosing the way in which a strategic decision should be formulated and announced, the institution's management will consider the desirability of making it publicly known. As a rule management institutions will be able and interested to convey details of their strategy to a wider public than business corporations would normally do. In many cases it may be very useful to inform not only the constituents but also the whole client base about strategy. However, the management of institutions operating under competition or struggling with major internal weaknesses may prefer to classify certain strategic decisions as confidential for obvious reasons.

2.3 Strategic plan

Planning is an essential feature and tool of strategic management. It helps to apply strategic management in a structured manner, with due regard to proportions and coherence between the institution's objectives, programmes, outputs and resources. A strategic plan can be used as a general reference document for further management action as well as for orienting every individual. That is why quite a few institutions have introduced strategic planning.

This being said, the reader should recall that not every planning for three, five or more years ahead deserves to be called strategic. If mere extrapolation is used to produce a plan instead of creative thinking based on thorough analysis of facts, or if analysis is overdone but does not help to find and take new opportunities, such planning cannot normally be considered strategic.[1]

The aim of this section is not to review planning methodology in every detail, but to point out specific questions faced by institutions that have decided to apply some sort of strategic planning. For instance institutions have to choose what to plan and for how long, in what degree of detail, whether the targets will be indicative or imperative and so on.

Many institutions in both centrally planned and market economies are requested by their parent bodies to use a particular plan structure and methodology, as a rule because their planning has to be harmonised with

---

[1] Cf. J.Q. Hunzinger: "The malaise of strategic planning", in Management Review, Mar. 1980, pp. 9-14.

sectoral plans embracing many other organisations. Such
binding methodology may be different from what certain
institutions consider to be an effective structure for
their own strategic plan. Double planning, i.e. preparing one plan for superior bodies and a different one for
the institution itself, is not a good solution and can
cause a lot of confusion. A compromise can be found by
supplementing the official plan, which enters the sectoral planning and control circuits, with internal documents
covering different or additional strategically important
aspects of the institution's development.

Time-horizon

In many cases institutions accept more or less automatically the time-horizon for planning given to them by
a superior body. Probably more from mere habit than for
valid objective reasons five-year plans are used in most
cases. Given the choice, at the present time of rapid
change institutions sometimes prefer to use a three-year
period for complete and comprehensive plans. In such
plans, numbers are tabulated year by year.

Selected aspects (e.g. building new facilities, preparing for the opening of a masters' programme and attaining its planned size, or establishing a geographically
detached and technically independent sub-centre in a
remote area) are normally planned within the time-horizons
judged necessary for their implementation.

Rolling plans (e.g. up-dating a three-year plan
annually by adding another year) are used in many institutions, but they can easily degenerate into mere extra-
polations as institutions cannot, as will be discussed
later in this chapter, afford to review their strategy in
depth every year.

Planning outputs and activities

In planning outputs and activities, the institution
will determine its product mix, key programmes to be
introduced or phased out, output volumes to be attained,
and other objectives (including qualitative ones) to be
achieved in its main areas of activity.

As regards its product mix - namely programmes serving a variety of clients from one or more of the undergraduate, postgraduate, doctoral studies and post-experience areas - the institution will, as a result of its
regular review and monitoring processes, wish to make
changes from time to time. These changes may result from
moving into new markets and perhaps relinquishing existing markets, and/or from a wish to serve present clients

more effectively. They may involve not only alterations in content but in structure too.

Planning for such developments can be a lengthy process involving the design of curricula, approval by university committees, centre councils or other sponsors, negotiating for the necessary resources and so on. Lead times of between 1 and 3 years (between recognising the market need and implementation) are quite common in universities and polytechnics for new first degree and masters' programmes. In post-experience areas, however, changes in the portfolio can be made much more speedily and, although most will be made on a year-by-year cyclic basis, it is not uncommon for new courses and seminars to be inserted in a current year with as little as 3 months lead time.[1] Consequently, a strategic plan will list individual important programme changes the preparation of which requires a long lead time, while changes in the portfolio of short post-experience courses will be planned in terms of the number of courses to be renewed every year, or the share of participants coming from particular sectors.

In post-experience work, the product life cycle concept is particularly relevant to such planning. As figure 3 illustrates, management courses and seminars may have a similar profile to consumer products. In the 1960s the Bradford Management Centre developed a one-week course "management science for managers" which ran once or twice a year for several years, starting with 10 participants and peaking at 30; it was withdrawn in the early 70s when firm applications had fallen to half a dozen. By that time other management science courses of a more specialised type had been planned and had replaced the introductory and more general course. Thus, in a similar fashion to an industrial enterprise, the institution must continuously monitor its product mix and plan for new products well ahead of the decline of existing ones. In some countries the typical pattern in centres with a substantial post-experience training programme is that one-third of all courses in a given year will be new and the remaining two-thirds will be repeats with some degree of up-dating and relatively minor rather than radical modifications in structure, content, and choice of speakers.

Within the post-experience area, one major product-mix decision has confronted many institutions in recent years, namely what should be the relative effort devoted to external and internal training respectively? In other words, how much of the institution's resources should be

---

[1] See also section 6.1.

Figure 3 Product life cycle concept

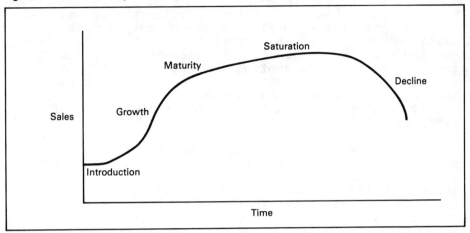

allocated to open market courses and how much to programmes for specific organisations or groups of organisations? The market has created a substantial shift towards internal training for many management centres which
began on a purely open market basis and figures of 20-30%
of total post-experience activity are now commonplace.
At the same time the development of more active learning[1]
methods for practising managers, such as action learning
or the Manchester Business School's "joint development
activity", can influence the post-experience product-mix
very significantly.

There is also, at strategic planning level, a
broader product-mix issue as already discussed in section
1.3: what is the appropriate balance for the centre at
various points in time between teaching, training, consulting and research activities? Most institutions are
launched with fairly immediate course commitments, but
the development of any substantial research effort, if
this is an objective, will be a matter of years rather
than months. Consultancy, too, takes a fair amount of
time to build up. In short, therefore, strategic planning must encompass questions concerning the long-term
development of both teaching programmes and research and
consultancy such as: In what areas do we currently
possess strengths, actual and potential? What areas
would we wish to enter? How will research and consultancy efforts complement and strengthen our teaching?

_____

[1] See R.W. Revans: <u>Action learning: New techniques</u>
<u>for management</u> (London, Blond and Briggs, 1980).

Planning people

The main task of personnel planning is to make sure that the institution will have enough people with the right technical profile, experience and training to carry out the required jobs. In a management institution this presupposes that its choices concerning the type and volume of planned activities are expressed in terms of manpower requirements and compared with the staff currently available, account being taken of unavoidable staff departures.

In developing countries, where professional staff are not readily available in adequate numbers, planning may have to take into account the lead time needed to sponsor suitable candidates for further training or to prepare them within the institution to become fully operational. A period of 3 to 5 years may elapse in such cases before a fully trained faculty member becomes available to an institution. The planning horizon, for this reason alone, will call for a minimum of 5 years. The estimation of requirements should also take into account the fact that at any time some proportion of the faculty may be away on leave or in developmental programmes. In order to avoid a tight supply situation, the forecast should make an appropriate allowance for this factor.

The following strategic choices will be reflected in personnel planning:

(1) the range of expertise, theoretical and practical, that the institution wants to establish, maintain and develop;

(2) the portfolio of action means to be used (proportions between teaching, training, consulting and research and the ways in which faculty is to carry them out);

(3) the standard faculty workload.

As regards the latter, it will be examined in chapter 6. Without going into detail, strategic planning needs global workload indicators (e.g. a faculty member has to devote 250 hours to class-room work, or direct contact with students, per year).

In some cases relatively simple global ratios are used, such as the staff/student ratio. For example the typical British university will expect its management centre to accept the same staff/student ratio as the rest of the university, e.g. in the University of Bradford the figure is 1:12. But this measure shows an enormous range of values from university to university. Even in the United Kingdom, a recent survey of 17 university manage-

70

ment schools, including all the major ones, produced figures ranging from 1:5.6 to 1:20. Staff/student ratios have limitations because the over-all figure for a centre will depend on the mix of types of course, e.g. undergraduates are less labour-intensive to teach than doctoral students, and the mix of educational and learning methods, e.g. small group tutorials consume more teaching resources than lectures to large groups.

Since management institutions are highly labour-intensive, a series of successive approximations with the financial (income/expenditure) plan will be necessary.

Planning facilities: buildings and equipment

Determining teaching and office space is not a difficult exercise if growth figures concerning the volume of work and staff are available and if consideration is given to programme changes likely to increase space requirements (e.g. more work in small groups). The exercise will confirm whether existing facilities will suffice or supplementary space will be needed. Problems may be faced by institutions that have attained full occupancy of facilities and therefore have to decide whether teaching or office space will be considered as a factor that stops further growth. In some institutions residential accommodation may be the limiting factor.

Interim solutions may be found in renting additional space. However, in certain cases further growth may be feasible only if new buildings are planned. The moment has to be properly chosen in the light of the institution's over-all development prospects and growth strategy, so as to ensure that the high investment expenditure is justified.

Thus, just as production executives have to plan for new plant and equipment so do management centre directors. Few engaged in such roles in the last decade can have avoided involvement in the planning of new buildings. The role of the director and the institution's management team may vary but as a minimum they must specify the broad parameters, e.g. how many students or trainees are to be accommodated and how many staff offices are required, and deal with specific issues such as what audio-visual aids will be provided and what computer system installed. A new site may have to be found; the strategic importance of such a choice has already been emphasised in chapter 1. Clearly expert advice will be sought and one of the many advantages of a large institution will be the existence of specialists in such areas as educational technology and computer systems. Many institutions have had excellent experience with a building committee. The director or his deputies will get involved

in more detailed aspects such as the mix of teaching
rooms and the teaching resources available, both human
and technological. Whatever level of detail the direct-
or prefers to work at, he must establish a harmonious
relationship with the architect. Their choices will be
constrained by economic and other factors such as legislation concerning health, safety and welfare, standard
space allowances per student and per staff member (e.g.
12 m^2 per faculty member and 6-8 m^2 per administrative
employee), or maximum building costs authorised by a parent body.

Once the basic design has been agreed, the director
will be well advised to monitor the development of the
detailed plans: even though he may not choose to concern
himself with detail, changes can occur at a higher level,
e.g. the positioning of the computer terminal room,
which he should be made aware of and have an opportunity
to influence if he so wishes.

The choice of contractor may or may not be a decision with which the director of the institution is concerned; in a university he will often not be, but in an
independent centre he probably will. It should always
be recognised, however, that the director has some degree
of responsibility not only for the outcome of the building programme but for the funds used for the purpose. He
will therefore be concerned with planning and monitoring
the progress of the building programme, and with prompt-
ing the architect, contractor or others involved.

As with any building programme, certain planning
techniques are useful. Gannt charts and critical path
methods are commonplace and the director, although not
primarily concerned in this aspect, may well receive
copies of these in addition to the basic building draw-
ings. Depending on the organisational context and the
method of funding, a careful eye may have to be kept on
the cash flow, a point to which further reference will be
made later.[1] The whole process is summarised in figure 4.

Planning finance

Whatever the particular financial structure and
degree of autonomy, all institutions must carry out some
form of long-term financial planning; many of the guiding
principles are not dissimilar to those applicable to a
business. The institution will wish to make projections
several years ahead of its income and recurrent expenditure, to estimate any capital expenditure for a time-

---

[1] Sections 6.4 and 6.5.

Figure 4 Main phases in planning and monitoring a building project

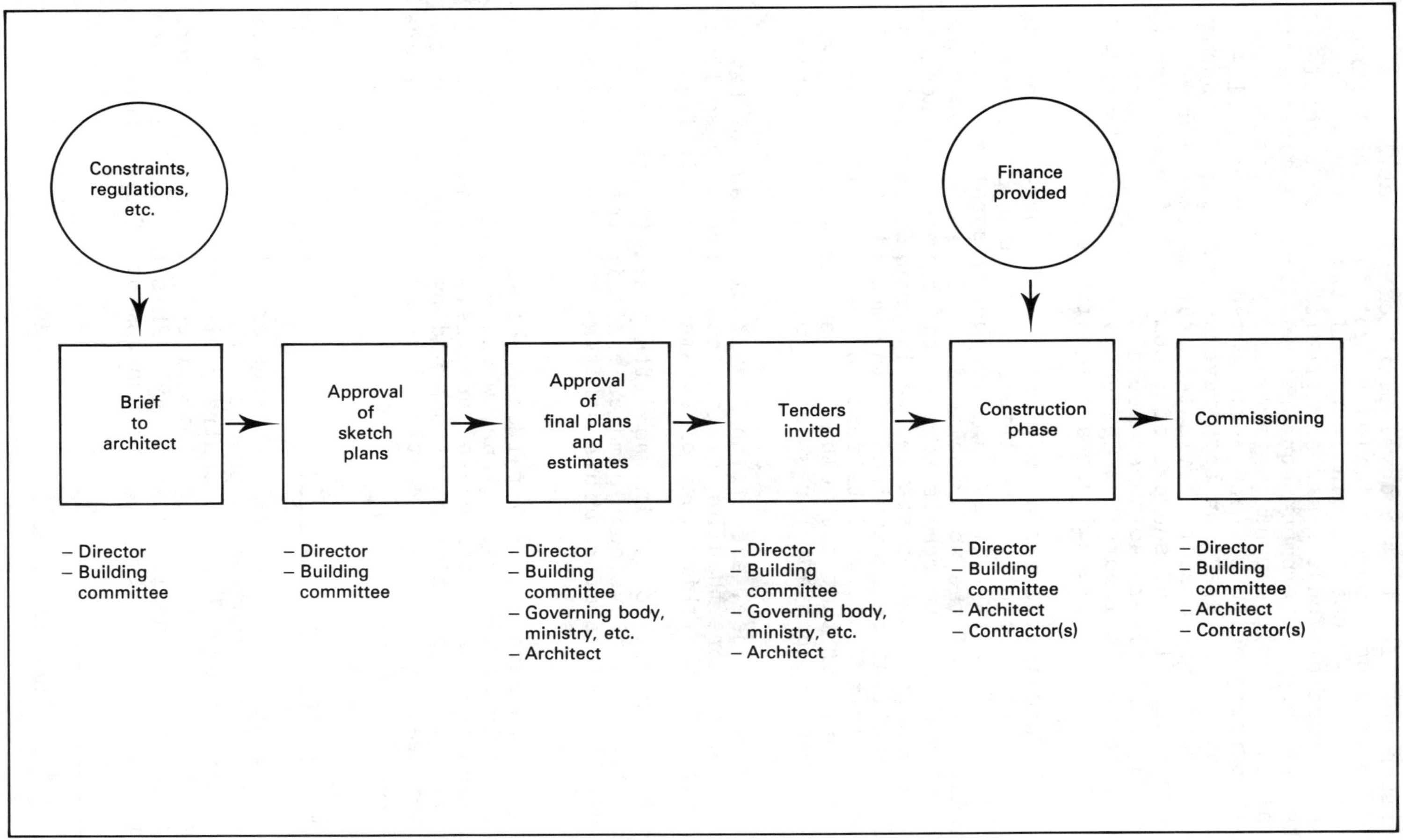

Constraints, regulations, etc.

Brief to architect
– Director
– Building committee

Approval of sketch plans
– Director
– Building committee

Approval of final plans and estimates
– Director
– Building committee
– Governing body, ministry, etc.
– Architect

Tenders invited
– Director
– Building committee
– Governing body, ministry, etc.
– Architect

Finance provided

Construction phase
– Director
– Building committee
– Architect
– Contractor(s)

Commissioning
– Director
– Building committee
– Architect
– Contractor(s)

horizon relative to the development of its facilities and to produce a more detailed budget for the next financial year.[1] These calculations will take account of: the sources of funding and any predictable or possible changes (e.g. government squeezes and their influence on real resources), demand patterns and their relationships with pricing policies, and anticipated rates of inflation and their impact on both revenue and costs. Income and expenditure must be estimated year by year and a clear indication of sources of income both for recurrent and for capital expenditure should be given, for example as indicated in figure 5. There may be a separate budget for capital expenditure and its financing.

A fundamental issue is planning the long-term shifts in the portfolio of the institution's financial resources. On the surface it is very easy to choose strategy and produce data of the sort included in figure 6. However, planning should be realistic and action needed to achieve major changes must be started early enough, in particular if an institution is advised at the moment of its creation that certain funds will be forthcoming for a limited period only or that the volume of certain grants is likely to remain constant irrespective of the institution's growth.

For instance, even if an institution does not have to generate more than 10% of its total income by selling services in the third year of existence and this figure

is to be raised to 25% in the fifth year, it may be impossible to achieve such a major shift in the financial portfolio unless appropriate strategy has been followed right from the outset.

There have been several cases of institutions, particularly in developing regions, whose serious financial difficulties have been caused precisely by the absence of realism in financial projections and by their failure to start searching for alternative sources of finance before it was too late.

2.4 Implementing strategy

If decisions on basic choices are the culmination of the strategic management process, they are by no means its final stage. On the contrary, the main task of management is to put strategy into effect, which may be more difficult than defining strategy. This has been foreseen in general terms: indeed, the assessment of institutional

---

[1] See section 6.4.

Figure 5 Basic financial budget structure

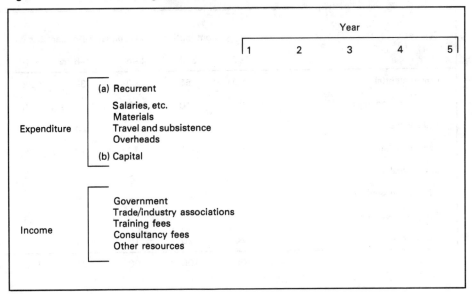

strengths and weaknesses should have answered the question about the institution's ability to implement particular strategies. This, however, does not reduce the amount of managerial and staff effort needed after the basic decisions have been taken.

It is well known that in every management institution there are centrifugal forces and tendencies and individuals often wish to do things that are inconsistent with strategic choices. In hundreds of cases someone will have to consider whether a particular assignment should be accepted. Organisational structure may have to be adjusted to strategy and staff members may be asked to tackle new problem areas and even to reorient their work quite substantially. This will be much easier, if as will be discussed below, strategy has been developed with full staff involvement and is not perceived by professionals within the institution as a constraint imposed by management.

Operational management

Making sure that human and financial resources are acquired, distributed and utilised and activities programmed and carried out in accordance with strategic decisions will be the principal task of operational programme planning and management. If this is agreed to, operational management will not be seen as an antipode of strategic management, but as its prolongation and executive

75

Figure 6   Projected shifts in financial resources

Sources	Contribution to total budget (%) in year				
	1–2	3–4	5–6	7–8	9–10
Government(s)	60	55	50	38	28
Trade and employers	20	10	7	7	5
Training fees	–	8	15	24	28
Consulting fees	–	5	10	17	20
Contractual research	–	2	5	7	9
Information services	–	–	3	3	4
Computing services	–	–	–	4	6
Foreign aid	20	20	10	0	0
Total	100	100	100	100	100

arm. However, operational management is not just a tool for implementing strategy. It has to ensure the smooth running of the whole institution, including areas for which no strategy has been established, and also react to demands and immediate opportunities that were not foreseen by particular strategic choices. It serves as a source of information and suggestions for future strategy.[1]

Reviewing implementation

Strategy implementation should be subjected to periodic reviews, to make sure that deviations from strategic decisions are detected and analysed and facts and ideas examined that might call for revision of strategy. For convenience, such review exercises will be made to coincide with the preparation of periodic (annual or biennial) reports on the institution or with the development planning cycle provided there is no dramatic change in the environment. Should these periods be too long or too short, the institution will choose its own timing. Rigidity is undesirable - no institution should continue

---

[1] For a detailed discussion of short-term operational programme planning, budgeting, control and monitoring, see chapter 6.

to stick to an obsolete strategic plan merely because,[1] once approved, it is regarded as an untouchable dogma.

Reviews of strategy implementation, like strategic analysis, can refer to the outline of a strategic audit provided in appendix 1.

2.5 Organising for strategic management

The commitment, competence and perseverance of the head of the institution will determine whether strategic management will be effectively applied. He has to be the leader when the process is being started, as well as the guardian of its continuity and survival. If the director ignores approved strategy or prefers to avoid making important choices, everybody in the institution will tend to substitute improvisation for strategy.

Involving professional staff

However, this top management responsibility does not preclude intensive staff involvement. On the contrary, the magnitude of the problems to be considered and the broad range of opportunities to be explored require the mobilisation of all available brainpower and experience.

This general principle has to be put into effect in organising work on various aspects of strategy. For example individuals or teams can be asked to explore trends and opportunities in certain sectors of the economy. Others can review strategies applied by similar institutions. As a rule, giving people specific tasks of strategic analysis is a more productive approach than merely circulating draft reports and proposals for information and comments. Not only can more expertise be tapped in this way, but working on strategy generates a quite different commitment to the decisions that will be made.

---

[1] A recently published witty review of corporate management realities makes the following comments on plan implementation: "Planning cannot possibly foresee all that actually can happen in the future ... Plans often must be disregarded or altered if they are not to be restrictive, or if one is to take advantage of unforeseen opportunities ... The fact that results closely approximated plans could merely mean that the planning called for less-than-optimum performance." A. Highman and Ch. de Limur: The Highman - de Limur hypotheses (Chicago, Nelson-Hall, 1980), pp. 133-138.

Brainstorming, working parties and other methods of generating ideas can be used in identifying opportunities and new types of institutional action. The PIP method[1] can be used to involve staff in the set of operations starting with an examination of the institution's effectiveness and leading to the clarification of new strategy and of action plans for putting it into effect.

Working on strategy is an interesting learning experience for the whole institution. In this respect management institutions are better off than many other institutions, as they can practice fact-finding, analytical, forecasting, planning and decision-making skills with which they are already familiar. These skills will be sharpened. However, the main benefits are in team-building, improved communication and better understanding of how others see the future of the institution and how people working in different disciplines or functions of management can aim at common goals.[2]

Organising external inputs

Essential inputs into strategy have to come from the external environment - the constituents, the clients and other stakeholders who possess information needed for strategic choices and will be interested in their implementation. Whatever the autonomy of the institution and its formal links with constituents and clients, it should associate them as closely as possible with strategic analysis and consult with them on the choices to be made. Several ways in which this can be done are described in chapter 3: "Links with the environment". The institution's governing body or council is a particularly suitable platform.

---

[1] See R. Abramson and W. Halset: Planning for improved enterprise performance: A guide for managers and consultants (Geneva, International Labour Office, 1979).

[2] According to Mintzberg, professionals working in organisations prefer to define and follow their own personal strategies and those of professional associations of which they are members. It seems to us that management development institutions tend to constitute an exception to this rule. As management is the very object of their professional endeavour, professionals in these institutions are more receptive to thinking in terms of collective institutional strategy than the members of other professions (cf. H. Mintzberg: The structuring of organisations: A synthesis of research (Englewood Cliffs, New Jersey, Prentice-Hall, 1979), pp. 363-366.

Some institution heads see a conflict between the need for strategic management as perceived by the institution and their actual decision-making authority. They are afraid that the parent body controlling the institution could interpret any attempt to raise issues of strategic significance as an encroachment on its own authority. In some cases these worries have not been unjustified. However, this is essentially a matter of tactics and relations. If the basic idea that strategic management is good for institutions is accepted, suitable ways for putting it into effect should be sought even in situations where institutions enjoy restricted autonomy. For example the parent body and the institution can organise a joint strategic planning exercise without challenging the authority of the former.

A delicate situation is one of conflict at the moment of strategic choices. For example a ministry may reject the idea of sectoral diversification of programmes if this means "sharing" the institution with another ministry, and the like. No recipe can be given for such situations; the institution's ability to "sell" the new idea to its constituency will determine the outcome.

When and how to start

In order to explain its internal logic, we have described the main components of the strategic management process in a general way, unrelated to any particular development stage of an institution or to the already existing planning and management systems. Clearly, there will be a wide variety of situations in which institutions or their constituencies will decide to apply strategic management.

If a new institution is to be established, following the process outlined in this chapter helps to prepare a meaningful feasibility study and take decisions on the purpose, objectives, programmes and resources of the institution. Thorough strategic analysis will identify alternatives that could otherwise be ignored or suppressed prematurely. On the other hand, many assumptions will have to be made, for example in assessing whether the new institution will be able to build the competence required by particular opportunities. Experience has shown that in such a case it may be more appropriate not to develop a complete and fully elaborated strategy beforehand, as it will probably require early corrections in any event. As already mentioned, certain strategic choices can be postponed. Some objectives can be defined rather generally, anticipating that after some time experience will make it possible to correct them.

Various opportunities and causes may trigger off strategic management in an existing institution. The impetus may be external or internal; the immediate cause may be severe criticism of the institution's performance, a financial crisis, a new opportunity created by a major development in the environment, a higher-level decision to introduce a new planning system, the need to submit justified proposals for new buildings to the parent body or, last but not least, the staff's and management's determination to make the institution more effective. The immediate trigger will influence the atmosphere in which the process of strategic management is launched, the commitment of management and faculty, and the level and amount of creative thinking that will go into the exercise. Even if an institution is compelled by events to re-examining its strategy, the exercise needs to be approached with a positive attitude.

The guidelines provided in appendix 1 can also be used for preparing and introducing strategic management in an existing institution.

Examples from institutions

The Escuela Superior de Aministración y Dirección de Empresas (ESADE) in Barcelona carried out a carefully structured strategic planning exercise under the title "Proyecto ESADE 80's".[1]

In the first step all faculty members, including part-time staff, were individually invited to give thought to trends in the school's environment and to prepare written comments. This was followed by three-day meetings organised in five groups mixing faculty from various disciplines (about 10 in each group). The discussions focused on assessing the importance and probability of changes that could be foreseen in Spain and in the Common Market countries. In the second step individuals and groups turned to management knowledge and attitudes, trying to make specific suggestions on knowledge areas and on attitudes which the school should try to influence. The third step was used to examine threats and opportunities for the school.

Conclusions from the three steps were then summarised by the planning committee of the school and discussed with representatives from business, political parties, trade unions, etc. Again the results of the discussions

---

[1] See Proyecto ESADE 80's (Barcelona, ESADE, mimeographed, 1979).

were summarised and circulated to all faculty members for comments. Finally, the planning committee prepared summary proposals for the approval of ESADE's management.

The Centre d'Etudes Industrielles (CEI) in Geneva[1] undertook a confidential internal planning exercise entitled "The CEI in the year 2000" during the academic year 1978-79. Some fifty aspects of the centre's existence, relationships, successes and problems were examined in a working paper, comparing the years 1956 (when the centre was established as a legally independent entity), 1978 (the current year) and 2000. Discussions at the centre were pursued for several months. Finally, the director prepared a summary document which was again discussed with faculty and reviewed by the board. It is being used as a broad framework and policy guide for orienting the centre's management as well as the work of individual faculty members.

In a different context, a strategic review of the Kenya Institute of Administration (KIA) was carried out also in 1978-79.[2] The Government opted for an "external and independent review of the institute's performance and effectiveness" by appointing a review committee headed by W.N. Wamalwa. The principal and the senior staff of the institute were interviewed and could make a number of suggestions, but no one from the institute was officially a member of the review committee. The committee proceeded very systematically starting by analysing achievements, comparing results with the institute's role and targets as defined by previous reviews and various ministerial decisions, and examining the present profile and facilities of the institute. This was followed by environmental analysis, paying particular attention to the countrt's development policies and to the need for making the public service more development oriented and receptive to modern management concepts. This led to proposals concerning the KIA's future "leadership role in over-all training in public management" and to a set of strategies concerning its clientèle, programmes, training methods, staffing and facilities. Last but not least, the committee underlined that the KIA should "be given the widest latitude possible in its operations" and, in particular, that "its contacts and relations with client organisations should be unfettered".

---

[1] See also chapter 7.

[2] See Report of the Committee of Review into the Kenya Institute of Administration 1978-79 (Nairobi, Government Printer, 1979).

Some more detailed examples showing how various institutions approached strategic analysis and planning can be found in the case studies in chapters 7 to 10.

LINKS WITH THE ENVIRONMENT

3

The fact that a management institution does not live in a vacuum but exists and operates within a particular environment, seems to be self-evident. Indeed, it is widely recognised[1]. However, a great many problems are quickly revealed if a closer look is taken at what different institutions regard as their environment, what their real links with this environment are and how these links are managed. There is a great deal of confusion. This is perhaps the area in which the heads of institutions experience the greatest difficulties for various reasons. This chapter will attempt, therefore, to give an over-all picture of the institutional environment and map out the various types of links that are to be understood, developed and controlled. It will thus pursue in greater detail and depth the discussion already opened in chapter 1, which inevitably had to touch upon several strategic aspects of links with the environment.

3.1 Understanding the environment

It is very difficult to produce a meaningful description of a complex environment and classify its components. It can even be debated what is to be regarded

---

[1] "All organisations are open systems: they are influenced by and they in turn influence the environment in which they are embedded"; C. Argyris: Integrating the individual and the organisation (New York, Wiley, 1964). "The institutionalised organisation does not exist in isolation; it must establish and maintain a network of complementarities in its environment in order to survive and to function. The environment, in turn, is not regarded as a generalised mass, but rather as a set of discrete structures with which the subject institution must interact"; M.J. Esman: "The elements of institution building", in J.W. Eaton (ed.): Institution building and development (Beverly Hills, Sage Publications, 1972), p. 23.

as the environment of a management institution and what is not. For example, does the military belong to this environment in general, everywhere, or only in countries where the army is in power, a state of affairs that obviously influences government policies, sometimes places high-ranking officers in managerial positions in public enterprises and so on? In Switzerland, for example, there is no military government, but the hierarchical position attained by an individual in military service is said to have a bearing on advancement in managerial careers.[1] Is such an environmental factor of relevance to local management institutions or can they ignore it?

There are no ready-made answers and no recipes to follow. Factors whose importance is paramount in one country (e.g. religion) or in relation to one particular objective (e.g. improving the management of rural projects) may be absent or negligible in another country. In France, for example, the "apprenticeship tax" is a key legal and financial dimension for the strategy of management education and training institutions. It has a peculiar feature: enterprises may choose to pay it directly to an educational establishment of their preference. Needless to add how important this feature is to institutions' links with the business community.

Every institution should try to analyse and understand its own environment, which requires information, experience, hard work and, above all, immersion in the life of the environment. "The main way in which an organisation can get access to the information and skill that is stored and transmitted by a social system is to participate in that social system".[2]

Despite this variety of situations, we must try to provide some guidance. As regards the general approach, two points can be made. Firstly, a management institution will be interested in the environment of the management process in the sectors to which its action is

---

[1] "Training in command, as conceived and applied in our army, has always had considerable impact on the management of civilian enterprises ...", H. Wildbolz in Schweizer Soldat, No. 10, 1976. See also R. Mabillard: "Citoyen-soldat: à qui profite la formation?" (Citizen-soldier: who benefits from training?), in Chefs, June 1981.

[2] H.A. Simon: "The business school: A problem in organisational design", in Journal of Management Studies, Feb. 1967, p. 3.

directed. Secondly, it will be concerned with its own immediate environment, which will include all sources from which the institution draws its input resources, knowledge and expertise, the organisations and public to which it supplies its outputs, and the factors that have a bearing on its structuring and operation. Factors that do not fall within one of these two environmental categories can in principle be viewed as being outside the management institution's environment.[1]

Components of a complex environment

The minimum check-list that follows indicates the sort of factors that influence management processes, as well as the creation and operation of the institution itself. It is not very important how the factors are grouped: the main objective is not to overlook factors whose impact on management and the institution is essential. The check-list concerns an inter-sectoral national management institution; other institutions (international, sectoral, etc.) will need to adapt it to their setting.

(1) Economic environment:

- Broad economic setting
- Population and employment
- Sectoral and organisational structure of economy
- Development level and trends
- Country's economic wealth, its distribution and ownership patterns
- Structure of markets, competition
- International economic and trade relations
- Financial systems
- Remuneration structure and levels
- Income distribution, purchasing power
- Standards of living.

(2) Geographic and physical environment:

- Size and geographic location of country
- Distances
- Natural resources: deposits, status of exploitation

---

[1] See also R.M. Thorpe: "The external environments of organisations", in Management Bibliographies and Reviews, Vol. I (Bradford, MCB Books, 1975).

- Energy situation
- Transport and communication networks
- Climate.

(3) Technological environment:

- Level of technological development in various sectors
- Technological expertise, know-how
- Research and development: efforts, institutions
- Communication and infrastructure technologies
- Technology in management: computers, microprocessors, office and control technologies.

(4) Political and legal environment:

- Political system, forces, parties, practices
- Centres of power
- Impact of politics on management
- Structure, goals and stability of government
- Government role, policies and interventions in economic and social development
- Legislation (related to business, labour, education, etc.)
- Taxation
- Structure and health of public finance

(5) Socio-cultural environment:

- Structure of society: classes, ethnic groups, minorities
- Influence and pressure groups
- Social attitudes and values (related to work, business, leadership, authority, seniority, etc.)
- Cultural traditions
- Religious beliefs, organisations, traditions
- Social organisations (employers, workers): orientation, role, influence
- Industrial relations.

(6) Educational environment:

- General education: systems, levels attained
- Technical and commercial education and training

- Financing of education and training
- University: structure and traditions
- Studies and institutions in social sciences and engineering.

(7) <u>Managerial environment</u>:

- Ways of doing business, entrepreneurship
- Management systems and patterns: organisational, sectoral, nation-wide
- Educational background and practical competence of managers
- Social background and attitudes of managers
- Motivation and remuneration of managers
- Management theories and their practical application
- Availability of information (local and foreign) on developments in management
- Management development and similar institutions and programmes, other services to management.

<u>Micro- and macroenvironment</u>

A useful perspective is one that differentiates the micro- and the macroenvironment in the above-mentioned groups of components. For a management development institution, the microenvironment will be one with which it interacts directly through a dynamic process of exchanges, transactions and mutual influence. Institutional links, which will be discussed below, concern institutions, organisations, groups and individuals within the microenvironment first of all. The ultimate purpose of the institution - the change to be achieved - will normally concern changes in its microenvironment.

But here again, everything is relative: what is macroenvironment to one institution may be microenvironment for another one (for an international management centre, for example). Furthermore, the borderline between what can be qualified as micro- and macro- is not static and may be fairly diffuse. It may be difficult to classify a particular factor. Changes in the macroenvironment are reflected in the institutional microenvironment (e.g. the world energy situation influences the energy problems, costs, and management in particular organisations) and in certain cases the reverse may also be true: numerous and important changes in the microenvironment will eventually reshape the macroenvironment.

Information about the environment

Interaction with the environment imposes a major information task on institutions, which can hope to be effective only if they have enough information about various environmental components. If collecting and evaluating such information is left until the beginning of a major strategic planning exercise, the task may be unmanageable: there will simply be neither the time and the energy to gather and screen the vast amount of information required. True, not all environmental information lends itself to collecting and processing in a formalised way. Information on social values, traditions, power groups and the like is not acquired by any formal information gathering and surveys, but over years of interaction with various social groups and institutions; it is the product of experience, stored in the memories of people. However, in many institutions there are quite essential gaps in that part of environmental information which needs to be treated in an organised manner. For example only a few management institutions serving the public sector in developing countries maintain up-to-date files on the main public enterprises in the country, although these constitute the main if not the sole clients for their training and consulting services.

What can be suggested to improve this situation? Necessary environmental information might be sorted out in three groups:

(1) Information to be collected and processed systematically (information on the client base, organisations supporting the institution, changes in legislation and regulations, government policy statements of interest to management and so on). Up-dating this information continuously is a must, not only for strategic decisions, but also for current operations. Some institutions call this activity "screening the environment for programme innovation".

(2) Information to be collected and processed ad-hoc, through special surveys or campaigns (information needed for revisions of strategy, e.g. on new sectors to be served or on important unforeseen developments that may trigger off new institutional interventions).

(3) Information to be obtained in processed form from other sources. While (1) and (2) concern primarily information on the microenvironment, the third group embraces information on both environments (e.g. statistics), but relates mainly to the macroenvironment.

The institution has to organise itself, in co-operation with its clients and constituents and with other

88

institutions, to acquire and analyse information under
(1) and (2) above. As for group (3), in this area management institutions need help since the vast majority of
them lack resources for collecting, surveying and analysing all important information on the macroenvironment.
This affects their strategic decisions, which are often
based on fragmented and partial information.

Examples of help to institutions in reviewing
environmental trends and challenges are provided by several recent studies of the European Foundation for Management Development. In 1977 the Foundation completed and
distributed a study of needs of European managers.[1]
This was followed by a major joint project with the
American Assembly of Collegiate Schools of Business on
"management and management education in a world of changing expectations". The final report was distributed to
the members of both associations.[2]

Some examples of national studies can also be given.
Using the above-mentioned studies as one of the starting
points, the Dansk Management Centre initiated a project
"Danish management 1990 in an international perspective".
This activity aims at improving the co-operation between
managers from the private and the public sector, management researchers, educators and trade organisations, and
at formulating conditions and opportunities on the basis
of international and Danish perspectives.

In December 1980 the Norwegian Council for Management Development completed and officially presented a
report on social change and management education and
training. In the same year the Centre for Management in
Nigeria issued a report on the management research agenda
for the country, based on a comprehensive survey of needs
and priorities as viewed by Nigerian managers in the
public and private sectors.

An example of an area where many institutions (particularly those in developing countries) will need more
help with collecting and analysing macroenvironmental
information is provided by various studies of future
trends and problems of world development (the Club of
Rome and New International Economic Order reports, studies of future trends in management and education and

---

[1] Education and training needs of European managers
(Brussels, European Foundation for Management Development,
1977).

[2] Cf. Managers for the XXI century: Their education
and development (Brussels, European Foundation for Management Development, 1981).

other similar **studies**). Their complexity and volume make it impossible for a single management institution to follow and digest them, yet they provide a number of ideas for reflection and essential data to be explored in thinking about each institution's future.[1]

Insight into linkages

Generally speaking, institutional links are contacts and exchanges with organisations, institutions, groups and individuals in the institution's environment. They can be formal or informal, more or less regular. They concern matters of common interest, which does not mean that there must be complete identity of opinion or interest on every matter.

The world of management development being what it is, institutional links represent a rather complex network in any particular case. Most strategic choices made by the institution will require a particular type of link to be established and developed. To control this network and utilise it to achieve the institution's purpose is a key management function.

In practice, every institution maintains some formal or informal links with its environment. But a question concerning the real value of these links and possible improvements is seldom asked. If there is a desire to get a deeper insight into linkages and make a better use of them, it might be useful to follow the 7-step approach described below.

(1) Identifying existing and missing links:

With whom are links maintained and why? What missing links are to be established? A summary checklist, attempting to relate the main purposes of environmental linkages to partners with whom these links are maintained, is provided on figure 7 in a matrix form.[2] Should an

---

[1] Selected published studies are listed in the bibliography to chapter 1 (see appendix 3).

[2] Various attempts to classify institutional linkages have been made. For example the institution-building perspective refers to "enabling linkages" (providing authority to operate and access to resources), "functional linkages" (input and output exchanges with other organisations), "normative linkages" (with organisations sharing an interest in common social values) and "diffuse linkages" (any important relationships that cannot be associated with formal organisations and groups).Cf.J.W. Eaton (ed.): Institution building and development: From concepts to application (Beverly Hills, Sage Publications, 1972).

Figure 7 Matrix of institutional links

Purpose (why?) / Partners (with whom?)		Constituents	Other sponsors	Clients: business	Clients: public organisations	Clients: individuals	Social institutions and local community	Public information media	University and other institutions
Supports and inputs	Mandate and orientation	•••	••	•••	•••	••	••	•	••
	Acceptance and political support	•••	••	••	••	••	•••	••	••
	Resources (financial, human)	•••	••	••	••	••	•	•	••
	Expertise and information	••	••	•••	•••	•••	••	••	•••
	Demand for services	••	•	•••	•••	•••	••	••	•
Outputs	Transferring technical expertise	••	•	•••	•••	•••	••	••	••
	Transferring norms and values	••	•	•••	•••	•••	••	••	••
Closing the loop	Feedback	••	•	•••	•••	•••	••	•	••

••• essential; •• important; • less important

institution find it useful, it might develop its own matrix of links and also rate their relative importance in its own setting. Our hypothetical matrix shows that, as a rule, every purpose requires links with several partners or their groups.

(2) Assigning relative importance:

Essential linkages have to be determined and distinguished from less important and marginal ones. Essential will be those with the so-called "stakeholders" - organisations and individuals having a direct interest in the existence, outputs and performance of the institution. Constituents and clients are the main stakeholders. In many cases (e.g. institutions established as membership organisations) the same organisations will appear in the constituents' and in the clients' roles but it is always useful to see the difference between these two roles.

(3) Defining the form of links:

A wide range of forms can be used, from informal personal contacts, ad hoc meetings and consultations to very formal arrangements (contracts, committees, etc.) concerning various exchanges and services.

(4) Assessing the current status:

An evaluation is needed of how useful and productive particular links have been, what effort they have required and what problems they have given rise to.

(5) Considering links between links:

"The fact that an institute's linkages are also linked is important: because of this, the individual linkages are not separate and independent. They are interdependent. A change in the state of one linkage is likely to affect the future state of one or more other linkages."[1]

Institutions know that some critical links are outside their control: between government and private business, between ministries (e.g. industry, labour and education), between different segments of business, between private and public enterprises and so on. Some of these links are shown in figure 8.

---

[1] W.J. Siffin: "Factors involved in the evaluation of management training institutions", in Inayatullah (ed.) Management training for development: The Asian experience (Kuala Lumpur, Asian Centre for Development Administration, 1975), p. 269.

Figure 8   Selected linkages within the environment of a management development institution

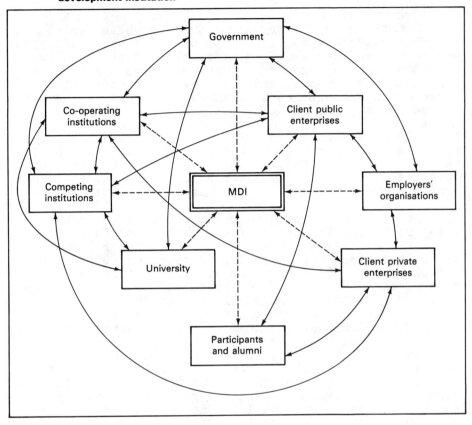

(6) Determining the approach and tactics for each link:

It will be important to decide whether and how a link should be nurtured and strengthened, maintained at the same level, played down or discontinued.

(7) Distributing responsibility within the institution:

As already mentioned, the management of key external links is one of the major responsibilities of the institution's head. In any event, there will be certain critical links (for example with the main stakeholders) requiring his personal involvement. However, he should not try to monopolise all links. This is not only a question of time. Some faculty members may have better personal qualifications to handle certain types of links. In addition, the institution's authority grows if faculty members demonstrate their ability to handle important external links.

3.2 Managing various links

Constituents

Constituents are organisations or publics which are most interested in the institution's existence and impact and therefore play a determining role in establishing, orienting and supporting it. There may be some formal legal link: the constituents may own the institution, the director may be appointed by them and report to them, they may have a majority control of the governing body, they may be members of the institution, and so on.[1] There is is a financial link, too: as a rule, constituents provide a considerable part of finance, in particular at the formative stage, when the ability to generate income from services is small. As mentioned in chapter 1, there are many different degrees of dependence on constituents.

In the overwhelming majority of cases the constituents are the government and/or the local business circles. Their respective shares and roles will differ from case to case: extreme cases are institutions established by either government or business solely, without any involvement of the other party. Business may be represented by employers or trade organisations. In France, for example the chambers of commerce are constituents of a vast network of private business schools and management centres.

Healthy relations with constituents are a key management issue. The real interest of constituents and their role vis-à-vis the institution may be changing with time. Figure 9 shows a case in which a government and an employers' confederation play a major role at the beginning but gradually reduce their involvement. Simultaneously, direct interaction with the clients keeps gaining importance.

While supporting the institution in principle, constituents may have different expectations. Within government, the ministry of industry may want something else than the ministry of labour; within business, large enterprises tend to require other services than small enterprise owners. The institution must try to understand the expectations of each constituent and "talk their language", i.e. present objectives, achievements and requirements in a way likely to be understood and well received by the given constituent.

The need for the closest interaction with constituents at the formative stage cannot be overemphasised.

_____

[1] Boards and governing bodies, which constitute a major formal link between institutions and their environment, are examined in detail in section 5.5.

Figure 9   Changing roles of constituents and clients

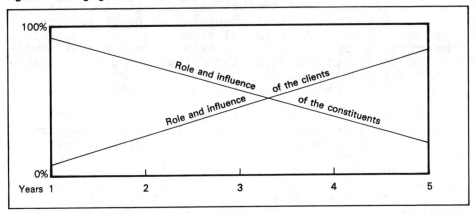

This is the stage when institutions depend heavily on
constituents. However, even if this dependence diminish-
es, as shown in figure 9, the main constituents should be
kept informed and sounded out on changes in orientation
and strategy. Also, opportunities should be taken to
render various services to constituents (ad-hoc technical
advice, examining reports, helping in preparing policy
documents, active participation in planning and similar
committees). This is not only an expression of responsibility and recognition but also a demonstration of interest in matters seen as being of importance by a constituent.

Direct membership constitutes a special case of constituents' relations with "their" institution. The members are not only the constituents of the institution and
its main clients: they are the institution. For example
in some countries of the Commonwealth the national institutes of management are private membership organisations
(management associations). The usual internal arrangement is that for policy matters the membership base uses
a committee (board) which, in turn, recruits and appoints
permanent staff for technical services and daily affairs
of the institute. The linkage institution-constituents
will thus exist within the institution, between its permanent staff and membership base.

Other sponsors

Many institutions enjoy the support and sponsorship
of some other organisations in addition to their constituents. Such sponsors view the institution as an appropriate instrument for achieving their objectives and are
therefore prepared to join the constituents in supporting
it. Support may be focused on strengthening the institution as a whole. It may be forthcoming from chambers of

commerce, private or official foundations, training and development funds or international organisations. For example UNDP/ILO technical co-operation projects have been used to provide technical expertise and financial resources in order to build up over 100 management institutions in developing countries. And a number of management faculties and schools have been developed with the support of the Ford Foundation and other private agencies.

In other cases sponsorship is tied to a specific work area and objective, such as establishing programmes for construction or population management. The United Nations Environmental Programme has sponsored the development of environment-related management training programmes at the CEI in Geneva and the introduction of environmental components into management courses through the ILO Management Development Programme. This Programme, in turn, has worked with the business schools of the Ateneo and de la Salle Universities in Manila and with the CEI for developing curricula, case studies and other training materials in environmental management for developing countries.

It is known that "other sponsors " have their own procedures for negotiating and approving grants and projects. Government ministries have an important role in this process: as a rule, formal negotiations pass through them and they determine national priorities.

Nevertheless, management institutions should have an active policy for developing links with organisations representing potential sponsors. It is essential to find out who the potential sponsors are for specific purposes and what their priorities and procedures are. Providing such sponsors with information on the institution and maintaining contacts that give evidence of the institution's competence and sound future plans can be very useful. Last but not least, any such sponsor, national or international, appreciates receiving objective information on what his grant has helped to achieve.

Clients: business

The institution's links with client business organisations are fundamental. It is with these clients that institutions have the overwhelming majority of transactions: they provide most services to them and in turn not only receive fees, but acquire essential information and knowledge of business and managerial practice. The views and priorities of business are determinant in programme planning and in evaluating the real impact of services. The more mature and independent the institution is, the greater is normally the importance of its relations with business clients.

Institutional strategy includes decisions on the particular sector or sort of business enterprises that the institution intends to serve. This segment will become the main part of its microenvironment; links with business will concern these client groups first of all.

Service planning and delivery, including their marketing, constitute the kernel of these links. Any institution would therefore have particularly close collaboration links with the client organisations for which it runs tailor-made in-plant training and organisation development programmes. However it is important to note that confining links with clients to the selling and delivery of training and consulting services would be an unduly narrow approach. For example, if an institution wanted to establish relations with top management, it might have to adopt another approach, e.g. by providing the sort of information in which top managers are actually interested, arranging conferences, meetings and briefing sessions for board members and managing directors, making personal visits at an appropriate level and so on. Basically, business leaders must be convinced that the institution lives with their day-to-day problems and is in a position to do more than organise courses and seminars. They must believe that they can trust the institution technically and make management information available to it without any risk. After all, in many countries the links between business on the one hand and educational and training establishments on the other, do not have any long tradition and many misgivings have to be overcome if effective working relationships are to be established.[1]

Many types of support are normally sought from business clients in addition to demand and payment for services, for example:

- information for developing cases and other teaching materials, and for research;

- opportunities for field projects and in-plant training of students;

- part-time teaching;

- assistance with student and participant selection;

- help with recruiting staff with business experience;

- membership in examination boards;

- feedback and advice on programme design.

---

[1] Cf. section 1.5, "Image of the institution".

Important clients, and organisations representing clients, may be particularly helpful in negotiations on the role and position of the institution.

Some institutions have had success with the so-called "business associates". This arrangement links the institution to a group of business firms that formally are not its direct members (constituents), but make considerable use of its service and want to see it prosper. Business associates are offered certain privileges, such as special information services or rebates on course fees and other services. The institution expects some regular financial contribution from them and would normally turn primarily to them when seeking support in the areas mentioned above.

An employment service for graduates is another way of liaising with business clients, used successfully by many business schools and management faculties. It helps clients to identify and recruit graduates with good qualifications for managerial jobs, and the institution to make sure that its graduates will be employed in areas for which they have studied. In addition, their training can be made more practically oriented in its final stage.

Clients: public organisations

A great deal of what has been said about links with business organisations also applies to public sector clients. We can, therefore, limit ourselves to commenting on what is specific.

If an institution wants to work for both sectors,[1] as is the case with many relatively independent institutions in Western industrialised and some developing countries, links with public organisations have to be based on a sound understanding of what really is similar or different in the management process. A priori judgements are not helpful. Not only the programme content, but also the way in which it is presented have to appeal to public managers. They must be convinced that the institution understands their specific conditions of action, objectives assigned to public organisations by government, problems of decision making, centralisation and decentralisation, political criteria and influences that cannot be avoided, and so on. If this is overlooked, an institution may be seen as irrelevant despite its excellent potential for helping public sector clients.

A special effort may be necessary to review programme proposals directly with groups of managers from

------

[1] See also sections 1.3 and 1.4.

public organisations and with units and departments that
have over-all responsibility for improving management and
administrative practices and for training managerial
cadres in the public sector. In every country there is
a wide spectrum of governmental departments and agencies;
they may have many different objectives, legal and operational autonomy, management systems and approaches to
improving performance. This will influence their links
with management institutions.

As for links with individual public enterprises, it
would be an error to believe that productive relations
can be instituted by decree: they have to be built on
competence and confidence, as in any other case. Public
enterprises that are under the pressure of multiple
social and economic objectives and from which higher performance is required, know very well that only high-
quality training and consulting services are of use to
them. If they have the right to choose, they will go to
institutions viewed as best. They are also keen to see
that confidentiality is respected and that an institution
is not used by a ministry to collect management information indirectly instead of obtaining it from public enterprise managers themselves.

Clients: individuals

Direct relations with individuals participating in
the institution's programmes have some particular aspects;
to manage them is not exactly the same thing as managing
links with client organisations, public or private. When
participating in training programmes, managers pursue
personal objectives in addition to organisational objectives. For example a general manager will be judging an
institution not only on the basis of assignments and contacts with his organisation, but very much on the basis
of the personal benefits drawn from seminars or other
events in which he himself has been involved.

Links with individuals are established and maintained in three stages.

In the first stage, potential clients are the target
group. The institution seeks the most effective way of
conveying its "message" and information on specific programmes to the management public in sectors it has to
cover, bearing in mind the managers' habits. For example
if it is known that practising managers do not read academic journals but do browse through the weekly business
annex of the local newspaper, this suggests where to
publish course announcements. Also, such announcements
should use a language appealing to practitioners, indicating to what sort of concrete problems the training event
is related.

Schools and faculties offering complete university-level management education recruit the major part of their students among the graduates of secondary schools, i.e. young men and women without practical experience. Their practices for informing and recruiting future students would differ from case to case. For example, the Ecole Supérieure de Commerce in Lyons organises briefing sessions directly at secondary schools and also information meetings for parents of potential students. As the ratio of applicants to accepted students is about 10:1 in this particular case and at some other management schools enjoying a good reputation in the country, there is also a system of relatively difficult admission tests. Intensive information and recruitment is thus combined with severe selection.

In the second stage, potential clients become participants. The main link will be provided by the teaching or training process itself: participants judge the institution by the quality of its technical activity first of all; if this quality is satisfactory it is much easier to establish long-term contacts with participants. If senior managers gather at the institution for shorter or longer periods, this provides an invaluable opportunity to tighten the links through personal discussion, consultation and social contacts outside the scope of the formal sessions.

Participants in longer programmes (management studies and some post-experience programmes) often organise themselves by electing a committee or appointing representatives for formal contacts with the institution's management in matters seen as important. In a management school this might concern the relevance of the curriculum to business practice and the placement of graduates after the completion of their studies. In programmes for practitioners, which tend to be shorter, this can help to create a pleasant work atmosphere quickly and provide feedback so that immediate improvements can be made.

In the third stage, the institution will have transactions with its alumni. If the concept of life-long education is accepted, and since many alumni continue to advance in their careers, they are at the same time potential clients for refresher and more advanced programmes. They are a source of demand for training, consulting and other work for their organisations. They are instrumental in strengthening the links with business and government and providing the institution with feedback, as mentioned above. Immediately, and in the long run, many alumni become key "supporters" of the institutions. Indeed, quite a few institutions could tell how helpful it had been when their alumni became minister or president of a major company, and had not lost personal interest in the institution!

The profiles and conditions of operation of various institutions being different there is no one standard way for liaising with the alumni. It is very common to keep them informed about activities and programmes. Many of them appreciate invitations to information sessions and conferences on business and management topics.

A strategic issue is whether to establish an association of alumni. There are quite a few such associations in Europe and North America and some institutions in developing countries have also created one. Such an association may strengthen the link with alumni and underline their belonging to a professional group that wants to support the institution. It provides a formal platform for interaction among the alumni themselves. On the other hand, it requires some organisational and administrative work. Travel cost may be considerable. As managers are busy people, they quickly lose interest if the association cannot offer very useful opportunities for technical self-development and social contacts. This has been the cause of decay of some alumni associations. Other problems have arisen in some associations of alumni attached to management schools granting diplomas and degrees: there may be generation conflicts within such associations and the whole association or part of it may become a pressure group engaged in defending an obsolete diploma and opposing change in the institution's profile and policy.

In a number of countries managers have established various associations where they meet for discussion and in order to deal with matters concerning their profession. In addition to general (inter-functional) management associations, there are specialised associations in virtually all functional areas of management, although a complete spectrum is found only in certain countries. It need hardly be emphasised that close contact with management associations is of great importance to management centres or schools and that many of the questions discussed in previous paragraphs can be handled through and with the support of management associations.

Social institutions and the local community

Any institution needs to interact with its social environment for several reasons: to enhance its understanding of social needs, values and aspirations, prevent a misinterpretation of its own objectives, enlist political support and get advice on how to introduce new concepts and methods that may affect social values and beliefs. Such links may be delicate and difficult to establish. Official decrees and decisions are not enough to overcome the initial mistrust and to get a new institution accepted politically and socially.

It is impossible to provide general advice on the contacts that should be maintained and how to go about it. This requires an in-depth appraisal of the political and social situation and forces, as well as an identification of cultural factors that are related to management and to the operation of a management institution.

In this area informal links will often prevail and be used to explain what the institution is, discuss potential problems and seek advice. In other cases the institution's staff should be seen participating in important social activities and events, thus giving evidence of their commitment and belonging to the social environment. Goodwill and involvement can also be demonstrated by helping social organisations to understand and resolve their own internal organisational and managerial problems. Quite a few management institutions have helped trade unions, voluntary associations, local municipalities, community bodies and other social groups to review their administration and organised information sessions and seminars on management for their members and permanent officials. In general, it is useful to demonstrate that management development and improvement is not an activity reserved to small élites in business and government, but a concept of interest to society at large, and useful wherever people co-operate for a common purpose.

The local community within which the institution is physically located, and where its staff members live, may be seen as unimportant by some institutions whose market is national or international and which, therefore, have limited dealings within the district. Such an attitude overlooks the fact that the local community is not only an external factor: it is also within the institution since the thinking and feelings of its staff tend to be strongly influenced by the value system and social relations characteristic of the community. In addition, any institution may need the local community's help on matters such as finding suitable buildings, expanding facilities, seeking accommodation for staff and participants, recruiting administrative and auxiliary staff, or arranging for various supplies and services.

Full participation in the life of the community becomes critical if the institution aims at improving management in traditional economic sectors and in social development programmes. In the words of a manager whose institution has been involved in such programmes, "... in this new world, management teachers do not deal with well-educated enterprise managers whose task is to allocate among a multitude of opportunities the abundant resources of large multi-national companies; rather they have to understand the problems of and to develop managerial approaches for development managers who must operate

within the culture of poverty, who must marshal government resources for the farmers, package them in ways that
they can accept, co-ordinate and orchestrate the efforts
of other development managers over whom they have no
authority, teach the farmers how to manage themselves,
and then, walk away." [1]

Public information media

In principle, an institution would use public information media to diffuse information that is not intended
for a restricted public (one client, constituents, members, etc.). Professional media (journals, information
systems and services) are suitable for disseminating
technical information to managers and other institutions,
general public media (daily press, radio and television,
etc.) for conveying information to the general public.

Although information media are a powerful tool for
forging links with the environment, in most institutions
this is a weak point of linkage management. Media are
used for announcing programmes and vacancies. Beyond
that, cases of close and fruitful contact with the media
are not many.

Many institutions contribute only very little to
professional information media. There are objective
reasons for this, such as the short experience of staff
or the fact that most good periodicals and information
services cover, in fact, only a limited number of industrialised countries. But it also is a question of linkage management: what is the institution's policy for
supplying inputs to professional information networks and
how does the staff apply this policy?

General public media could be used more actively for
informing the wide public of interesting innovations and
successes as well as problems and difficulties in the
management and training field. Editors should be able to
count on the institution if asked to write about various
economic and administrative issues. Periodic press conferences might be useful too.

3.3 Links with other institutions

The environment in which a management institution
operates includes other institutions that are active in

---

[1] G.A. Mendoza, President of the Asian Institute of
Management, in his foreword to D.C. Korten and
F.B. Alfonso: Bureaucracy and the poor: Closing the gap
Singapore, McGraw-Hill, 1981), p. ix.

the same or in closely related technical areas. This raises two questions of strategic importance.

First, at some point every institution is likely to ask itself what it knows about other institutions whose profiles and activities are similar or somehow relevant to its own programmes. Who are they? What do they do? Do they have their own client base or do they work for the same clients as we do? What are their objectives and strategies, strengths and weaknesses?

Once an institution starts getting and analysing information about other institutions, it cannot avoid the second question which concerns the relationship to be established and fostered. Should we ignore other institutions and behave as if they did not exist? Should we view them as competitors or as partners with whom cooperation is not only possible but necessary? Can we cooperate in ways from which both they and we will benefit?

Partners of interest

The first group of such institutions includes those pursuing the same ultimate purpose of developing management competence and improving management in practice. Some of them may be real competitors offering identical or similar services to the same clientèle. Others may engage in complementary activities: such is the case of a university-based school of graduate studies of management and of a training centre for management practitioners, or of a training institution and a consulting organisation. Yet others do similar work in other sectors or geographic areas or within large public or private organisations (in-company management centres and services). A management institution will be interested in this group of institutions above all. This is where most other members of the management development professions are employed and where the greatest potential for interinstitutional co-operation lies.

The second group includes institutions that are the homes of the various scientific disciplines, such as economics, psychology, sociology, mathematics, statistics, information science and others. Management institutions not only draw knowledge from these disciplines, but also directly employ faculty members whose primary training has been in one of these disciplines. Links with this group of institutions, which are normally located at universities, feed managerial institutions with a continuous flow of research findings and help to keep individual faculty members in touch with their basic disciplines. On the other hand, researchers and teachers in various scientific disciplines can learn a good deal and get new inspiration from exposure to practical problems.

Professional associations and scientific societies
also belong to this second group. As a rule, staff members adhere to such associations on an individual basis
because this helps them to keep abreast of developments
and in touch with colleagues employed at other institutions. Most institutions encourage such membership, in
particular for their senior staff.[1]

The third group includes a wide range of institutions and organisations whose primary field of action is
neither management development nor any basic discipline
from which the science and art of management draws, but
areas such as technological research and development,
quality testing and improvement, energy saving, regional
development, development planning, market and feasibility
studies, computing and communication services, office
equipment and organisation, finance and credit and so on.
In these and similar fields there are many instances of
developments that imply changes in management, and require
some retraining of managers, or where a service to
clients can be considerably more effective if technological, organisational, financial and managerial problems
are not handled separately. A management institution
may find it unrealistic to try to keep informed about
many different areas where developments could conceivably
influence management or require support through management training. However, it should be interested in wider
aspects of economic and social development as well as
technological and other innovations occurring in the
given environment. A narrow approach, e.g. viewing the
institution's role as merely providing courses in management techniques, can be best avoided if the institution
is in touch with the total development process and aims
at harmonising its activities with the endeavours of
other important institutions and social organisations.

In the three groups described above, the institutions of interest may be local ones, but they may also be
institutions in other countries and regions. Local contacts are essential if management institutions are to
improve the services rendered to the microenvironment, as
we have called it in section 3.1 above. However, links
across national and other borders are essential owing to
the nature of the management development profession,
which uses circulation of information from country to
country and international transfer of management expertise as universal tools that make it progress. Clearly,
the choice between national and international institutional contacts will be very much influenced by the size
and degree of development of the country and by the profile of the institution itself.

---

[1] See also section 4.4.

Rational approach to co-operation

Cases where a management institution would view other institutions as competitors only and intentionally refrain from maintaining links with them are very rare. Even institutions that serve basically the same market, as some international management institutes do, realise that the market is large enough and that even between competitors there is some scope for interinstitutional co-operation. However, the prevailing trend is rapid development of co-operation among institutions that have no major conflicting interests and are fully aware of the benefits to be drawn from co-operation. Of course, in a concrete case, every institution would decide how far to go in developing links with others. No one can afford to establish numerous and complex contacts and make commitments that would become a burden rather than a help.

A sound approach seems to be one in which an institution views co-operation with other institutions as a long-term strategic choice, thanks to which it will be able to achieve results unattainable otherwise. In this way it is possible to determine priority areas for co-operation, desirable partners, and methods to be used as well as resources earmarked for co-operation. A cost/benefit analysis will indicate whether particular co-operation ideas or offers are worth pursuing, bearing in mind that some long-term benefits are difficult to quantify. For example quite a few young institutions in developing countries have used long-term twinning arrangements with an American or European management school to build professional expertise and credibility and enhance their image with local management publics.

It should not be overlooked that real co-operation is a two-way process. Thus, while some very young and financially weak institutions may be looking primarily for help from others, there should be more and more instances of institutions that are simultaneously in the role of receivers and donors. These roles can concern different topics and partners.[1]

Some methods of co-operation

A variety of co-operation methods is available to institutions interested in helping each other. Figure 10

---

[1] See also Opportunities and priorities for co-operation, Report of the global meeting on co-operation among management development institutions, Geneva, 9-12 December 1980 (Geneva, International Labour Office, 1981).

gives a summary checklist of such methods with brief comments on their use and effectiveness. Some methods, such as meetings of institution heads and exchange of information on programmes, have been widely used. In many cases several methods have been applied simultaneously. On the other hand, certain methods are rarely used, although, if asked, institution heads seem to like them. For example many meetings have claimed more professional staff exchange between institutions, but in concrete cases institutions, especially in developing countries, have rarely been able to overcome technical, administrative, financial and other barriers. Also, joint programmes and services prepared, sponsored and managed by two or more institutions in order to pool resources and increase impact are little used.

An example of joint interinstitutional activity is provided by the International Teachers Programme (ITP), an intensive 8-week residential programme for professional management teachers and trainers run annually by a consortium of 8 management institutions from various countries. From a legal viewpoint, the programme is managed by a separate organisation established jointly by these institutions. Each member organises the programme once or twice and then the next member takes over.

An example of a joint service from the management information sphere is provided by the European Index of Management Periodicals (SCIMP) created by a group of 13 librarians of European management schools. The SCIMP selects and indexes articles from leading management periodicals, distributes them to subscribers in printed form and provides information on-line.

The Management Institutes Working Group on Social Development is worth mentioning, too. It grew from informal contacts between two Asian and two Latin American institutions.[1] Originally established for preparing managers for the modern economic sectors, these management institutes have become increasingly interested in management aspects of rural and social development. This being largely unexplored territory, they agreed on the regular exchange of field experience and the sharing of the results of action research concerned with new approaches to social development management.

---

[1] The Asian Institute of Management in Manila, the Indian Institute of Management in Ahmedabad, the Instituto Centroamericano de Administración de Empresas in Managua and the Instituto de Estudios Superiores de Administración in Caracas. See also chapter 10.

Figure 10　Interinstitutional co-operation: checklist of methods

Method	Comments
1. Meetings of institutions (contacts, experience exchange)	easy; good starter; not always well focused
2. Visits and study tours	easy; useful if properly prepared
3. Newsletters	useful if exchanged and read regularly
4. Exchange of publications	easy; interesting if systematic
5. Exchange of teaching and methodological materials (unpublished)	not too difficult; so far poorly organised; need to define what can be used
6. Fellowships for staff development (individual or interinstitutional programmes)	extensively used between developing and developed countries, less within developing countries
7. Student exchange	not difficult; useful if clear objectives pursued
8. Staff exchange	difficult; institutions hesitate
9. Using foreign teachers and consultants	very commun; useful at beginning, later to be confined to selected areas
10. Co-operative or joint research	popular at present; not all projects are effective; findings rarely applied and tested
11. Joint training programmes	could be used more frequently in new areas
12. Joint consulting and similar assignments	difficult; rarely used
13. Joint information and documentation services	promising but virtually non-existent; deserve attention
14. Joint design and development of new programmes and materials of common interest	promising; deserve attention; excellent planning and co-ordination is a must
15. Twinning arrangements (multipurpose)	very effective if partners well chosen; deserve attention
16. Programme co-ordination (division of tasks)	mutual confidence required; could be used more

A useful framework for stimulating co-operation and helping institutions to find suitable co-operation partners can be provided by associations of institutions. For example this has been the primary function of the European Foundation for Management Development (EFMD). To this effect the Foundation organises annual professional conferences (open to the wide management public in addition to members) and annual meetings of directors of member institutions. As mentioned in section 3.1 above, it helps members to study and understand trends of environmental change. It has also sponsored several studies into other matters of priority interest to European institutions as well as workshops and meetings on specific topics. Further examples are provided by the Asian Productivity Organisation (APO) and some other membership organisations serving management institutions.

Co-ordination efforts

In most countries, both developed and developing, a number of institutions have been established to provide management education, external management training, in-house training, consulting and other professional services to management in the private and public sectors of the national economy. In the overwhelming majority of cases, these institutions were created one by one, to meet a defined segment of national needs, as perceived by the constituents of a particular institution. Quite often, a constituent preferred to establish his own new institution, be it a small one, rather than to negotiate a reorientation or expansion of an existing one.

It is only natural that some division of labour between institutions tended to be installed. This may have reflected the original decision about the institution's sectoral focus, functional specialisation, types of educational and training programmes and so on. Some institutions have established their position and occupied a major segment of the market by giving evidence of professional competence and performance. However, it is also true that, in the course of time, many institutions have departed from their original mandates in searching for new opportunities and new types of services to offer to clients. At the same time management development and similar services to certain sectors, or in areas seen as too difficult and less attractive, have tended to be avoided by quite a few institutions. All in all, although there are fairly dense networks of management institutions in some countries, it would be difficult to define them as well balanced, harmonised and integrated.

The need for some degree of co-ordination is therefore increasingly recognised and various co-ordination schemes have already been installed.[1] The arrangements used include national management development councils or foundations, committees and boards for management studies, associations of business schools and other professional institutions, associations of management teachers, and so on. A distinctive feature of formalised arrangements that seem to operate effectively is that they involve the key stakeholders alongside the management institutions themselves. In some cases, for example when the Fondation Industrie-Université pour le Perfectionnement des Dirigeants d'Entreprise was first established in Belgium in 1955, the main initiative came from industry. In developing countries, governments have tended to take the lead, as in the case of the Nigerian Council for Management Education and Training, but full support and active involvement of industry, university and professional institutions is usually considered necessary.

In individual cases, the constituents may co-ordinate management education and training by instructing an institution to prepare a new type of programme by a given date or, on the contrary, to limit its growth or to refrain from entering a new field. This may be necessary if university-level management studies start proliferating beyond justified needs and beyond the parent universities' capacity to sponsor high quality departments of management. However, the prevailing trend is co-ordination by dialogue and consensus, whereby professional institutions, their constituents and their clients try to define their specific and mutually-related roles and agree on effective ways in which not only individual management institutions, but whole national or sectoral networks of institutions should develop.

The conclusions reached may take the form of joint decisions, recommendations to institutions, universities, governments and industry, analytical reports pointing out desirable trends, and so on. Selective financial grants, for instance for developing and introducing new types of programmes, have been applied in several countries. Focus tends to be on quality rather than on quantity: on the recruitment, training and remuneration of management teachers and trainers, the ways in which institutions can strengthen their links with the client base, the quality standards to be achieved by particular programme types, the research needed to develop training programmes adapted to local needs, or the performance standards to be attained by various institutions.

---

[1] Cf. Kubr M.: "Trends in co-ordination and planning of management education", in Management International Review, No. 1, 1974.

It is very likely that management development institutions will increasingly view voluntary and conscious co-ordination with other institutions as an integral part of their strategic management.

ATTRACTING AND DEVELOPING PROFESSIONAL STAFF

4

The quality of professional staff is a factor which many would regard as the most critical determinant of the effectiveness of any management development institution. In this chapter we shall explore a wide range of issues relevant to staff selection, appraisal and development.

The term "professional staff" or "faculty" refers to the institution's staff who initiate and conduct training, research, consulting and related professional activities. The administrative staff provide a variety of support services which facilitate the performance of professional tasks. The two groups complement each other, although in the management institution the pro-active role is played chiefly by the faculty or professional staff.

This chapter is divided into four sections. The first examines the links between institutional tasks, manpower planning and the mix of professional staff required. The search for and recruitment of professional staff are discussed in section 4.2. Problems in the appraisal and development of staff are examined in section 4.3. Finally, section 4.4 focuses on motivating performance.

4.1 Institutional tasks and professional staff

Professional staff requirements

The nature of professional staff requirements may vary from one institution to another for several reasons. First of all, it depends on the institution's particular mix of teaching, training, consulting, research and other tasks. Second, whether an institution is new or old and well established is an important consideration. A new institution must face the complex task of selecting and developing a faculty group capable of dealing with the entire range of the relevant functional and discipline-based subjects whereas an established institute may have to cope with only marginal additions to its faculty or occasional replacements in selected subjects. Though a new centre cannot hope to accomplish this task all at once, it must have a well thought out strategy capable of being implemented over a reasonable period of time. Third, institutions which are university departments offering long-term academic degree programmes will have faculty needs different from those of independent institutions emphasising post-experience programmes. The former will favour full-time, more academically oriented faculty, whereas the latter may make greater use of part-time and more practically oriented faculty. Fourth, to the extent that institutions specialise in the problems of specific industries or sectors in the economy, they will need to attract professional staff who combine substantive capabilities in the field of management with knowledge of the sectors concerned.

In all these respects, management development institutions in developing countries face more difficult problems in selecting and developing faculy than their counterparts in developed countries. Manpower shortages, constraints imposed by traditional educational systems and limited resource all contribute to this comparative disadvantage.

These differences aside, there are some basic considerations relevant to the selection and development of professional staff whuch are common to all management institutions:

(1) Management education, being an applied field, calls for a blend of theory and practice. The selection of faculty should be guided by the fundamental need to impart a professional orientation to its diverse activities.

(2) Given the interdisciplinary nature of management, management development institutions need to maintain a diversity of professional talents in the relevant subject areas and provide for the integration of the diverse functions through appropriate forms of faculty interaction.

(3) Professional staff can be drawn from two complementary sources, i.e. the relevant academic disciplines and the community of practitioners. The synergy of this combination can provide a significant reinforcement to the blend of theory and practice.

(4) The faculty mix referred to above makes it imperative for institutions to articulate their purpose and mission so as to act as a force that motivates and

114

integrates the **professional staff.** In the absence of a common approach and philosophy, faculty diversity could be a source of disharmony.

(5) Given the manpower shortages in the management field, it is essential for institutions to have their own strategies for faculty development and to remain sensitive towards the need to renew faculty. While some measure of staff turnover is to be welcomed, significant losses of this scarce input can be costly and difficult to replace. A stimulating and supportive environment within the institution is thus a necessary condition for attracting and retaining a good professional staff.

Appropriate staff profile

On the basis of the foregoing considerations, it is possible to present a broad sketch of the appropriate staff profile:

(1) A strong practical bias. The professional staff will have a strong commitment to the application of concepts and analytical tools to the real world problems of practising managers. They will view theories and concepts as a means of solving problems rather than as an end in themselves. Irrespective of their functional or disciplinary specialisations, they should be willing to play an active role as "users" of knowledge.

(2) An interdisciplinary orientation. Knowing that managerial problem-solving requires cutting across the boundaries of disciplines and functions, the staff will take a broader view of the links they should maintain with related fields of study and the need to work in teams to accomplish institutional tasks. A major implication of this attitude is that they will not remain narrow specialists, but will endeavour to understand and make use of the knowledge being generated in fields of study related to their own.[1]

(3) A commitment to improving management practices. The staff will view teaching, research and consultancy as institutional means of influencing and improving the

---

[1] "The one says here are my tools, where is a problem to which I may apply them. The other says here is an interesting problem, what tools might be appropriate to its solution. The distinction between a discipline-centred and a problem-centred professional identity is critical in the selection of faculty ..." D.C. Korten and F.B. Alfonso: Bureaucracy and the poor: Closing the gap (Singapore, McGraw-Hill, 1981), p. 233.

practice of management. They would therefore be client-oriented in their behaviour and innovative and receptive to ideas in accomplishing the institutional tasks assigned to them. Both practical bias and an interdisciplinary orientation are designed to strengthen this commitment.

Though the professional staff will be drawn from a variety of functional and disciplinary specialisations, the institution will be greatly strengthened if the foregoing characteristics are widely shared by its staff. The selection process could be used to attract persons who have similar preferences and to develop the desired commitment through appropriate induction experiences. Lack of a common understanding of institutional goals and unwillingness to work together to achieve them, owing to conflicting perceptions of goals and preferences on the part of the professional staff, are major reasons for the indifferent performance of many management schools and centres. Achieving a proper "fit" between institutional tasks and priorities on the one hand, and the faculty on the other, should be a major objective of strategic planning.

Main categories of staff

Unless a management institution pursues a single activity or uses a single means of action (e.g. teaching, but no research), its requirements will be for a mix of professional staff with skills in teaching, research and consultancy. Our assumption throughout this chapter is that most institutions engage in all three of these major activities although,as discussed in chapter 1, it is possible to start out with training programmes alone and later on branch out into research and consulting. On the other hand, some institutions may choose to stay in training only.

Institutions that use the full range of intervention do face a major choice which has a direct bearing on the categories of faculty required and the manner of recruiting them. Activities such as teaching and research could be organised either as separate divisions with their own full-time staff or as programmes in which all faculty members participate by allocating a part of their time to each activity.[1] In the former case, which we shall call the "single activity approach", those who teach or train engage only in that activity and nothing else. In the latter, which we shall call the "multiple activity approach", those who teach may also undertake research or consulting work. This may be done either simultaneously (e.g. 50% of the time for teaching and 50%

---

[1] See also section 5.2.

116

for research), or sequentially (e.g. two years of teaching followed by a year of research or consulting). The choice between these alternatives is a critical one and must be made deliberately. Generally speaking, smaller institutions will find it difficult to have separate divisions with staff who specialise only in one activity all the time. Larger institutes, on the other hand, may find it easier to assign specialised professional staff on a permanent basis to the different divisions because they are better able to maintain sufficient professional staff for each activity. Even so, there are many large institutions which have consciously decided against the single activity approach involving the permanent allocation of staff to different divisions or task groups for reasons already discussed in chapter 1.

These alternatives have important implications for the kinds of professional staff to be recruited, their evaluation and the developmental opportunities and career patterns to be planned for them. In the single activity approach, the endeavour may be to attract faculty who have expertise only in the activity for which they are being recruited. If the multiple activity approach is adopted, it is important to search for staff who are competent in more than one activity or who could eventually become so. The selection and development of multiple purpose staff will involve more complex inputs and processes. For example, those who are hired to do teaching, research and consulting simultaneously may be expected to have research degrees or publications to their credit and consultancy experience in addition to purely teaching or industry work experience. The assessment of these qualifications is clearly more difficult and complex. Special attention has therefore to be given to the criteria and processes used in the selection, evaluation and development of professional staff engaged in multiple activities.

Core faculty

Irrespective of the approach adopted, every institution should carefully select and nurture a small core whom the leadership can count on. In any institution there will be a number of persons who are new or inexperienced. There will undoubtedly be some staff turnover. Given such problems, the director of a management institution will need to depend on a core group who regularly share the burden of building and managing the major institutional tasks with him. There is, of course, a danger that a core group which takes on an air of permanence might degenerate into a clique or an élite resented by others. It is the mark of a good leader that he chooses and uses his close colleagues carefully without threatening the rest of his staff in the process.

Part-time faculty

It is common practice in management development institutions all over the world to use part-time faculty (external faculty, external collaborators, etc.) in addition to full-time staff. Some do it mainly because they cannot find good candidates willing to join the institution for full-time employment. However, the use of part-time staff is more and more part of a deliberate personnel policy. In particular, part-time faculty helps maintain flexibility in programme planning,[1] plays a significant role in establishing and maintaining links with the environment and provides access to special expertise unavailable in any other way. Some institutions have found that part-time staff is the best source for recruiting full-time faculty while avoiding the risk that new staff will be unable to transfer their experience to others.

There are two basically different types of part-time staff. Professionals employed at other institutions (universities, research institutes, etc.) help to keep the management institution in touch with developments in various basic disciplines and handle specific teaching or other tasks that do not justify a full-time appointment (in smaller institutions in particular). Professionals from business and government administration are used mainly to enhance the practical bias of training programmes.

Some institutions fail to work effectively with part-time faculty: an external collaborator may come once a week to deliver a lecture or case, and then go. However, more and more institutions tend to involve part-time faculty members in various aspects of the institution's work and life to enhance their feeling of belonging to the institution's total team, help in their professional development and use their experience beyond the mere delivery of teaching. Thus the various ideas and experiences discussed in the following sections of this chapter can in many cases also be applied with imagination to part-time faculty.

4.2 Search and selection: processes and problems

We have already noted the importance of manpower planning as a basis for estimating the amount and quality professional staff needed, as well as the fact that the types of faculty needed and their skill mix will depend upon the choice between the single activity and the multiple activity approaches discussed above. Against this background, we shall now present five strategic

---

[1] See also sections 6.1 and 6.4.

considerations relevant to the selection of professional
staff in management development institutions.

An active search strategy

In both developed and developing countries, the
supply of professional staff of the requisite quality
often falls short of demand. An aggressive policy of
search should therefore be an important part of institutional strategy. The conventional approach of advertising in the press and recruiting persons solely on the
basis of the response of applicants is unlikely to yield
satisfactory results in most cases. If there is excess
demand for the few who are well qualified, they may not
necessarily respond to such advertisements. On the other
hand, many who are not suitable may apply and a selection
may have to be made from among sub-standard candidates.

Some institutions have found it useful to adopt a
"push and pull" strategy for attracting high quality professional staff. They use public advertisements and
announcements to make known their recruitment efforts.
They then follow this up by contacting institutions and
persons in touch with potential faculty to recommend suitable candidates and persuade the latter to apply for the
positions announced. They might even informally meet
with some of these candidates to disseminate information
and interest them in joining their institutions. This is
in contrast to the passive approach adopted by many educational institutions who depend solely on impersonal advertisements and interviews to attract professional
staff. In some countries, institutions may be required
by their boards or governments to announce or advertise
their job vacancies publicly. But there is nothing to
prevent them from taking steps to improve the response
to the advertisements. The more aggressive institutions
not only take advantage of the "push" effects of public
announcements, but also use the "pull" effects of personal and institutional contacts and persuasion to draw out
candidates who might otherwise not have evinced any interest in the selection process. An active search policy
calls for a willingness to go beyond formal selection
procedures and experiment with innovative approaches.

A strategy to develop and adapt faculty

Reference has been made to the shortages of professional management trainers and consultants in many countries. In most developing countries there is the added
problem that the profession of management itself is new,
so that the available stock of trainers, researchers and
consultants in this field is meagre. Under these circumstances, management institutions need to follow a deliberate strategy of selecting young professionals with high

potential and **investing in their development, using faci-**
lities within the country or abroad. Many institutions
that have adopted this approach have found that younger
people are more flexible than older ones who are already
established in their professions. Knowledge of the functional areas of management (marketing, finance, etc.) and
the relations between diverse functions are new aspects
of learning to be acquired by selected faculty who may
have been trained in traditional disciplines only. Some,
who may have had academic training, may need to be exposed to real-life management problems by placement in industry for short periods as part of the faculty development
programme. This is an investment with potentially high
returns provided the trainees have been selected carefully and the educational or training programmes have
been well planned.

A major limitation of this strategy, apart from its
high cost, is that the new faculty become productive only
at the end of the developmental period. In the long run,
however, this is not a drawback as the alternative would
have been to depend on others, possibly older professionals who may be ill-equipped to deal with the new educational or research tasks and whose adaptability is limited. New institutions, in particular, should weigh the
costs and benefits of the alternatives carefully. On balance, they may find the strategy of selecting and investing in younger and well motivated professionals a more
desirable approach in spite of the added costs and the
waiting period involved.

Links with sources of recruitment

For the search policy to be effective, first of all,
management institutions should be able to identify and
cultivate important sources of supply of professional manpower. Three sources of recruitment have been found useful by many institutions:

- domestic academic institutions;

- foreign academic institutions;

- the world of practice (industry, government, etc.).

Academic institutions in the country (including other
management institutions!) are an important source of recruitment. Both experienced staff as well as fresh graduates who may need further training could be recruited
from this source. Where discipline-oriented and conceptual strength is being sought, this source has much to
offer. Economics, behavioural sciences and operations
research are examples of subjects in which young persons
with advanced degrees may be readily available. In many

developed countries, professionals with advanced degrees
in management and its functional areas can also be recruited from these institutions.

Foreign institutions constitute another important
source. Some management institutions in developing countries find it useful to attract foreign nationals for
varying periods until their own professionals are ready
to take over. Many smaller countries may find it necessary to tap this source on a long-term basis. Foreign
universities, foundations and international aid agencies
have facilitated the forging of links with foreign management institutions in many countries.

A more important use of this source has been in the
training and development of the nationals of the developing countries. In recent years, institutions in the
United States and Europe have trained a fair number of
young professionals from developing countries who were
subsequently recruited by institutions in their home
countries. Some management schools and centres have
found it worthwhile to visit foreign institutions, interview candidates and offer them jobs. Recruitment campaigns need not be confined to the home country provided
prior efforts are made to scan foreign academic institutions and locate potential faculty efficiently.

The world of practice, including industrial enterprises, government agencies and other organisations, has
professionally trained staff with considerable experience
and expertise in areas of interest to management development institutions. Many of them, expecially those specialising in post-experience programmes and consultancy,
often want a significant proportion of their professional
staff to have practical management experience. For such
institutions the world of practice is an important recruitment source, complementary in many ways to the first
two sources discussed above.

An active search policy includes establishing close
and personal links with all of these recruitment sources.
Through correspondence, personal visits, exchange of lit-
erature and joint training, research and problem-solving
activities, these links can be kept alive and made mutually rewarding. Management institutions should take the
initiative to keep these sources informed of their progress, opportunities and interests so that they can respond expeditiously and keep potential candidates within
their territories adequately briefed.

The use of a variety of recruitment sources, rather
than total dependence on a single source, facilitates a
more effective cross-fertilisation of ideas and experi-

ences. Different sources tend to complement one another and bring about a useful blend of theory and practice.

Role of professionals in selection

The participation of professional staff in the selection of their colleagues is very important. The concern here is not about the selection procedures used, but rather with the philosophy underlying the entire process of search and selection. When a new institution is established, it is natural that its constituent or governing body has to interview and select its first few professional staff members. In many countries members of such boards or councils are prominent citizens who may not have the expertise needed to assess the competence of the specialists being recruited. As a management institution grows, the task of selecting professional staff should be increasingly transferred to the competent professionals within the institution, with assistance from external experts if necessary. Through informal processes or formal staff selection committees, they can do an excellent job of assessing the worth of the candidates under consideration and recommending those who deserve to be appointed. In developing countries in particular, this approach should be encouraged so that internal professional capabilities in seeking and selecting competent staff are developed. The delineation of the relative roles of the parent bodies, the boards and the faculties of institutions in respect of selection therefore deserves careful consideration.

Financing search and selection

An active search strategy, the nurturing of links with diverse recruitment sources and investment in faculty development are activities that cannot be sustained without adequate funding. Unfortunately, funds for these purposes are not easy to come by unless the management of the institution takes an active interest and raises funds, by seeking external assistance if necessary. Government, foundations and international aid agencies are among the sources used by some institutions in the past to finance their search and selection efforts. The point to remember is that an active search and selection policy can be planned and implemented effectively only when adequate funding has been provided to finance it as part of a continuing institutional strategy.

There are obviously many other factors, in addition to the five strategic considerations discussed above, which are germane to the search and selection process. The work environment provided to the faculty, the administrative services available, the professionalism in the management of the institution and opportunities for

growth are among factors that prospective faculty are
likely to consider in making their choice. It is important therefore that management institutions, especially
newer ones, disseminate information about their activities, facilities and opportunities as widely as possible.
This is an effort in which not only the director, but
also all professional staff can participate. The image
thus built will be a critical factor in attracting high
quality professionals.

4.3 Appraisal and development

Problems of appraisal, development and motivation
of people touch some of the most sensitive spots in any
organisation. It is difficult to evolve standardised
approaches to deal with these issues in the context of
management institutions, whose outputs, inputs and con-
version processes do not normally lend themselves to easy
measurement. Even so, it is useful to define the problems and present the broad alternatives which deserve to
be considered in this highly complex area.

Career planning

Professional staff need to be told at the time of
their recruitment about their career prospects and the
opportunities for growth and development they can expect
to have if they perform well. In professional institutions it is movement up the professional ladder rather
than the administrative or managerial ladder that should
interest staff. Openings in the purely managerial field
will be few. On the other hand, opportunities for advancement in the professional sphere can be greater and
the institution can be so structured that professional
advancement receives appropriate pecuniary rewards, with
the result that professionals do not look to managerial
posts in order to improve their economic condition. The
kinds of organisational structure and scales of pay which
are conducive to the accomplishment of this goal are to
be considered very seriously.

The professional grades and designations used by
management institutions vary a good deal, but most of
them would fall into one of two distinct patterns. University based institutions tend to use academic grades
and designations (e.g. assistant professor, reader,
associate professor, professor) whereas some industry or
government sponsored centres use other designations (e.g.
training officer, senior training officer, research officer, chief consultant). Generally speaking, it is better
to limit the number of grades so that the scope for hierarchical thinking and conduct is minimised. An operating
culture that respects professional peer authority rather
than administrative hierarchy is more functional from the

standpoint of work and morale. In explaining career prospects to new faculty members, it is this outlook that they should be encouraged to adopt and live by.

The problems of career planning will also differ depending on whether the institution follows the single-activity or the multiple-activity approach. If the professional staff are engaged only in a single activity (full-time teaching, for example), their growth path is relatively straightforward. If they engage in multiple activities, they could move up through different routes and the planning of their career becomes more complex.

Staff appraisal

A critical institutional function that has a direct bearing on the career planning, development and motivation of professional staff is the appraisal of their performance. In spite of the importance of this function, there are management institutions which do not have formal appraisal systems. Periodic appraisal or evaluation of individual performance serves a threefold objective:

(1) it generates useful information on the individual's contribution to the accomplishment of institutional goals;

(2) it aids the process of controlling performance and offers a basis for rewarding or penalising the individual depending on his performance; and

(3) it provides feedback to the individual on his work and helps to plan his career development.

Various approaches to staff appraisal are in vogue. One is to review the performance of a person only when he is considered for promotion to a vacant post. If such an occasion does not arise, the person's work is not evaluated. In a pyramidal structure with very few senior positions, occasions for individual appraisal may thus arise only when senior professionals retire or leave the institution for good. This is common in universities in many countries where each department may have only one professor. Most staff may remain as lecturers for years. Some may leave in frustration, seeing no career prospects ahead. Management institutions with structures similar to bureaucratic hierarchies also tend to follow the same pattern.

Second, in institutions where the staff are employed on a renewable contract basis, a person's work could be evaluated when his contract comes up for renewal. In this system, once a person gets tenure (e.g. becomes a professor in a university), his performance does not get evaluated any longer.

124

A third alternative is to appraise a person's work every year on the basis of what he had planned and accomplished. Though he cannot be rewarded or penalised every year, the cumulative inputs from annual appraisal can be used in deciding on promotion or other appropriate steps for his career advancement if the practice of annual evaluation is followed by a medium-term appraisal (e.g. at the end of three years).

Of the three alternatives, it is the third which comes closest to fulfilling the threefold objective of appraisal in a management development institution. However, if this approach is to succeed, a number of conditions must be met:

(1) There should be a well developed internal system for activity planning, monitoring and review. Each individual's work for the year ahead should be planned and the resources and support services he needs to complete it should be provided.

(2) There should be generally accepted standards of faculty workload which could be used in the process of planning and negotiation with individuals. While in the training sphere this is feasible, in activities such as research, norms can be evolved only through mutual negotiation and agreement.[1]

(3) The institution should have greater flexibility in the promotions it can grant and the resources it needs to sustain a reward and penalty system capable of motivating its staff. Clearly, a pyramidal structure for professional staff makes this approach difficult.

(4) As a number of activities will have a planning horizon exceeding a year (e.g. research projects, course development), a qualitative assessment of such activities should be attempted only as part of a more comprehensive evaluation of performance once every three years or so. The periodicity of this comprehensive medium-term review should be linked to the mix and duration of activities assigned to the individual and need not be standardised for all staff.

For all these reasons, management institutions need to be clear about what they wish to accomplish through staff appraisal and satisfy themselves about the appropriateness of the structure, criteria and process of appraisal underlying their approach.

---

[1] See section 6.2, "Faculty workload".

Criteria and process of appraisal

The annual and medium-term appraisals will naturally differ somewhat in their structure and content. The annual review's thrust will be on the quantum of work done in relation to the annual work plan, whereas the medium-term appraisal will focus on both quality and quantity as well as the individual's progress over time. One year is too short a period to evaluate quality and its improvement over time, though some inputs on quality can be generated on a yearly basis too, especially where teaching has been a person's prime responsibility (e.g. through evaluation sheets filled in by participants). In general, however, assessment of the qualitative dimensions of work is a more complex and time-consuming process and cannot be attempted meaningfully every year. All components of the activities and responsibilities assigned to the individual for the period under review should be fully reflected in the appraisal structure.

As regards criteria, there are important differences between short-term (annual) and medium-term appraisal. The dominant criterion for short-term appraisal will be one of efficiency, i.e. the degree of achievement of the targets for the activities which were mutually agreed upon between the individual and the institution. Teaching of specific courses, development of cases and other teaching materials and consulting assignments lend themselves to this type of assessment. While the physical completion of targets could be measured in this fashion, this criterion cannot be of much assistance in evaluating the effectiveness of the activities completed in terms of their expected impact on client groups (e.g. students, industry) and relevance and professional contribution (in research, for example) as judged by peers (e.g. other faculty, outside experts). The application of effectiveness criteria makes sense only in the medium-term appraisal since the inputs required involve an assessment of quality and take a longer span of time to generate and process.

In spite of the refinements which can be introduced into an appraisal system, there is no way of avoiding the use of judgement by evaluators. The reasons for this are not far to seek. While activities can be planned explicitly, and criteria stated objectively, the actual application of the criteria and the measurement of outputs in specific cases do involve subjective assessments and a pooling of judgements by the peers, clients and supervisors involved in the process. All professional staff are not engaged in the same mix of activities and so inter-personal comparisons become even more complex. These are problems which can shake the confidence of those being evaluated in the fairness and reliability of

the system. It is for this reason that the process of
appraisal assumes special significance in the context of
a management institution. Briefly stated, the process
should be such as to increase the confidence of those
being evaluated and give them a sense of participation
so that they respond constructively to the signals given
by the appraisal.

In specific terms, the process of appraisal should
be explained clearly to all concerned and an explicit
statement made on (1) what is to be evaluated, (2) how it
is to be evaluated, and (3) who will do the evaluation.
It is equally important that those being evaluated have
opportunities to provide inputs to the evaluating authority and have recourse to appeal in case they are dissatis-
fied. While confidentiality of personal data and inter-
personal comparisons needs to be maintained, secrecy on
the processes being used and total lack of communication
can be disruptive and harmful to the motivation and morale of the professional staff. Policy statements on appraisal have been prepared and circulated by several management institutions to their staff. In some cases the
staff are invited to discuss the criteria and processes
and offer suggestions for improvement.

The effectiveness of staff appraisal will depend a
great deal on what is done on the basis of its findings.
Where appraisal is made only for purposes of promotion,
the feedback to the individual is quick and telling. In
other cases appropriate feedback on performance has to be
provided to the staff involved and followed up with rewards and penalties designed to motivate staff to improve
their performance. Rewards need not in all cases be pecuniary in nature. Public recognition of exceptional
efforts and outputs, elevation in terms of wider responsibilities, prestigious assignments and nominations, further
opportunities for personal development and accelerated
salary increments are all part of the wider set of options
that institutional management has at its disposal to inspire professional staff to perform better.

Development: needs and options

There are different phases in the career growth of
professional staff. We have seen how in the initial
phase that follows recruitment new staff need to be offered certain development opportunities to make them more
effective in their new roles. These opportunities may be
quite different from those required by staff who have
spent a few years at the institution and whose work has
been appraised. The post-appraisal phase represents a
more mature stage in an individual's career compared to
his post-recruitment phase. Though staff development is

a continuous process, we shall examine it in terms of
these two phases for the sake of convenience.

Post-recruitment phase: focus on formal training

The most appropriate time to assess the initial development needs of a new staff member is when he is recruited. It is rare for a new staff member to be able to
reach his full productive potential without some early
efforts to strengthen him in certain areas. Even older
and more experienced recruits usually need some help and
guidance to adapt them to their new tasks.

Development in the post-recruitment phase can be
usefully tailored to the background and experience of the
new staff member on the one hand and institutional require
ments on the other. In particular, a difference should
be made between those who have had formal management education and those who have not had any such formal education, but have had either training in a relevant discipline or useful experience as a practitioner.

The development of staff who have had formal management education can be classified in three categories:

(1) Some of them may not have been exposed to the entire
range of activities of a management development institution. For example an individual may be familiar with
teaching, but not at all with consulting or research. The
development opportunities he needs are research and consulting assignments in which he can work with senior staff
or as a member of a team with others from whom he can
learn. A scheme of job rotation for a period with senior
persons who have been made responsible for his development would be appropriate for this person.

(2) Though formally trained in management, some new staff
members may need to be strengthened in pedagogical methods. If the institution wishes to use the case method
extensively, they will have to be given a chance to master it either through formal workshops or programmes or
through field work in collaboration with more experienced
professionals. An institution which intends to use pedagogical methods unknown to its new recruits should provide
them systematic opportunities to acquire the necessary
skills and experience.

(3) Some of the new staff, though well versed in concepts
and theories, may be unfamiliar with the problems of the
world of practice. In order to strengthen their practical capabilities, it may be useful to place them in organisations (industry, government, etc.) to work with managers on real life problems for a reasonable length of
time (e.g. one year). Such assignments, to be effective,

need to be planned and monitored as part of the professional development of the persons concerned.

The development needs of faculty who have had no
formal management education may also be met in some of
the ways discussed above. However, a more important possibility that merits consideration is formal training in
management. In particular, if the new faculty members'
training is in narrow disciplines such as mathematics,
economics or accounting, it is too much to expect them to
acquire systematic knowledge about management on their
own through informal means. Several options are available. Their full-time enrolment in MBA or PhD programmes
could be sponsored by the institution. Alternatively,
they could be sent to specially designed faculty development programmes.[1] Those who have been drawn from the
world of practice and need conceptual strengthening will
also find such specially designed programmes useful for
their development.

Post-appraisal phase: need for self-development

It has been emphasised in the preceding section that
the process of periodic staff appraisal should lead,
among other things, to the identification of the development needs of the staff at different stages in their
career. As a person grows in maturity, the nature of his
needs will also change. While at the entry point, he
needed formal training or participation in team efforts
as part of the learning process, as he matures he will
need opportunities for individual study, self-development,
and a change of pace from his routine activities. In
other cases, he may need to get updated on new developments in a specialised subject, or enhance his competence
through self-development.

Obviously, development opportunities in the post-
appraisal phase will have to be more individually tailored. There are several possibilities.[2] First of all
it is possible, through the annual work planning exercise

---

[1] For example to the International Teachers Programme (ITP). A one-year faculty development programme
was introduced in 1979 at the Indian Institute of Management in Ahmedabad. Section 11.1 of Management, administration and productivity: International directory of institutions and information sources (Geneva, ILO, 1981) lists
a number of national and regional directories of training
institutions and programmes of interest to new faculty
members.

[2] See also sections 6.1 and 6.2 dealing with work
scheduling and standards of faculty workload.

to earmark a part of the time each year for self-development. The practice of giving longer summer vacations to professional staff is derived partly from this consideration. Some institutions build in time for self-development in the work plan of the faculty. Second, once in six or seven years, professional staff may be permitted to take a year off from their regular duties in order to undertake research or practical work which contributes to their development. This scheme of granting sabbatical leave to professional staff may be more common at universities. In all cases, the cost of the sabbatical (salary of the staff) is borne by the institution concerned. Third, the staff member may be encouraged to go on an exchange visit to another institution or granted special leave to accept a fixed-term, external assignment for a year or two. This again provides a change of pace and opportunities to acquire new experiences.

Of these options, it is only the sabbatical leave that can be institutionalised and practised with regularity. Other options such as exchange and visiting assignments or study leave for updating and self-development are less predictable in terms of the opportunities institutions can offer to their staff. There is therefore all the more reason why the identification of development needs should be tied to the process of appraisal, so that a conscious search for development opportunities is initiated by both the institution and the staff concerned.

One of the benefits of a carefully planned faculty development programme is that it will provide unusual opportunities for job enrichment. Management institutions with multiple activities have a built-in facility to let their faculty choose and vary the mix of activities that they would like to engage in at a given time, subject to institutional needs and priorities. Institutions which are predominantly concerned with only one activity such as teaching or consulting are more limited in this respect. They should therefore deliberately seek ways and means of encouraging their staff to develop new and innovative activities or programmes since they may otherwise normally not get such opportunities. A number of suggestions for faculty development offered in this section, if implemented, will also contribute to job enrichment in the process.

4.4 Motivating performance: strategic elements

A well conceived strategy for the appraisal and development of professional staff will undoubtedly have a positive influence on their motivation to contribute their best to the institution. The important role that a reward and penalty system plays in this context has already been commented upon. The appraisal process should have a strong active component in order to make its impact felt on future performance.

It would be naive, however, to assume that the motivation of staff can be controlled solely by systems of appraisal and development. A good deal of the work of professional staff in management institutions does not lend itself to direct supervision and day-to-day control. Incentive systems cannot be designed and practised in the same fashion as is common in manufacturing enterprises. The appraisal system should therefore be reinforced by other elements which, along with appraisal, should constitute a comprehensive strategy for motivating professional staff.

Healthy compensation policies are essential. However, no less important are some other factors, which will also be reviewed in this section.

Compensation policies

Institutions set up under private auspices normally have greater flexibility in the use of monetary incentives. They can adopt salary structures that are competitive with other organisations, especially business enterprises, which seek to recruit their staff from the same pool. In most developing countries, however, management institutions are set up under state auspices or with substantial state support, and there is an unmistakable trend to bring their compensation policies into line with those of the civil service. It is not uncommon for faculty salary scales to be pegged a bit below the scales of senior civil servants and in any case not to let them exceed the civil service scales. The civil servants who are influential in formulating these policies are normally averse to the idea of building into the system the concept of monetary incentives and disincentives on the basis of staff performance. The end result is that the management institution's staff becomes yet another component in the civil service or closely allied to it, with very little built-in pressure for innovation and improved performance.

There are several reasons why this trend has to be reversed. First of all, the nature of the tasks performed by professionals at management institutions is quite different from that of the conventional civil servant. Second, the kinds of skills and qualities required of them are quite different. Third, the alternative opportunities and rewards available to them in other sectors may be much greater than those available to the average civil servant. For all these reasons, there is a strong case for delinking the salary structures of management institutions from those of the civil service and for

building into their compensation policies a system of
financial rewards and penalties based on performance.
Salary scales should be such that they attract well
qualified and talented professionals who will be creative
and innovative in the performance of their institutional
tasks.

Monetary rewards alone cannot ensure that staff will
be innovative and well motivated. Professionals are
certainly influenced by the quality of their work environment, and a host of other non-pecuniary factors. Even so,
when their compensation falls below a certain threshold,
the quality of their work and their sense of motivation
tend to suffer. It is for this reason that serious
attention should be given to the formulation of appropriate compensation policies at the stage of strategic planning with a view to giving the institution competitive
edge in attracting and retaining suitable staff. For
example in several institutions faculty members are permitted to retain the consultancy income that they earn
in full or in part. This provides an element of flexibility in their compensation and a visible link to performance. It does represent a departure from civil service norms and at least in part offsets the disadvantage
of the faculty salary scales being tied rigidly to government scales.

When competitive salary structures are adopted,
institutions have a corresponding responsibility to demand good performance from their staff and to penalise
those who do not measure up. In other words compensation
and evaluation policies should be such that those who do
well are rewarded and those who perform poorly on the
basis of accepted criteria are penalised and, if necessary,
made to leave. The excessive sense of job security that
is often associated with government service is not something to be cultivated in institutions that place a pre-
mium on innovation and creativity.

Leadership and direction

A major factor determining the performance of professional staff is the quality of the leadership of the
institution. It is top management that sets the goals
and pace of work for the staff. The sense of direction
that the leadership provides and the institutional environment and processes it fosters have a bearing on the creativity and innovativeness that characterise an effective professional institution. A leadership that is ob-
sessed with procedural and hierarchical controls is likely to encourage organisational rigidities and stifle creativity. On the other hand, a leadership that is accessible to the staff, receptive to ideas and encourages
experimentation, questioning and risk-taking will tend to

stimulate innovativeness and commitment on the part of
the faculty. Exciting ideas, programmes and projects
have often emerged through the process of close interaction between the faculty and those who direct them, and
the interest of senior members of the faculty in nurturing and inspiring younger ones in their creative efforts.

Participation in institution-building and operational management

A participative role for the professional staff in
institution-building is another factor that contributes
to better motivation. Teaching, research and consulting
are creative endeavours in which those who carry them out
should feel completely involved. A strong sense of
involvement will exist only when they have a decisive
role in designing, planning, and conducting the programmes. They should be encouraged to participate in the
strategic planning processes of their institutions[1] so
that they can contribute new ideas and commit themselves
to the new goals and tasks being evolved as a guide to
future action. Management development institutions should
foster an operating culture in which responsibility for
planning and implementing all the tasks involved is given
to the faculty groups concerned. The urge to be creative
and to excel will be strengthened when the professional
staff is made to play an active role in the affairs of
the institution. It is common practice in management
institutions in several countries to have staff committees
to develop policies and plans for all major institutional
activities and to oversee the management of programmes.
Heads of activity groups and departments also tend to be
appointed for specified periods and not on a permanent
basis so that new ideas get injected and different persons
get opportunities to influence programme conduct.[2]

Job enrichment

A considerable advantage of working with a professional institution is a steadily evolving work content,
due to changes in the wide range of factors affecting
management in practice and to the development of management theory. In addition, there are considerable opportunities for job enrichment such as pioneering development work in new areas and sectors that the institution
intends to enter. It might often be more productive to
entrust such new assignments to competent faculty members

---

[1] See also section 2.5.

[2] For a more detailed discussion of the organisation
al patterns used see chapter 5.

than to recruit new people for this purpose. The motivational effects of such job enrichment can be very strong.

Commitment to the profession

In the final analysis, it is the faculty's commitment to their profession which constitutes the foundation of their motivation. No one will become a good teacher or consultant if he joins the institution and stays with it only because of a good salary and job security. Working with a management institution is demanding on time and intellect; only those who like teaching and consulting and are committed to "their" institution are likely to be successful and find their job satisfying.

Given a set of activities the outputs of which is not easy to measure and the supervision and control of which are exceedingly complex, the quality of the staff and their inner urge to maintain high professional standards give the best assurance of performance. A sound appraisal policy and good leadership are not substitutes for professional quality and commitment to institutional tasks. As we have noted before, quality control is best exercised at the entry point. It is, therefore, at the stage of the search and selection process that the foundation is laid to ensure that the faculty will be potentially creative and innovative.

Commitment to the profession can be enhanced and the quality of staff increased through active involvement in professional associations and societies. Some of these associations accept only members meeting certain professional criteria or have several categories of membership reflecting such criteria. They are a meeting place for individual professionals from various institutions and an important source of technical information and ideas. Senior staff in particular should be encouraged to be active members of such associations within the possibilities that the institution is able to offer.[1]

---

[1] See also section 3.4.

ORGANISING THE INSTITUTION

5

Organisational structure refers to the more or less fixed and formal relationship of roles and tasks to be performed in achieving organisational goals, the grouping of activities and people, the delegation of authority and the vertical and horizontal information flows in the organisation.

It is generally recognised that any complex social organisation, including organisations whose "business" is developing knowledge and helping to implement change, needs an appropriate organisational structure to operate effectively and efficiently. It is also generally recognised that there are no universally valid organisational solutions and that structure must never become an end in itself.

However, in organisational practice there is often a tendency to choose from a limited number of models and apply principles whose origin is, as a rule, in traditional manufacturing industry or in public administration. This reflects the fact that organisational theory has focused on these two sectors and drawn primarily from their experience. It is only recently that high technology industries, research and development organisations, information processing and generating organisations, adult education and training establishments and similar entities started being seen as organisations that may have their own, very particular, organisational problems and needs.

Management institutions have not escaped these pitfalls. For example many of them aim at applying some form of matrix management, but simultaneously try to stick to the "golden rule" whereby every subordinate should be assigned to a single boss.

There is a need to give more consideration to what processes and people in management institutions require in order to be provided with an effective and healthy organisational framework. Instead of reviewing organisational theory and practice in general, this chapter will therefore start by examining those characteristics of management institutions whose influence on organisation is essential. In the subsequent sections, an attempt will be made to describe and explain organisational arrangements that tend to prevail in the current practice of management institutions.

5.1 Factors affecting structure

Nature of tasks and people performing them

There is, first of all, the nature of the basic tasks in a management institution: of the teaching, training, research, advisory, consulting, systems development, information, and similar tasks. They have a high intellectual content and require the application of considerable individual judgement. They include only few routine elements and it is difficult to programme them in detail and standardise them. Hence they need a form of organisation in which the work assigned to individuals is defined in rather broad terms, on a relatively long-term basis, eliminating the need for frequent controls and detailed instructions by a superior. The individual is given considerable freedom to decide how best to perform his task and co-ordinate his work directly with that of colleagues performing similar tasks. He works relatively independently of his colleagues, but closely with the clients he serves.[1] He is encouraged to show initiative.

The profiles of people in such an organisation reflect the nature of the tasks: they are highly educated and skilled professionals who do not need detailed instructions and guidance, perhaps with the exception of junior staff who have not yet attained a professional level of skill.

Organisational unity and coherence, and the possibility to carry out tasks requiring involvement of groups of professionals, are ensured by the standardisation of skills and knowledge, and also by induction training and indoctrination of new staff joining the institutions. As already mentioned, in developing countries, where most management institutions start their operations with less

---

[1] Cf. H. Mintzberg: The structuring of organisations: A synthesis of the research (Englewood Cliffs, New Jersey, Prentice-Hall, 1979), p. 349. Chapter 19 entitled "Professional bureaucracy" is particularly relevant.

experienced staff, a very solid initial staff training is an essential condition of establishing the institution as a really professional entity.

In such an organisation, job descriptions do not lose their function, but excessively detailed job descriptions are to be avoided. In particular, the requisite articulation of tasks and functions must not be allowed to develop into a bureaucratic structure where confidence, enthusiasm and initiative give way to formalisation and power struggles. A disorganised but committed and enthusiastic professional team can be more productive than a bureaucracy perfect in appearance but out of line with the nature of work and objectives of a management institution! For such institutions, organisational rigidity kills creativity.

Providing information on the institution's objectives and policies to individuals enjoying a relatively high degree of work freedom is essential. Consultative/participative styles of management are a very good way of providing this information and helping every individual to see and perform his particular task in the wider context of the institution's programmes and strategies.

The tasks and people described above constitute the professional core of a management institution; some basic approaches to organising this professional core will be discussed below in section 5.2. However, in addition to the core tasks there is a range of support tasks that have to be performed in a management institution as in any modern organisation: they provide the necessary administrative, logistic and other support to the basic missions of the institution carried out by the professional core.

The range of these tasks depends on many factors. In particular, it reflects the size and complexity of the institution and its conception of functional independence. Besides internal administration, management institutions may choose to build their own support services in areas such as printing and publishing, book selling, catering, accommodating participants and so on. Alternatively, such services may be purchased from external suppliers.

Some organisational principles for this area will be explored in section 5.3. At this point the different nature of administrative and support functions is to be noted. They consist, essentially, of routine tasks that can be relatively easily standardised. They do not require highly educated professionals, although they should be carried out by well trained, conscientious and reliable personnel.

Management institutions differ in one important respect from other professional institutions as far as the relations between the professional core and the support services are concerned. In nuclear physics or micro-biology institutions, for example, there is a mental gulf between these two wings. Special efforts have to be made so that they can understand each other. In management institutions some of the functions performed by support services are also treated by the professional core in their teaching or consulting assignments. A management institution can effectively organise its own accounting and budgeting, record keeping, personnel administration and so on, and staff in support services often has more than basic notions of what the professional core does. This should ease mutual understanding and co-ordination.

Disciplines, functions and types of service

The practice of management is inter-disciplinary and multifunctional, and so is the total programme of a typical management development institution. However, every teaching, research or other task is not immediately inter-disciplinary and many programmes or activities are limited to one functional area only. Also, most faculty members will be professionals educated and trained in one particular discipline (e.g. psychology or computer science), or their training and experience may be primarily in one functional area (e.g. marketing or production engineering and management).

The various services offered by a management institution complete this already fairly complex picture. These services are represented by teaching and training programmes, organisation development programmes, research or consulting activities addressing a specific clientèle, sector, organisation, group of organisations or geographic area, and so on.

Thus, structuring a management institution for effective programme delivery and resource utilisation involves combining disciplinary, functional and service criteria in grouping tasks, creating teams and organisational units, linking them to each other, and applying programme guidance and co-ordination within units between them. Achieving a balanced interdisciplinary and multifunctional approach in all programmes and activities of an institution is a major task of professional management, one that is far beyond the possibilities of organisational structure. However, the internal structuring of any institution can make this task easier or more difficult to perform.

In most cases tasks and people cannot be grouped according to the same criteria. Individual tasks have to

be grouped into activities and programmes to achieve particular purposes. Several tasks falling under different
disciplines and functions will normally be combined to
deliver one service or product. For example, a consulting assignment may require interventions in various functional areas of management and even some special disciplines, e.g. statistics or operations research.

Only relatively constant services that demand a
sufficiently high volume of activity permit a primary
grouping of professional staff into units according to
type of service. In such cases the common purpose pursued tends to impinge strongly on the profile of the unit
thus created, simplify co-ordination and provide positive
motivation. However, professionals tend to be isolated
from colleagues in the same discipline or functional area
and certain service-oriented units may be losers in the
game if the more competent and dynamic staff is fully absorbed by another unit.

In most management institutions the basic grouping
of individuals tends to be by disciplines or functions or
their various combinations. This makes it possible to
create homogeneous and technically strong specialist teams,
including leading and senior professionals alongside the
more junior ones. The total workload can be flexibly re-
arranged within the group, whose primary loyalty is to
the professional discipline or functional area. The group
tends to consider itself as part of a particular discipline and maintain professional contacts outside the
institution.[1]

But this arrangement involves considerable risks.
The involvement of disciplinary or functional groups in
preparing and providing various services requires a great
deal of planning and co-ordination not only in terms of
time and resources, but also in technical terms. It requires an elaborate co-ordination machinery. Some aspects
of co-ordination may have to be handled centrally, which
restricts the possibilities of delegation. This question
is so important that we shall return to it in the next
section and also in the last chapter of the book.

Even more dangerous is excessive departmentalisation,
in which the department is perceived by its members as
more important than the whole institution and a unilateral
approach to management problems tends to develop. "Departmental structures must not be allowed to develop within
the professional school or, if they are unavoidable, their
importance must be minimised ... Curricula planning, too,
can best be done by groups that cut across disciplinary

---

[1] See also chapter 3, "Links with the environment".

boundaries ... **It is not important what particular** techniques come into play in a particular case. What is
important is that the administration of the professional
school take the lowering of barriers as a major goal of
its policy."[1]

Strategy

Strategy and structure are intimately related.
A.D. Chandler's studies[2] demonstrated that a company's
strategy in time determined its structure, while to some
extent structure influenced strategy because of time lags,
inflexibility and inertia.

In a management institution the strategic dimension
is not necessarily respected if organisational structure
is built on the logic of work-flows or on the disciplinary
and functional mix of current activities. As a rule,
important strategic decisions cannot be put into effect
without reallocating resources and without deliberate
managerial and staff effort. If structure hampers instead
of facilitating strategic change, the whole process may
slow down and eventually stop completely. But the strategic behaviour of an institution does not start with the
application of a set of strategic decisions. As already
mentioned in chapter 2, strategic decisions are by no
means the starting phase of the strategic management
process: they are prepared by analytical, conceptual and
planning work involving not only the institution's management, but a considerable part of its total professional
staff. Structuring the institution for strategy therefore includes structuring it for strategic planning and
management, as well as adopting a structure that will
facilitate and stimulate the implementation of the decisions made.

The structural aspects of strategy definition and
planning were explained in chapter 2 and there is no need
to repeat them. As for structural measures in support of
strategic choices, there can be a variety of them and
each situation will have to be examined on its merits
before a decision is made.

In nearly every institution, one of the basic strategic choices concerns the use of a particular portfolio

[1] H.A. Simon: "The business school: A problem in
organisational design", in Journal of Management Studies,
Feb. 1967, pp. 13-14.

[2] A.D. Chandler: Strategy and structure: Chapters
in the history of the American industrial enterprise
(Cambridge, Massachusetts, MIT Press, 1962).

140

of means of **action: teaching, training, consulting, re-**
search, etc. Organisational structure should be congruent
with the strategic choices made. For example, if an
institution perceives the need to make a major sustained
effort in research, suitable structural arrangements need
to be envisaged. These may involve the establishment of
a research department with full-time research staff, or
faculty members may divide their time between teaching,
consulting and research tasks. If a high teaching load
is maintained, if faculty members find private consulting
assignments technically and financially more rewarding
than research, or if a research co-ordinator is appointed
but given no resources and no power, it is unlikely that
important research activity will get off ground.

To give another example, a frequent case (in developing countries in particular) is that of a management institution which has been commissioned, or has itself decided,
to initiate and implement a major programme for improving
management in a priority economic sector. This will require a whole range of new activities and adequate resources. But it will be some time before the volume of
services to this sector attains its maximum level and it
may be difficult to foresee not only when and how this
maximum will be attained, but also the exact portfolio of
means of action to be applied (how much research, teaching,
advisory and consulting work, and how each is to be combined with the others).

The question is whether and when to establish a
special unit in the institution to serve the target
sector. If it is established too early, it may be difficult to staff it and determine the work content effectively. If too late, momentum may be lost and objectives
never attained. But is a new unit really the best solution? Would not a task force or a special committee manage such a programme with better results and at a lower
cost? And if a special unit is established, should it
include all staff working for the given sector, or only
staff performing certain core activities, or should it be
essentially a programming and co-ordinating unit, drawing
expertise for specific tasks from other units? Many
factors will influence the decision. Among others, the
institution will have to consider the desirability and
feasibility of fully specialising certain faculty members
in the management and related problems of one sector. In
some sectors (often in construction), such specialisation
may be seen as necessary by the clients. But in other
sectors this is not the case.

Size of institution

Size affects structure in any organisation. In management institutions, where the operating core is made up

of professional faculty and the use of material resources
is limited to teaching facilities (and in some cases residential and catering facilities), the number of faculty
members is probably the most accurate indicator of size.[1]

As the institution grows, some of its programmes
tend not only to grow in volume but to become relatively
stabilised - hence a greater use of specialisation by
types of service in internal structure. In large institutions such units may become very independent, be granted considerable financial autonomy, and even organise
their own auxiliary services.

The number of rungs in the management ladder has a
general tendency to grow with the organisation's size.
In management institutions, however, this growth does not
seem to be linear. As the professionals in the faculty
are largely autonomous and do not require constant supervision, the span of control can be wider, the middle line
can be kept very small and the whole structure will be
rather flat, even in larger institutions. Steep hierarchies of managers and long chains of command are not
found in effectively structured professional institutions,
irrespective of their size.

The content of managerial jobs, too, changes with
size. The larger and more complex the institution, the
more planning, technical guidance and co-ordination will
be required from the institution head and other managers,
and the less time they will have for personal professional work other than managerial. A full-time concentration
on institutional management may become inevitable at some
point. However, here again one important feature of professional organisations has to be pointed out: the perception of managers by the professionals in their organisation. The managers' full-time concentration on managing must be perceived as professionally desirable and
in the interest of the whole institution. To avoid any
misunderstanding, in many institutions, including large
ones, the director does a certain minimum of teaching.
In some cases this has been instituted as a rule that
even the director has to observe. It is a good one.

The proportion between managerial duties and direct
professional work is even more delicate in the case of
other management positions within the institution. In
principle, every effort should be made to find structures
and co-ordination arrangements that permit departmental
heads and similar officials in the professional core to
spend anything from 30 to 70% of their time in direct
professional work. An unhealthy practice has developed

---

[1] Cf. section 1.4.

in certain institutions in developing countries, where
departmental heads feel that their job consists merely of
distributing and controlling the work of others.

Parent body

Many institutions are not totally free in choosing
optimum organisation; the over-all institutional set-up
within which they are established may impose a rigidity
of structure.

For example a centre established within a university
or polytechnic may find that it is constrained to a
certain form of departmental structure which is very
hierarchical - director or chairman, professors, senior
lecturers, lecturers, etc. - and to lengths of courses
which are inviolable. It may be impossible to establish
a separate governing body for the institution and the
director's decision-making powers may be fairly limited.
A university rector or senate may be the authorities to
which important decisions have to be referred, although
a senate's conception of what a management institution
should do may have a strong academic bias and its members'
knowledge of management practice may be very limited.[1]

Some public administration and management institutes
were first established as sections within government departments. They were subject to the same rules and procedures applicable in the rest of the country's civil
service in such important matters as budgeting or staff
recruitment, promotion, discipline and professional development.[2]

When the specific organisational problems and needs
of a new management institution are first discussed,
there often appears to be a conflict since the organisation and management style of the parent body are viewed
as sacrosanct. But such conflict may not be inevitable.
The parent body may be free to relax the rigid structure.
It should be prepared to do so if it is keen to establish
an effective management institution. Imagination helps
to find solutions even in situations that look hopeless
at the outset! If there is no possibility and no will to

---

[1] See also chapter 6: "Governance in higher education", in E. Rausch (ed.): Management in institutions of
higher learning (Lexington, Massachusetts, Lexington
Books, 1980).

[2] See e.g. Report of the Committee of Review into
the Kenya Institute of Administration 1978-79 (Nairobi,
Government Printer, 1979), pp. 14 and 42.

seek acceptable solutions, it might be better to conclude
that the university or other organisation in question is
unsuitable as a parent body for a management school or
centre.[1]

Culture

The way we organise ourselves depends not only on
the task at hand but also on the collective programming
of our minds and on the system of our collectively held
values, i.e. on culture.[2] However, the influence of
culture on the structure of a management institution and
on the style of managing it in a particular environment
is not simple and straightforward. It may be very difficult to perceive for people who have always lived and
worked in the same cultural environment. The opportunity
to compare with other cultural environments appears to be
a prerequisite for relating various organisational and
managerial concepts to a given cultural environment.

An institution's organisation is affected by local
culture or even a set of cultures in a country embracing
several social groups with important ethnic, language,
religious and other differences. The culture or cultures
of an institution's direct environment will have a bearing on the distribution of power and authority, centralisation and decentralisation, sharing of information, decision-making procedures, communication channels, preference
for working individually or in groups, and so on.

The organisation and functioning of an institution
is also influenced by the particular culture of the professions represented by its staff. This is a phenomenon
that crosses the limits of local and traditional cultures
and its impact in a particular case depends very much on
the intensity of links (both institutional and individual)
with the professional world. As already mentioned in
chapter 3, these links may not be as strong in the case
of management development professionals as in some older
and well established professions. In some developing
countries their impact may be fairly limited at the outset but it will tend to get stronger with the passage of
time.

Useful comments on culture in professional organisations were made by C. Handy of the London Business
School. Using the term "organisations of consent" he

---

[1] See also section 1.4.

[2] See e.g. G. Hofstede: "Culture and organisations",
in International Studies of Management and Organisation,
Winter 1980-81, pp. 15-41.

144

points out that the psychological contract between the individual and the organisation has a different slant in such an organisation. The individual tends to see himself as a valuable resource which the organisation ought to cherish. He is very much an individual with personality and with individual rights and must be so regarded. The contract includes some deep beliefs about the way people should relate to each other: hierarchy is bad, argument is good. While in the hierarchical state authority is conferred by those above, in an organisation of consent real authority is granted by those below - they recognise that management and co-ordination are needed, but the person who seeks to manage them must win their confidence and consent.[1]

Last but not least, the institution's own culture has to be mentioned. There may be no such phenomenon in a newly established institution, but experience confirmed by research has shown that it does not take too long for an organisation to develop its peculiar values and behavioural patterns which will influence its structure and management style. For example unwritten rules may exist on the sort of matters that the head of the institution would not decide without a consensus of senior staff, or on matters that would be reviewed in restricted confidential meetings instead of being publicly discussed with all employees.

In organising an institution, these various cultural influences have to be weighed. If it is decided to choose a solution unusual in the given cultural set-up this might lead to a cleavage between officially adopted rules and the way things work in reality. Or the institution's management will face the problem of changing established values and behavioural patterns, which, though not impossible, is never easy.

A general model

Figure 11 compares a typical organisational model used by management development institutions to a model prevailing in manufacturing enterprises.[2] It shows, in a condensed form, the salient features of organisation in management institutions: its flat structure, the absence of the middle management group, the amalgamation of

---

[1] See C. Handy: "The organisations of consent", in D.W. Piper and R. Glatter (eds.): The changing university (Windsor, NFER Publishing Co., 1975).

[2] Adapted from H. Mintzberg: The structuring of organisations: A synthesis of the research (Englewood Cliffs, New Jersey, Prentice-Hall, 1979).

Figure 11   Two models of organisation

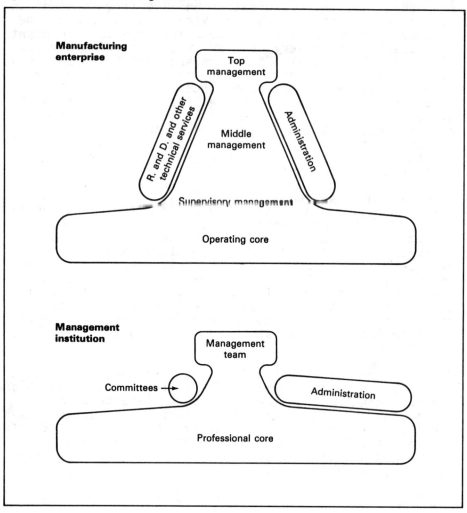

Manufacturing enterprise

Top management

R. and D. and other technical services

Middle management

Administration

Supervisory management

Operating core

Management institution

Management team

Committees →

Administration

Professional core

research and technical services with the operating core in one professional core that interacts directly with the client base, and an extensive use of committees.

5.2 Organising the professional core

How are the main factors discussed in the previous sections applied in organising the professional part of management development institutions? It would be impossible to review all the alternatives. We shall, therefore, try to point to some typical arrangements which have been adopted by many institutions.

Two caveats have to be made at the outset. Firstly, organisational charts and denominations of units within institutions require careful examination before any attempt is made to classify and assess the institution's organisation. For example there may be a "consulting division", but it will be important to find out what is meant by consulting, whether this unit actually does or only negotiates and co-ordinates consulting, whether it has staff fully assigned to it or uses staff from a central professional pool, what its degree of autonomy is within the institution's structure, and so on. Secondly, searching for "pure" structural solutions and trying to apply a few simple models to all situations would lead to a dead end. The environments, purposes and resources of management institutions are so diverse that in practice the overwhelming majority has recourse to hybrid structures.

The professional core as a single entity

At one end of the spectrum there is the institution that does not find it necessary to divide its professional staff into separate units. The whole faculty constitutes one team including faculty members of different professional profiles.

This arrangement is typical of smaller institutions providing a limited number of rather homogeneous services. Since virtually all institutions work with a small faculty in the first period after their establishment, they normally use this organisational type before deciding to adopt another structural pattern required by growth and programme diversification. However, even some mature institutions have retained this model for its simplicity, its flexibility and the absence of the internal organisational barriers that tend to appear as soon as distinct units are established and start growing within the institution.

For example, with a faculty of 18, and part-time faculty bearing some 15-20% of the teaching load, the Centre d'Etudes Industrielles (CEI) in Geneva is structured in this way. Its organisation is based on informal and flexible arrangements that have developed over time, the only formal text being the three-page statutes establishing the CEI as a foundation and defining the role of its board.

Programme co-ordinators

Programme planning and co-ordination will be discussed in detail in chapter 6. However, in this chapter we cannot avoid mentioning the structural aspects of co-ordination.

Even smaller institutions organised as one single
team tend to use a conspicuous management function whose
various alternatives are found in management institutions
of all types and sizes: a programme co-ordinator. He is
a sort of project manager, responsible for the planning,
preparation and delivery of a particular teaching, training, research, consulting, or other programme. It is a
part-time job carried out by experienced faculty members,
who, in addition to their teaching and other assignments,
co-ordinate the inputs of other faculty members in order
to deliver a balanced inter-disciplinary and inter-functional programme.

Thus, elements of matrix management appear even in
smaller institutions with no formalised matrix structure.
This reflects the nature of their tasks and the profile
of the professionals they employ rather than other factors.
In theory, there is an alternative way: direct internal
co-ordination of all programmes by the institution's
management. In practice, such an arrangement is rarely
used and central management tends to limit itself to
ensuring co-ordination between the different programmes
and rectifying disproportions and errors in individual
cases.

Functional organisation

A typical functional structure is one in which professionals are grouped into units (departments, sections,
etc.) using the management function or discipline to
which they belong as a basic criterion. For example there
may be functional departments of general management and
business policy, finance and accounting, marketing, production management and personnel. Turning to disciplines
applied in various areas of management, there may be departments of statistics, operations research, applied
economics, law, behavioural science (or sociology and
psychology), computer science and information systems,
languages and other.

Functionally specialised units can be found in management institutions of any type if their faculty has
attained a certain size and has had to be subdivided in
distinct units. Units specialised by discipline are
normally found at business schools and faculties where
major courses in such disciplines are taught to undergraduate or graduate students.

The general problems and pitfalls inherent in a
structure based on disciplines and functions were mentioned in section 5.1.

Notwithstanding these, a functional structure is
frequently used by management institutions since in many

cases the functional areas covered constitute a more constant feature than various programmes (which can change on relatively short notice) and the volume of individual programmes does not justify the establishment of special service (product, programme) oriented units. However, there seems to be a tendency to keep the number of functional units rather small to avoid fragmentation.

The approach to programme co-ordination tends to be about the same as described above. Either programme co-ordinators are used or it has to be the institution's general management (e.g. a director of studies, director of research, etc.) that co-ordinates the functional departments' inputs to various programmes. As functional units also organise programmes that lie primarily within their technical area (e.g. marketing management programmes are organised by a marketing department), a considerable amount of programme co-ordination can take place within such units.

Service-oriented organisation

A management institution has a service-oriented structure if its professional core is organised in units defined by the institution's products or services rather than by functions or disciplines. Various aspects of the institution's service portfolio can be used as bases for establishing organisation.

(1) Intervention means:

Units typically established in this case are for training, consulting, research, information, and so forth. Each unit is supposed to have the multidisciplinary and multifunctional staff it needs for programme delivery. In addition, this form of organisation assumes that individual staff members will use primarily one particular means of action - they will work as trainers, or researchers, but not both. Such arrangement will have to be maintained at least for a certain period of time, at the end of which some staff may rotate between units.[1]

Consequently, this arrangement is not used by institutions in which one means of action strongly dominates the others (e.g. where an institution is primarily a teaching or a consulting establishment) or if individual faculty members are expected to make parallel use of the various means of action and could not be assigned full-time to one division.

Cf. section 4.1.

Divisions specialised by intervention means can embrace a wide range of programmes (e.g. all training programmes) or only a certain programme type (undergraduate studies are normally organised in a different unit from post-experience management training, etc.).

Within service-oriented departments, in larger units in particular, functional specialisation is often chosen for grouping professional staff.

(2) Client sectors:

Unit specialisation by client sectors is quite popular; we have already explained that the decision may be a strategic one. In both training and consulting organisations sectoral units tend to be seen as an efficient vehicle for developing sectoral expertise and programmes, establishing close relationships with firms and organisations in a particular sector and generally increasing the chances of having a good impact on that sector.

(3) Geographic regions:

In developing countries there is a tendency to establish regionally specialised units within institutions if a particular region has its own management development needs that have not received enough attention. As a rule, this also implies physical decentralisation. A question to be asked is whether it is more advantageous to decentralise certain technical and support services, but maintain a strong link with the institution's central office, or to establish a separate institution.

In some cases geographic specialisation is used without physical decentralisation. For example, the INSEAD in Fontainebleau has established a special unit for promoting and organising co-operation programmes with Asian institutions, while a similar unit attached to the CESA in Jouy-en-Josas aims at developing programmes with Arab states.

Figure 12 shows the internal organisation used for a number of years by the Institut National de la Productivité et du Développement Industriel (INPED) in Algeria, one of the largest management development institutions in the world. The main technical departments are consistently service-oriented, although several different criteria have been combined in specialising the departments. The five detached units are regarded as parts of the Department of Regional Development. About 170 professional staff members and 40 foreign consultants worked with the INPED when the organisational structure reproduced in figure 12 was introduced. The existence of two departments dealing with research and studies (the DEIT

150

Figure 12   Organisation chart of the INPED

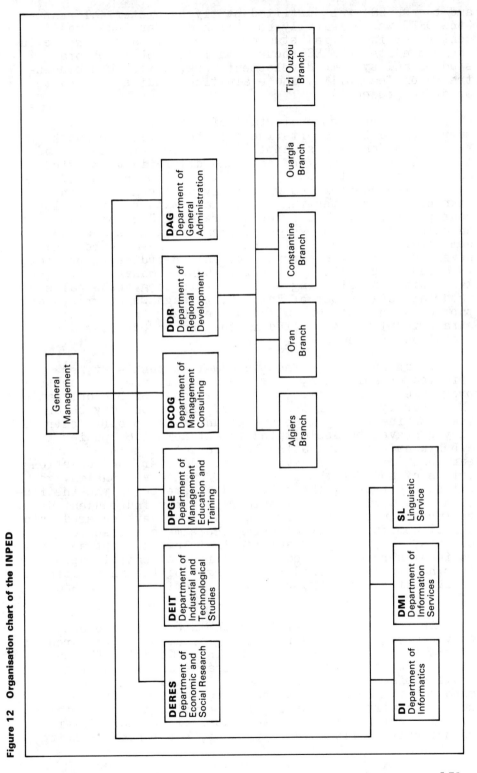

and the DERES) was justified partly by historical reasons
(the DEIT was originally established as an independent
centre for industrial studies); partly by a difference in
their mandates (DERES focused on more global sectoral
studies and systems development work, while DEIT concen-
trated on feasibility and evaluation studies related to
specific projects).

With a professional staff of not more than 14,
supplemented by 10 part-time collaborators, the Dansk
Management Centre also applies a service-oriented structure. However, this reflects the diversity of missions
and methods of its four basic units. The Internal Training Section co-operates with individual companies in designing and implementing tailor-made management development programmes. The External Training Section organises
an eight-week executive development programme and short
seminars, all in general management. The Research and
Development Section carries out and co-ordinates projects
in areas of priority interest to Danish management. The
last unit, the Planning Section, acts as a technical secretariat to a number of "clubs", through which groups of
public and private organisations exchange experience of
strategic planning applied in the Danish business and
social environments.

If an institution adopts a well-thought-out service-
oriented organisation, this can not only simplify central
programme co-ordination, but allow considerable delegation
of authority to divisional heads. Divisions may be organised as financially independent units, as profit centres.
They can even be assimilated to autonomous companies in
a business group and authorised to retain part of their
earnings for further development. However, the question
arises of how far the autonomy of such divisions may go
without destroying the unity and coherence of the institution as a whole. For example relatively independent departments in several large institutions have entered into
direct competition by offering the same services to
clients, or started organising their own support and promotional services instead of calling on central support.
This has to be examined in the light of the institution's
management philosophy, bearing both effectiveness and
efficiency in mind.

An interesting example of the use of autonomous
service-oriented units is the organisation of research
institutes within the London Business School. The main
areas covered in 1981 include finance and accounting,
small business, economic forecasting and public sector
management. Such institutes are established if the volume and quality of research in a particular area attained
a sufficient level to attract external sponsors interested not only in financing a project, but in co-financing

the whole institute and its programmes. Some faculty members work part-time in these institutes but several full-time researchers are also employed on short-term contracts. These researchers could not normally be recruited by the School as faculty members. In 1981 the School employed 45 research workers on short-term contracts in addition to the same number of faculty members.

Another arrangement is the establishment of a legally separate entity for consulting work. For example the Centre d'Etudes et de Perfectionnement à la Direction et à la Gestion (CEPI) in Lille established a separate consulting organisation as a joint company owned by its staff, which is expected to devote 20% of its working time to assignments organised through this company. Income from consulting is divided as follows: 25% to the individual concerned, 25% to the Centre and 50% to the shareholders (i.e. individual staff members, including those who have a heavy teaching load and therefore less time for consulting).

Matrix organisation

Whether management institutions choose a functional or a divisional structure, they have to solve some important co-ordination problems in either case, perhaps with exception of small institutions providing a limited number of different services, or large institutions that can afford to be consistent in applying divisional structures and decentralisation. That is why, in recent years, so many management institutions have become interested in matrix management and started using it in one way or another. The fact that they employ management professionals, who should be able to understand and use the matrix approach to management more easily than other professionals or administrators, has undoubtedly played a role in this.

A great deal has been written about the advantages and difficulties of matrix management and we can assume that the reader is familiar with this material.[1]

---

[1] See, e.g. J.K. Galbraith: Designing complex organisations (Reading, Massachusetts, Addison-Wesley, 1973); K. Knight (ed.): Matrix management: A cross-functional approach to organisation (Westmead, Farnborough (UK), Gower Press, 1977); T. Peters: "Beyond the matrix organisation", in Business Horizons, Oct. 1979; or L.E. Greiner and V.E. Schein: "The paradox of managing a project oriented matrix: Establishing coherence within chaos", in Sloan Management Review, Winter 1981.

An example of a matrix structure is provided by the Ecole Supérieure de Commerce (ESC) group in Lyons (figure 13). The professional core is organised in functional departments (including a language department) and service-oriented centres. These centres include: a school of graduate business management studies (ESC), a special one-year programme of postgraduate studies (CESMA), a management training centre (CFP), a programme of doctoral studies organised in collaboration with Lyons University (PDG), an action-research programme organised jointly with the local chamber of commerce and a group of business firms (IRE) and a centre for international co-operation (CI). The centres are organised as internal units of the ESC group and have no legal status. The functional departments supply the centres with professional staff in various disciplines and functional areas; this includes numerous part-time staff, which, from the professional viewpoint, is selected and has its performance evaluated by the heads of departments.

At the present time, an analogous pattern can be found in many management schools, productivity centres, consulting organisations, etc. They use it in order to achieve a better interdisciplinary approach, and better coherence, staff-time utilisation, and involvement of individual professionals in programme management.[1]

However, it is important to understand the real relations in matrix structures in the particular case of management development institutions. In fact, these relations are more complex than a two-dimensional matrix can show. As we already know, in the overwhelming majority of cases managing a functional or purpose-oriented unit is not a full-time job. The direct teaching or consulting load of an individual with co-ordinating responsibilities in a matrix structure will differ from case to case, but there will be some. In these tasks he will be co-ordinated by other colleagues. A two-way co-ordination relationship between two colleagues is not unusual: in his capacity of director of a graduate programme, a member of a marketing department will co-ordinate and control his own department head. Furthermore, the two-boss model of matrix structure rarely applies, as faculty members normally intervene in several programme areas co-ordinated by different persons.

It might appear that this creates an inextricable and unmanageable grid of relations of authority and responsibility. Indeed, it would be impossible to use it in

---

[1] See e.g. the evolution of matrix organisation of the Cranfield School of Management in G. Wills: Continuing studies for managers (Bradford, MCB Publications, 1981).

Figure 13   Organisation chart of the ESC Lyons Group

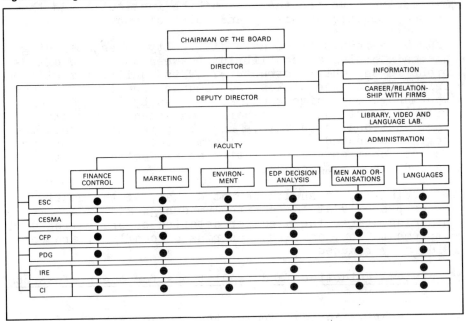

a traditional manufacturing firm or government department. But even in management education and training its
application is not easy and should be reserved for mature
institutions. While it is true that matrix management is
a challenging experience and a good way of learning more
about the institution and understanding its culture,
certain conditions should already exist, or the institution should at least be actively working to create them.

Matrix management cannot work without relatively
experienced and mature staff, able to understand and play
the various roles within the matrix structure. They have
to know and support the institution's management development philosophy and strategic objectives. Consequently,
matrix management is not suitable for "laissez-faire"
institutions, which have pushed the individuals' academic
freedom to an extreme, nor for institutions operating
without clear objectives and strategies.

Culture is an important factor, too. Matrix management requires a setting that permits a flexible interpretation of status, authority and lines of command and
communication. If it lives in a conservative local environment, the institution must consider whether its
internal culture has developed sufficiently to permit the
use of matrix management. Even if it has there may be
difficulties in organising contacts with the external
world. For example a matrix structure will give high

155

authority **to programme directors, but** the external world
may continue to see the head of the institution as the
only acceptable authority and point of contact.

Some institutions have difficulty in establishing
and maintaining an equilibrium between the basic dimensions in the matrix structure. This equilibrium will be
influenced by the status and remuneration level of those
who manage each dimension, as well as by their association
with the institution's general management. In some cases
the functional departments have less influence than the
service-oriented units, the former being viewed primarily
as cost centres and the latter as product-delivering and
income-generating centres.

Finally, it should be noted that, if the matrix functions properly at the curriculum design and programme
planning stage, the need for detailed co-ordination during
implementation, and also the risk of conflict, are considerably reduced.

Technical guidelines and regulations for the professional
core

In orienting and organising the activities of its
professional core, some institutions have found it useful
to issue guidelines and regulations for the preparation,
planning, organisation and delivery of particular professional services. For example the Centre for Management
Development in Nigeria has developed a series of brief
guidelines (three to ten pages each) for activities in
education and training, management research, consulting
work, institutional support provided by the Centre to
other management institutions in the country, technical
support services, and publications and library. The
Indian Institute of Management in Ahmedabad has combined
substantive and procedural aspects related to research in
a concise document entitled "Research and publications at
IIMA (objectives, policies and procedures)". It refers
to the main types of research carried out by faculty, the
functions of the Institute's research and publications
committee, the processing and preparation of research
proposals, as well as the publication and dissemination
of research results.

As a rule such documents are viewed as a useful
means of providing information about policies and achieving coherence of action in medium-sized and larger institutions and in institutions with a relatively high staff
turnover. But they are not a substitute for induction
training, indoctrination and professional guidance.
Furthermore, they should not try to regulate those

aspects of content and method of professional work which, as mentioned in section 5.1, do not lend themselves to standardisation.

5.3 Organising administrative and technical support functions

We saw in section 5.1 that, in parallel with its professional core, a management institution has to organise and operate a whole range of administrative and technical support services without which that core would be paralysed or its high skills and expensive time would have to be spent on routine support and office tasks. We shall now review the main organisational principles applying to this area.

Administrative and general support

Under this title we include functions and services such as accounting, budgeting and payroll, switchboard, mail, secretarial support, reproduction and printing, purchasing and storage, buildings administration, maintenance and cleaning, transportation; in some institutions also catering and living accommodation for participants and even for faculty are included. In developing countries additional services may have to be organised, such as reception of foreign visitors, an important transportation section or liaison with customs.

As a rule these services are organised in a separate sector: in one unit or several units, depending on their diversity and volume. Centralised arrangements prevail even in cases where a fairly decentralised pattern has been adopted for the professional core. However, this centralisation is seldom total. Direct secretarial support is normally decentralised to organisational units within the professional core. There may be some disagreement on how far such decentralisation should go. There is the criterion of administrative costs, which may be lower if centralisation is applied. However, due weight has to be given to flexibility of administrative support and the utilisation of professionals' time, which can be considerably increased by decentralisation of administrative support.

Some support services, such as residential and catering facilities, may develop into large entities, enjoying considerable autonomy within the institution's structure, working on the basis of a separate budget and fully equipped with their own internal administration and support.

Head of administration

The head of administration (administrative director, director of administration and support services, etc.) has tremendous influence on institutional efficiency. It is in the interest of every institution head to designate a competent, flexible and dynamic person, able to understand the differences and common points of professional and administrative work, and the various constraints under which management institutions operate. The better the head of administration, the smaller will be the number of purely administrative matters reaching the desk of the institution's director. Of course, the head of administration has to be granted adequate decision authority and the right of signature in all matters where personal involvement of the institution head or his deputy is not absolutely necessary.

Co-ordination with the professional core

Mutual understanding and smooth co-operation with the professional core do not develop automatically. Despite the comments on the nature of these two different sectors made in section 5.1 above, there are various risks of friction and conflict; they can cause major inefficiences if an atmosphere of good communication and mutual respect is not nurtured.

For example some professional trainers insist on receiving immediate and priority service, like to give orders even to administrative staff who do not report to them and look at administrative clerks with disrespect. Turning to administrative employees, some of them do not understand the nature of professional tasks, think that professionals do not have much to do, and are not prepared to consider any exception from regulations. Occasionally administrative employees in units where professionals have to go and ask for a service or clearance develop an arrogant attitude even to senior professionals. All these and similar situations require tactful handling by the institution's management.

Quantitative co-ordination is essential. Both understaffed and plethoric administrative services do a lot of harm.

Administrative regulations

To standardise administrative procedures and ensure that every staff member is fully informed about them, management institutions use various types of administrative norms such as staff regulations, organisation manuals, faculty handbooks, director's instructions or circulars, etc. These cover a wide range of organisational and administrative questions as in any other organisation.[1]

Administrative regulations define procedures to be followed by all staff of the institution. They constitute, in fact, one of the formalised links between the professional core and the administrative and technical support wing of the institution.

There are no two institutions that would view the use of internal administrative regulations in the same way. However, there is some consensus that a certain number of such regulations is necessary and healthy. On the other hand, an excess can have a negative effect and provoke major conflicts between the professional staff and the institution's general management. Or, what happens at best is that regulations are issued, but management does not have the courage to insist on applying them.

Experience has also shown that management institutions are well advised not to take the administrative regulations used in their parent bodies as a model since many such procedures have been devised for different work-processes and categories of personnel and would cause unnecessary paperwork in a management institution.

Technical support

Activities usually referred to as technical support in a management institution include public or client relations (promotional activities), a library service, audio-visual aids, editing and publishing, a computing centre, etc. They are defined as technical support as they do not directly provide services to the institution's clients, but their activities have some technical content and require personnel of an adequate technical background.

However, there are different situations. In a management institution established as an association with a large membership, client relations may be replaced by a department of membership services, which becomes a part of the professional core as it directly organises and provides services to the main clients - the institute's members.

The library may operate as a typical support service to the professional staff and course participants; but,

---

[1] Cf. also the University of Notre Dame studies in the management of not-for-profit institutions. The manuals published so far cover accounting procedure, management procedures and budgetary control procedures (see **bibliography** to chapter 6, appendix 3).

in another case, information services may be oriented mainly to external clients and their internal support function will be of secondary importance.

The position of a computing centre is similar. Its programming and computing functions related to teaching, consulting and research may become less important, while the share of training, systems design and data processing for clients increases.

These varying roles and conceptions of the above-mentioned and other technical services have structural implications. Basically, institutions have three choices:

(1) integrating technical support with internal adminis-tration;

(2) organising technical support as a separate area, re-porting to a member of the general management team;

(3) integrating technical support fully with the profes-sional core and treating it as one of the major client services in cases where external service prevails over the internal support function.

5.4 Organising general management

It is the responsibility of the institution's general management to pull all human and other resources together and to develop relations with the environment in defining and implementing strategy. The functions of general man-agement and their organisation will be most comprehensive in an autonomous institution, which has to generate and manage its own resources for survival and growth. But autonomous institutions use various types of legal set-up, and this affects general management considerably. In institutions belonging to a university, government depart-ment or other parent body general management organisation will involve links with these bodies, which, in turn, may decide to take care of some of the general management functions on the institution's behalf. As a result, a wide spectrum of organisational patterns can be found at the general management level.

The pattern of general management

Certain common trends tend to emerge from this diver-sity of patterns.

Very pronounced is the tendency to combine manage-ment by individuals with elements of collegiate manage-ment. Even if the external set-up (the parent body in particular) imposes a certain concept of general manage-ment, the institution will frequently make a serious and original attempt to give clearly defined managerial

160

responsibilities to individuals in cases where collegiate
management prevails, and to use internal collective consultative and even decision-making bodies when the parent
body insists on vesting responsibility in a single person
at the top.

This is very much a matter of the institution's internal management culture. Irrespective of what the statutes and organisation manuals require, institutions develop a tradition of handling certain matters collectively.
There may be no formal platform for this and no voting
procedure to define a majority; consensus is rather
achieved through a series of consultations and meetings
where alternatives are examined and objections discussed
and overcome.

Another important tendency is that of confiding
higher executive positions to management development professionals. The term "professional" is not interpreted
in a narrow way: experienced managers or administrators
selected outside the institution are eligible and are
even very welcome in certain situations. However, they
must have an appropriate educational background (though
not necessarily a PhD or master's degree!) and a personal
inclination towards educational, consulting and similar
activities if they are to get satisfaction from their job
and be accepted as leaders by the institution's team.

In more and more cases, management positions in institutions are being made elective. This is clearly an influence of university traditions, but it has even affected
institutions that are entirely independent of universities.
Only rarely is the institution's head elected by the staff,
except at some universities: this is usually the prerogative of a parent body or the institution's board. However,
faculty chairmen, deans and departmental heads are elected
in many institutions. In other cases, they are appointed
by the director from short-lists designated by the faculty,
or after consultations with senior faculty members or
official faculty representatives.

A logical result of the foregoing is a tendency towards job rotation in managerial positions. Senior management teachers and consultants are ever more prepared to
relinquish their positions and return to full-time teaching, consultancy and research. This, however, is not unrelated to questions of status and salary structures. If
promotion to a managerial position is the only way to
achieve higher status and better remuneration, job rotation becomes difficult if not impossible.

The chief executive officer

The institution's chief executive officer may be
called director, director general, general manager,

principal, chairman or dean, to mention only some of the
denominations given to this top position in various institutions. It is he who normally has the statutory responsibility to the board or to the parent body for the institution's total operation and development. This responsibility covers all aspects of management, with the exception of those where decisions have to be made either collectively by the board, or are within the authority of a
parent body to which the institution is accountable. But
even in such cases, the head of the institution will be
the person who submits and defends proposed decisions,
and who will play a leading role in carrying the decision
into effect once it has been taken. Indeed, the formal
aspect of decision-making must not be overestimated: it
is well known that in most cases neither a board nor a
parent body can make a good decision if the institution
concerned has not done a good job in preparing it.

At the risk of repeating what some readers may consider self-evident, certain functions of the institution
head have to be emphasised.

Firstly, operational co-ordination and short-term
monitoring are not the director's central functions. His
crucial function and responsibility is one of clarifying
and defining the institution's purpose and goals, its
management development philosophy and basic strategic
choices. This creates an absolutely essential framework
within which not only programme directors and other departmental managers, but also individual professionals
without direct management responsibilities will be able
to take programme decisions directly, without having to
refer them to the top manager in most cases.

Secondly, he has to maintain harmony and healthy
proportions in the institution's operations. This goes
far beyond programme planning and control and includes
questions such as to what units and programmes the best
people are assigned, what means of action and clientèle
are given priority, what initiatives are rewarded and
what criticised, and so on.

Thirdly, he provides for unity between external and
internal leadership, emphasising the former or the latter
as appropriate in the given environmental context and
stage of development of the institution.[1]

Fourthly, he and his personal deputy are the only
persons in institutional management who deal fully with
the wide range of both professional and administrative
questions. Even if administrative support services are

_____

[1] Cf.section 1.4.

162

well organised and controlled by competent people, many questions of co-ordination remain to be solved. Inadequate delegation may even bring to the director's desk matters that should have been ultimately resolved in another office. The institution's head may have to intervene to defend administration and lead his professional staff in observing rules and in matters of record keeping, document circulation, making commitments with financial implications, and so on.

Many institutions do not properly appreciate the role of a general deputy to the institution's head. There are some large institutions without such a position and if the head is absent or totally engaged in one important matter, no other matter can be dealt with at the senior management level.

The deputy director's job does not have to be full-time; many institutions have combined it with one of the executive positions that will be discussed below. In fact, the title "deputy" means, almost by definition, that he must have other substantive responsibilities otherwise the deputy would have work to do only when the director was away! It is essential that the deputy participates continuously in the top management process to be able to handle policy matters on behalf of the director, and that his role is recognised as such within and outside the institution.

Other members of the general management team

In management institutions that are primarily teaching and training establishments, a key internal management position is that of the faculty chairman, faculty dean or director of studies. His role may be emphasised by the fact that he also acts as a general deputy to the institution's head, but it does not have to be so in every case.

In most cases the faculty chairman guides and co-ordinates curriculum development and new programme design (focusing on content and methodology), as well as current course programming and programme delivery. He is also responsible for the development of the faculty. In an institution that has applied a fully developed matrix structure, he may act as the main co-ordinator of functional departments with service-oriented centres, using and chairing curriculum development and programme planning committees for this purpose. There are, however, cases where the scope of this function has been limited to representing the faculty within the institution's management committee and to managing and co-ordinating faculty development.

In addition to the faculty chairman or director of studies, other specialised director positions can be found in institutions with predominantly functional organisations of the professional core. In such instances, there may be a director of training, director of consulting, director of research, or the like, if in each of these action areas the institution has a sufficient volume of activity requiring external contacts, planning, co-ordination and evaluation.

If an institution uses a fully-fledged matrix structure, both the heads of functional departments and of the service-oriented divisions or centres are normally considered as members of the general management team and participate in both policy making and over-all co-ordination through the appropriate committees.

Committees

Committees, an old and well known tool of management, are used by most management development institutions for sharing information, co-ordinating plans and operations and organising the processes of consultation and decision-making. Both permanent and ad hoc committees are used. The over-all approach to organisation and the prevailing management style will determine the roles of committees: where decentralisation, participation and a matrix approach are fostered, the co-ordinating and decision-making roles of committees tend to grow. Where a centralised and autocratic model prevails, committees will still be used for information and consultation, but the institution's manager will not hesitate to overrule a committee's conclusions and recommendations. In many institutions, however, committees are directly used as decision-making bodies: decisions are made by consensus of senior professionals who sit on the committee, and the institution's head will rarely use his formal authority to alter such decisions.

Virtually every institution, even a small one, will have a general committee, which may be called a management committee, executive committee, co-ordinating committee or the like. Persons holding managerial positions are its members: the institution's head, his deputies and the faculty chairman in any case, departmental heads and directors of major programmes or centres in many cases. It is used for discussing all matters of importance to policy and co-ordination. Meetings are relatively frequent, once or even twice a month.

In many institutions the whole faculty is viewed as a consultative and policy-making body and plenary faculty meetings are used not only for exchanging information, but for collectively examining matters of importance to the institution's development. The formal rights of such faculty meetings or boards may be stipulated by the institution's statutes or general regulations. In university-based management institutions, there is a tradition that various academic matters will be discussed with the whole faculty before a decision is made, or it is the faculty meeting that decides.

In addition to general committees, management institutions also use various special-purpose committees. Their number tends to grow with the institution's size, but the organisational pattern used and the internal culture of the institution also influence the number and profiles of committees.

For example in some institutions major strategic planning exercises have been handled by a special ad hoc committee.

A curriculum committee deals with the design of the institution's programmes and focuses on programme content and methodology; as a rule, important changes and new programmes have to be submitted to this committee. In some institutions a separate pedagogic committee is established for every major programme to assist the programme coordinator in defining the curriculum and improving programme delivery.

In many cases there is a general programme planning and co-ordination committee; its main task is to prepare annual work programmes and make sure that the inputs and outputs of all units are properly co-ordinated and workload equally distributed.[1]

There may be committees for guiding and evaluating activities in particular work areas - e.g. a research (policy) committee, a library committee, a computer services committee and so on.

Some institutions, in particular the academic ones, have an appointments committee; its agreement is a condition for selecting and appointing new faculty members.

A building committee has been found indispensable by institutions with a major expansion and building programme planned and implemented alongside current operations.

There are no strict rules determining the number and profiles of committees to be established and some institution heads tend to be very tempted by the various advantages of this management tool. However, there are risks of inefficiency and even disorder if new committees are established light-heartedly, if the same people are

---

[1] See also chapter 6.

constantly called to meetings of different committees, if committees encroach on responsibilities of other committees or if the conclusions reached by committees are not taken seriously by the institution's head or governing body.

5.5 Boards and councils

Collective bodies through which management institutions are linked with their constituents and environment are an important part of their over-all structural set-up. In most cases there is such a collective body at the top: a governing body, board, board of trustees, board of directors, council, board of governors or the like. The head of the institution is appointed by this body and reports to it in most cases. In certain institutions such a collective body may have an advisory function. Yet in a smaller number of cases, the institution's director and the chairman of the board are the same person.

As a rule the existence of the board is required by the law on the basis of which the institution has been established or by the institution's own statutes. There are some substantial reasons behind this: the recognised need to use a wide range of experience in orienting the institution, to link it formally to other organisations in its environment and to ensure collective and relatively independent control. These reasons are strong enough to have led to the establishment of boards even in some institutions where they were not required from a strictly legal point of view.

Notwithstanding this, there are problems and short-comings in the functioning of many boards. Frequently a legalistic approach prevails: the board is seen as an inevitable formality from which no real benefit can be drawn. There are "sleeping" boards that never meet, as well as boards that would endorse anything submitted by the director.[1]

Main types of boards

Three basic types tend to emerge from the considerable variety of boards used in managing management institutions.

The first type represents constituents external to the institution: public or private organisations that have established it or should contribute to orienting its

---

[1] See also R.N. Anthony and R.E. Herzlinger: Management control in nonprofit organisations (Homewood, Illinois, Irwin, 1980), p. 47.

work. Their link with the institution may be very strong
(it may be defined as co-ownership, membership or administrative authority) and involves financial commitments
and responsibility in addition to the right to participate in collective debate and decision-making on programmes, budgets, etc. Members of such boards are appointed by organisations they represent or by a higher
authority (e.g. a minister).

For example the Council of the Dansk Management
Centre includes representatives of the Centre's major
"shareholders"; 25% of them represent the government, 50%
the federation of industries and employers and 25% various
professional bodies. The Board of Directors of the Management Development Centre in Khartoum has 11 members appointed by the Minister of Public Service and Administrative Reform; in 1981 it included four representatives
of government, three employers' representatives, one
trade union delegate, two members from within the Centre
(the director general and his deputy) and the Chief Technical Advisor of an ILO project attached to the Centre.

The second type of board represents "internal" constituents: it is elected according to certain rules by
members in an institution established as a management
association. The Irish Management Institute or the
Nigerian Institute of Management have such boards.

The third type of board can be found in a number of
autonomous institutions in various countries. As the
institution is legally independent, the board members do
not formally represent any other organisations, but are
chosen and act in their personal capacity. De facto,
most board members tend to be chosen because of their
association with important and influential businesses or
public organisations in the institution's environment.
As a rule such boards renew themselves periodically from
the inside: they themselves select and co-opt new members.
In fact it tends to be the head of the institution who
recommends new members to the board.

Boards of this type are to be found in institutions
organised as foundations, such as the Lembaga Pendidikan
Dan Pembinaan Manajemen in Jakarta or as companies limited by guarantee but not trading for profit, such as the
London Business School.[1]

[1] "The governing body is a self-perpetuating body
which itself fills vacancies in its own membership and appoints additional members. The membership is made up of
approximately equal numbers of those with academic experience on the one hand, and those with industrial, commercial or trades union experience on the other. All members
are appointed individually and not as representatives of
organisations." London Business School constitution, rules
and regulations (1981), p.6.

Composition and work methods of boards

The legal differences between various types of board play their role, but their importance should not be over-estimated. The main problems leading to inefficiencies in the functioning of boards are managerial and can be resolved within existing legal or statutory arrangements.

There is, above all, the problem of the boards' composition. Not only expertise and competence, but also sincere interest in the success of the institution are essential qualities of a board member. The board's composition has to reflect the institution's profile and orientation: for example an institution that aims to be international should not have a board consisting of nationals of one country only. The institution's clients have to be suitably represented on the board, preferably by individuals who will personally contribute to forging productive links between the institution and its environment. Many institutions have found it very useful to have on their boards representatives of workers' organisations and other important social groups, in addition to persons representing the views and experience of business and government.

Concerning the size of the board, there is no simple rule that would apply universally. Most boards tend to have between 11 and 25 members; if a larger board is deemed necessary, it usually has to organise its work differently, limiting the number of its meetings to one or two a year and electing an executive committee which meets more frequently.

What is really done at board meetings is a key issue. Boards that are used merely to endorse what the director has decided are not useful. They end up by being passive bodies and when the inevitable crisis strikes, they will abandon the institution's head and take to the hills. Confusion can also arise when a board member gets torn between representing a constituency and sharing collective responsibility for the institution. The boards of some international institutions pay much more attention to politics than to helping the institution to find the right orientation and solve its problems.

The institution's head must not try to dominate his board, he has to work with it in a competent manner. To obtain the board's advice and help, he has to ask meaningful questions at the right moment. Even the delicate question of who is to be delegated to the board can and has to be handled by the institution's head in cases when the board's role is clearly misunderstood or under-estimated by a constituent organisation. Also the institution's head should not isolate the board from the staff.

168

It may often be useful to invite senior staff (programme co-ordinators, department heads) to present reports or proposals to the board and also to involve board members in the institution's programmes. There has been a growing tendency to provide for faculty representation on the board, for example by the faculty chairman (dean) or another elected representative of the staff in addition to the institution's head, who attends the board meetings in any case and often is a regular member of the board.

OPERATIONAL PROGRAMME PLANNING AND CONTROL

6

As pointed out in chapter 1, in the long run a management development institution can hardly aspire to be effective without running its programmes and using its human, material and financial resources efficiently. Fundamental choices have to be translated into everyday action, work has to be distributed and controlled, operations have to be scheduled and monitored in accordance with changing reality and adjusted to new opportunities and constraints.

Useful experience acquired by institutions in managing operations will be the object of this chapter. Short-term programme planning and scheduling in the main areas of institutional activity will be examined in section 6.1. Section 6.2 will describe several approaches to determining and applying standards of faculty workload. Sections 6.3 and 6.4 will deal with operational aspects of costing, pricing and financial management. Finally, section 6.5 will review key aspects of monitoring programmes and operations.

Appendix 2 "Basic data and ratios for a management development institution" supplements this chapter by suggesting a range of indicators that can be used in operational planning and control.

6.1 Programme planning

Scope and objectives

Operational planning in our conception aims at establishing a detailed schedule of activities and work programmes for a particular period of time. Its purpose is to translate the major options and objectives of the strategic plan into operational decisions and measures and ensure a balanced workload and resource utilisation.

The **institution's strategic plan provides** the main orientation for operational programme planning by indicating the basic targets to be attained and relations to be respected, such as the proportions between training, research and consulting activities, their growth rates, sectoral focus, major new programmes to be launched and so on. Such targets and objectives are compared with the real resource situation: with human, financial and other resources that are available or can be generated by programmed activities. Realistic reassessment of demand is another essential input: it may lead to the conclusion that operational programmes will be at variance with the strategic plan, which has been devised for a longer period, using more global data and assumptions that may have changed in the meantime. Every programme planning exercise is an occasion to consider new opportunities, including those that were unknown when the institution drew up its strategic plan.

Time cycle

Most management institutions use annual programme planning (for calendar or academic years). Open programmes scheduled for a particular year are publicly announced and advertised, while other activities are scheduled in internal planning documents.

There is a tendency to prepare such programmes many months ahead of the programme period. For example, at the Ashridge Management College the 1982 programme was:

- discussed and agreed in principle in September 1980;
- adjusted and confirmed in detail in March 1981;
- published and advertised in July 1981.

If the demand and resource situation is not very clear and not sufficiently stabilised, institutions may prefer to announce programmes for six months only and prepare them less in advance of the programme period.

While annual activity plans and budgets constitute the backbone of the programme planning system in most institutions, it will be shown below that in certain cases operational management and monitoring require a quarterly or monthly break-down of annual plans, or even weekly work scheduling.

Programming teaching and training

In institutions with long programmes of management studies (undergraduate and graduate) an important part of teaching capacity is normally taken up by courses repeated every year, unless major changes are foreseen,

Figure 14 Checklist for training programme review

Criteria \ Programmes	A	B	C etc.
Introduced	1967	1979	1975
Demand	stable	low	high
Competition	growing	low	low
Participants' views	neutral	neutral	very positive
Our assessment	practically useful; some sections are getting obsolete	needs were not properly examined; course too theoretical	deals with burning issue adequately; perhaps too long
Profitability	good	low	satisfactory
Other comments	government subsidy will continue	programming failure	price can be increased
Decision	continue; immediate revision needed	drop	continue; up-date in 1983

such as an increase in the number of parallel classes or a reorganisation of the curriculum.

Turning to shorter training programmes, sometimes there is a tendency simply to schedule the same programme as the previous year, so long as the public is interested. However, institutional strategy may give some general guidelines for programme innovation. For example, the Lembaga Pendidikan dan Pembinaan Manajemen in Jakarta has decided that every year at least 10% of the training time should be devoted to new courses. Even if there is no such target it is essential to review all training programmes, proceeding roughly as suggested in figure 14 (using concrete data if possible).

In similar vein, new programme proposals are also very carefully reviewed by more and more institutions; the old practice of introducing many new short programmes on the basis of personal preferences of faculty members is disappearing. In addition to assessing demand and competition it is necessary to compare the investment to be made for the preparation of a new programme and the recurrent cost of running it with the price that can be charged and expected demand. Even in institutions that are less income-minded it is useful to compare the costs of new programmes with the expected benefits.

The share of tailor-made programmes organised for particular client organisations is often suggested by the strategic plan. It is surprising how high this figure can be in many independent institutions working primarily for the wide management public. Individual programmes are planned on the basis of a needs analysis and financial and administrative arrangements agreed to with particular clients. However, here again quite a few institutions have developed certain types of in-company management development and problem-solving programmes, which they try to sell to various clients without modifications or with only minor ones. A reassessment similar to that made in the case of public programmes may be imperative.

Programming consulting and research

The programming of consulting activity depends mainly on institutional policy regarding consulting and on the ways in which the faculty is involved in this activity. Consulting is not programmed if no more than minor assignments are undertaken by individuals on a personal basis. On the other hand, if consulting is a regular client service organised by the institution, it needs to be programmed though not in the same way as educational and training activities.

As a rule the basic pattern of consulting activity and its organisational and time implications can be globally determined by the annual work programme. Individual assignments are then included in the work programme case by case; their scheduling will depend mainly on the results of promotional activity, through which new assignments are identified and negotiated, and the staff time available for new consulting assignments.

Since the volume of consulting assignments tends to be strongly influenced by the volume and quality of promotional activity, including the preliminary diagnostic surveys which make clients aware of problems and of the type and importance of desirable interventions, particular attention should be paid to short-term programming and control of promotional activity.

If faculty members are to be involved both in training and in consulting assignments during a given period, the director or co-ordinator of consulting needs to know exactly when each individual will be available before he can schedule and confirm particular assignments.

For example, the Singapore National Productivity Board uses a three-month rolling operational plan, prepared each month, dropping a month and adding a new month. The schedule of consulting assignments is thus

174

kept up-to-date, responding to clients' requirements as rapidly as possible and trying to maintain an even distribution of workload among the consulting staff.

Turning to research, its scheduling in any period will also depend mainly on the institution's research policy and the sort of projects envisaged.

Action-oriented research undertaken on the basis of contracts with business and government clients can be assimilated, for the purpose of planning, to consulting assignments. Research undertaken on the institution's own initiative and financed by itself does not have to respect deadlines agreed with external clients: it can be scheduled as convenient, keeping in mind, of course, that it may be inefficient to extend a project over an excessively long period merely to fill the gaps in the faculty's time. The scheduling of smaller individual research projects is normally left to the discretion of faculty members, but in many cases the agreed completion date is included in the institution's work programme.

Individual work plans

Most management institutions have introduced some sort of work planning for individual faculty members. It is harmonised with the planning of programmes in respect of the plan period, the object of planning and the degree of detail. Its purpose is to distribute work evenly among individuals and give them sufficient advance information to enable them to organise their own work in the course of the year. Uncommitted time will also be shown, and the institution will be able to use this information later, in deciding whether to accept new unplanned commitments and to whom to assign them.

It is normal for every faculty member to prepare his own annual work plan. Standards of faculty workload and other directives and targets issued to this effect by the institution's management will set the quantitative framework; specific teaching and other tasks will be included after discussion with programme co-ordinators and departmental heads. The individual plans are normally prepared in parallel with the plans of the institution's principal programmes.

In planning teaching and training, programme co-ordinators approach individual faculty members to ask them to participate in particular programmes; they do this at their own discretion or in consultation with the heads of functional departments. Faculty members, in turn, may take the initiative and offer their services to programme co-ordinators. Gradually, individual work plans are thus filled with specific tasks. Both programme plans and individual work plans are mutually harmonised and the programme planning committee or the faculty chairman intervenes only to solve conflicts or correct errors. For example some faculty members may be less in demand for management seminars, whereas others may be quickly over-loaded. There is an understandable tendency on the part of programme co-ordinators to make sure that the best faculty members take part in their programmes, although this is not always possible. The whole exercise is sim-plified by the fact that quite a few programmes are re-peated every year and will be assigned to the same faculty members.

Major programme development work, such as new course design, case writing, preparing and testing business games, etc., is normally included in individual plans on the basis of suggestions made by programme co-ordinators and discussed with department heads.

Individual work plans will also indicate the faculty members' contribution to collective research projects being prepared by the director of research or project co-ordinators, and projects suggested by the faculty members themselves.

If consulting is an official institutional activity, an individual annual plan will seldom go beyond earmark-ing a certain number of days to it as particular assign-ments have normally to be scheduled for shorter periods and at shorter notice. Managerial and co-ordination duties will be included at the request of the institu-tion's head or management committee.

An outline of an annual work plan sheet is provided as figure 15. In reality this document provides more space for listing activities and covers from two to four pages. It may include a summary section indicating un-committed time, columns for recording real figures and comparing them to the work plan, and other information.

It is difficult to generalise about individual work schedules for periods shorter than one year. In some institutions quarterly or monthly work programmes of in-dividual faculty members are considered to be a useful tool of management control; where this is the case, depart-ment heads regularly discuss such programmes and their fulfilment with the members of their departments. In other institutions individuals are encouraged to use a formalised system for short-term work scheduling, but de-partmental heads are interested only in cases requiring co-ordination. Yet another group of institutions leaves short-term work scheduling completely to the discretion of individual faculty members, on the assumption that if the annual teaching load and other technical assignments

Figure 15   Annual work plan sheet

Annual work plan	Name:
Year:	Department:

I.   Teaching and training: courses

Course title	Days (hours)
Total	

II. Teaching and training: other duties

Activity	Days (hours)
Total	

III. Research and consulting

Projet	Days
Total	

IV. Management, coordination, self-development

Function or activity	Days (hours)
Total	

Summary

Activity area	Days (hours)
I. Courses	
II. Other teaching duties	
III. Research and consulting	
IV. Management etc.	
V. Unallocated balance	
Total	

are correctly defined and distributed, individuals should
be given full freedom in scheduling their work and co-
ordinating directly with colleagues within the general
framework of the annual programme.

Work plans of functional departments

Departmental work plans are a useful management tool
in institutions where functional departments are assigned
specific roles in developing particular technical fields
in addition to supplying manpower to programmes and projects. A departmental plan is more than a mere summary
of the individual plans of its members showing its total
contribution to the institution's work programme. In
particular, departmental plans express development objectives to be achieved in the given technical area, including the preparation of new courses and teaching materials,
research and publications, new staff recruitment, staff
development from junior to senior level, recruitment and
training of external faculty members, research for which
the department is responsible and so on. Departmental
plans show whether the institution is not neglecting the
development of a whole technical area because of the
heavy workload imposed by current programmes or for other
reasons.

The real importance attached to departmental plans
by institutions varies from case to case. For example in
the Cranfield School of Management the technical groups
are regarded as operating centres and their role in planning and budgeting is very important. They are allocated
resources depending on their teaching contribution to the
institution's programmes and have a great deal of autonomy in deciding on the use of external teachers and on research in their specific areas. In quite a few institutions, however, departmental plans are only a formality,
since the functional departments' role in management is
very limited.

Programme planning machinery

Programme planning is a structured exercise carried
out according to a common schedule. In most institutions
the responsibilities of programme co-ordinators, department heads and other managers also include specific planning tasks. In addition, there is a great deal of informal discussion and consultation involving the whole
faculty. The faculty participates in programme planning in every institution, although not to the same
degree.

The institution's management normally issues guidelines and indicative targets for every programme planning
exercise. The preparatory phase can thus start, in which

programme co-ordinators consult with department heads
and individual faculty members on how best to deliver the
programme in the forthcoming period. This is a major
matching exercise, involving many alternative choices of
an operational nature. Step by step, by successive approximations, both idle capacity and bottlenecks are
shown and divergent views or conflicts revealed and resolved. For example the proportions between training and
research are adjusted, or the contribution of external
faculty members increased or reduced as appropriate.

The preparation of the work programme is normally
co-ordinated by the institution's management - the faculty
chairman in most cases - using a programme planning committee or some other body for working with programme co-
ordinators and departmental heads. The Indian Institute
of Management in Ahmedabad even has a dean of planning
for this purpose. In some institutions a particular period (normally one of reduced teaching load) is declared
to be a "planning-exchange period", when all staff members
have to be present, participate in planning and thus
simplify the whole exercise.

In larger institutions running a number of parallel
programmes such co-ordination and matching exercises may
become quite complex. Microprocessors are increasingly
used for scheduling and timetabling and in some cases a
small administrative unit assists the faculty chairman
with this task.

6.2 Faculty workload

This is an area where most institutions find it useful to apply some quantitative standards to professional
work. Since the faculty members carry out various kinds
of task, an attempt is made to compare their time requirements and achieve some uniformity of load standards so as
to ensure that the distribution of workload among the
faculty is not unduly uneven. Such standards, even if
based on solid experience, are by necessity approximative.
They can immensely improve the quality of programme planning and control if used by competent institutional management. But they can do a lot of harm if copied from
other institutions regardless of different conditions and
imposed in a bureaucratic and mechanistic manner.

Rationale behind the standards

An example of the Centre d'Enseignement Supérieur
des Affaires (CESA) in Jouy-en-Josas will be used to
explain the rationale behind the standard faculty workload. At this institution the annual standard applied to
a faculty member is 180 hours. It is determined as
follows:

Effective working weeks to which the standard applies	— 40 weeks
Effective working days per week	— 4 days
Total number of days	— 160 days
Days reserved for developmental work	— 70 days
Number of days left for teaching	— 90 days

The time structure of a normal teaching day is:

Class-room teaching	— 2 hours
Preparation	— 3 hours
Other duties	— 3 hours

In this way the standard of 180 hours of teaching (90 days of two hours each) is established; it corresponds to a weekly load of 4.5 hours during the 40 effective working weeks, or eight hours if weeks reserved for developmental work are deducted.

At the CESA, the contract with faculty members is based on a four-day working week. The fifth day is left free for individual or group consulting, as well as for private teaching assignments outside the institution. Consulting is encouraged, but most of it is undertaken by individuals on a private basis. However, CESA allocates a considerable amount of time (70 days per year) to developmental work, such as new programme design, case writing and various research projects whose results will be utilised in teaching.

Alternative approaches

Every institution is a distinct case with its own particular programme structure, resources, profile and experience of faculty, conditions of employment of trainers, and so forth. It needs its own workload standards reflecting its particular potential and development needs. It is good to know the standards applied by others, but it would be dangerous to copy them without making allowance for different conditions.

Legally and financially independent institutions usually have a free hand in determining the standard faculty workload; in some cases they have developed a procedure of consultation or even a sort of collective bargaining whereby such norms are discussed and agreed to with the whole faculty or its representatives.

180

Institutions based on a university, or assimilated
to a university, may have to observe standards issued for
the whole sector of higher education, or negotiate excep-
tions with the university or their ministry before being
free to apply different standards.

Some alternative approaches corresponding to different situations are mentioned below.

Time for teaching and training

Particular teaching and training programmes are
normally rated in numbers of standard hours (or other
planning units) which correspond to real time, but ratios
may be used for some programmes requiring more preparatory time, those conducted outside the institute or in
evening courses, etc.

Some institutions stop at this and do not use any
other standards for related pedagogic duties, such as
tutoring, tests and examinations and so on. In other
cases there may be a very detailed list of standards for
supervising project work or the writing of theses and the
like. Some problems may have to be faced in both cases.
If no standard provision is made, faculty members may
give preference to work that counts for fulfilling the
standard load. On the other hand, if the provision is
too generous and applied mechanically, some faculty members may easily be able to meet the standards without
doing any class-room teaching and training.

Time for new programme development

As we have seen, CESA uses a standard of 70 days for
developmental work; unfortunately only a few institutions
can afford to budget such a high figure. Some proceed in
just the opposite way: for example the Ashridge Management College applies a standard workload of 450 hours
based on 43 weeks, i.e. a weekly load of 10.5 hours, assuming that about 30% of effective time is to be spent in
direct class-room work and the rest in preparing and ad-
ministering training programmes. If major programme development work has to be undertaken, the time required is
assessed and allocated case by case and deducted from the
total annual standard.

Some institutions have developed ratios for the preparation of new courses. For example they authorise two
hours for routine preparation, etc., of one hour of teaching, but between four and 20 hours for developing one
hour of a completely new programme. But even this does

not provide for preparing new case studies, business games, etc., for which time should be budgeted separately.[1]

Time for consulting and research

At the CESA consulting is predominantly a private matter for individuals; it also represents an interesting opportunity to earn additional income, which can be up to 40-45% of salary. But if the policy is to organise consulting as an institutional activity and if staff members are required to share their working time between consulting and teaching, the number of days to be spent in consulting should be determined as a standard.

Major research projects, in particular those requiring team work, should be treated in a similar way. Either there may be a standard which allocates time for research on an annual basis, or an adjustment of the general standard may be made each time there is a need to plan an important research project (mainly by adjusting downwards the standard teaching load). Minor and current research done individually in connection with teaching work is normally not accounted for in the standard load.

Time for staff development

Mature institutions with experienced staff (in particular academic institutions with long summer holidays) do not usually make a standard provision for staff development - it is considered that such provision is inbuilt within the total work organisation of the staff. If they can afford to, they often grant a sabbatical year after five to seven years of intensive teaching and training.

In young institutions, and for new and inexperienced faculty members, staff development time should be allocated on the basis of real needs and opportunities.

Time for management and co-ordination

In one way or another any institution will allow time for programme co-ordination. There may be a fully developed rating scale for different types of co-ordination and managerial tasks, or the managers of important programme areas and centres within the institution may be required to bear a considerably reduced standard teaching load. For example at the National Institute of Business Management in Colombo the heads of departments are supposed to spend 40% of their time in managerial and

---

[1] Cf. J.I. Reynolds: Case method in management development: Guide for effective use (Geneva, International Labour Office, 1980), Part IV.

administrative work and the rest in direct professional work. As already mentioned in chapter 5, many institutions have made a healthy decision that even their director has to devote a minimum amount of time to teaching or training.

For example the management of MBA programmes at the Cranfield School of Management is rated at 70 units out of an annual standard load of 240 to 250 units, i.e. about 29%. At the Indian Institute of Management in Ahmedabad a provision amounting to 50% of available time is made for this type of function, but the aim is to reduce it to 30%.

6.3 Costing and pricing

Many management institutions, including some that have to generate part of their own income, have only a vague notion of the real cost of their activities. The fees charged for various services are then arbitrarily set and bear no relation to actual costs. However, the recent recession and restrictions in public spending in many countries have induced a growing number of institutions to change this practice: it is not intellectual curiosity but stringent economic necessity that forces them to seek a deeper insight into the cost of their programmes and feasible ways of minimising costs without affecting quality. In some institutions this has become a question of survival.

Various programming decisions are difficult to make without a knowledge of the costs involved. It may be risky or even inefficient to authorise the preparation of new programmes without knowing their costs. A knowledge of costs is needed for planning, budgeting, and control and, last but not least, in order to justify requests for budgetary grants and subsidies. Even institutions whose total budget is sponsored by the government should be interested in the cost of various activities in order to increase internal efficiency and save public money.

Like businesses, management institutions can approach costing and cost control in various ways depending on the nature of their programmes and the desired degree of detail and precision.[1]

---

[1] See e.g. A recommended costing system for the CPC (Nicosia, Cyprus Productivity Centre, 1980) and pages 170-177 in G. Wills: Continuing studies for managers (Bradford, MCB Publications, 1981).

Basic approach

A simple example will be used to demonstrate basic costing considerations. Let us assume that the average annual salary of a professional faculty member is $20,000 and the average number of available working days 200. The institution's cost structure is 40% of professional salaries and 60% of administrative salaries and other general costs, i.e. the overhead charge will be 150% on every dollar of professional salary. The cost of one professional working day will thus be $100 + 150 = 250.

How can this cost be related to various activities? If consulting, research or other services are provided to external clients against payment, the institution knows that the minimum cost of a chargeable day is $250. The days allocated to such activities will be deducted from the total time-budget; if, say, 50 days are allocated, the time left for teaching and training will amount to 150 days.

Let us assume, further, that the standard teaching load corresponding to 150 days is 225 hours, i.e. 1.5 hour of direct teaching work per day, or 7.5 hours a week on the average. This includes a provision for current preparation, correction of exercises and tests, tutoring and individual advice, etc.

The cost of a one-week (five days) seminar (of six hours a day) would then be 5 x 4 x 250 = $5,000.

General administrative and promotional expenses have been included in the form of overhead. But there is no provision for developmental work, such as designing a new programme, case writing, preparing special handouts and exercises and so on. In this respect, there are two possibilities. Firstly, a provision for programme development work may be made by including it in one way or another in the standard cost of one professional day, which will then be higher than $250. Secondly, to arrive at a more accurate costing of individual activities, the related programme development work may be charged directly to each programme. If in our case 80 days of developmental time were budgeted and the programme is likely to be organised five times, the corresponding share of developmental cost is 16 x 250 = $4,000, and the total cost of one seminar $9,000.

Some refinements

Some further costs may be viewed as direct programme costs if greater precision is sought. Certain institutions prefer to consider programme promotion, participants' selection, and the cost of handouts and other training

184

materials as direct programme costs - if this achieves a useful purpose.

For example mail and non-local telephone costs can be charged to a particular management seminar to which they actually relate, but does this make sense? With this system a general promotional activity would be regarded as an overhead cost, but extensive promotion undertaken for a particular programme would not be charged to other programmes; this is only logical if there is a desire to know and manage costs.

Institutions also have some choice in distributing overhead costs. Different overhead rates may be established for different activities: for example, if general and administrative expenses are deemed to relate more to training activities than to research or consulting, this could be reflected in differentiated overhead rates. As regards the basis on which overhead is distributed, institutions normally choose between professional salaries and activity time, in particular if they use a more refined costing system in which professional time is costed separately for different staff categories (junior trainers or assistants, lecturers or operating consultants, professors or supervising consultants, external teachers, etc.). This may be useful in institutions offering programmes at several levels (e.g. top management, and supervisory and technician training) if the real cost of training or consulting staff is likely to be very different at each programme level for the same programme duration.

Price considerations

Returning to the example of our management seminar, if 15 participants are foreseen the institution could theoretically set the fee at $600 to break even. In real life, however, such simple arithmetic would seldom apply.

There is, first of all, the total budget and income structure and general pricing policy as defined by the institution's strategy and by a realistic assessment of its current financial position.[1] This will indicate the share of income to be generated by charging fees for client services. As a rule the institution will know from preliminary negotiations with its sponsoring or co-sponsoring bodies whether it can expect a budgetary allocation at an equal, reduced or increased level. Also, it may or may not be authorised to carry over a financial surplus to the next year's budget. If not, it is likely to endeavour to generate only as much income in the current year as it can really use for covering its

_____

[1] Cf. section 1.4.

expenditure, including the development cost that it is
authorised to finance from annual operating budgets.

However, even if there is a strong desire to charge
higher fees, this may not be so easy. The situation in
the local market of training and consulting services has
to be considered: the institution cannot normally charge
fees out of proportion with what others charge for comparable programmes and with what the clients are able and
willing to pay. Furthermore, clients expect some continuity and no radical changes in the pricing of professional services: even though they recognise the need to
adjust fees to inflation and to the cost of living, they
resent drastic increases due to internal policy decisions
of institutions.

6.4 Budgets and financial flows

A budget expresses in financial form the planned
programme of the institution. It is a statement of planned future results, which should be achieved if the work
plan is successfully implemented. It reflects, on the
one hand, the institution's financial strategy, and, on
the other hand, a realistic assessment of its ability to
achieve strategic objectives in the given budgetary period.

Management institutions normally have to present
their annual budgets to their parent body or board for approval and in support of requests for grants and subsidies
if the institution is not totally self-financing. Often,
the budget has therefore to be presented by a date and in
a form fixed by legislation or a parent body. However,
budgets should not be seen as a passive reflection of the
planned work programme and their preparation as a closing
phase of programme planning. Preliminary budgets should
be prepared in parallel with programme planning for the
main activity areas of the institution to show whether
the intended programme is financially feasible and to
permit corrections at a relatively early stage of programming. If it is anticipated that the financial situation is going to be difficult, financial targets and
expenditure limits may be prepared at the very beginning
of the programme planning exercise in order to indicate a
realistic financial framework for all programme planning
activities.

What can management institutions do to arrive at
balanced budgets providing for both quantitative and qualitative development and not just for sheer survival from
year to year? Of course, the total orientation of the
institution has some positive or negative budgetary implications, and basic choices cannot be changed in the short
run in connection with annual budgeting. However,
certain options remain open and are normally considered

during programme **planning**. **Several possibilities** are mentioned below.

<u>Increasing income</u>

(1) Increase demand through active programme promotion:

Many institutions can make a greater effort to inform the right people in client organisations about suitable training and other programmes. If a technically good programme does not appear to arouse enough interest, a special promotional campaign, using personal contacts with clients in addition to routine course announcements, may be necessary.

(2) Plan more income-generating work:

If the faculty does not grow this can be achieved by reducing or totally suppressing activities that would produce no income in the given budget period. Many autonomous institutions have had to do this to survive. However, this can mean that research, programme development or staff training are suppressed or that the faculty teaching load is set excessively high. Future consesequences may be disastrous.

(3) Favour programmes selling for higher prices:

Short top management programmes, or courses reacting to burning topics normally produce more income per time unit than other programmes. But the institution's ability to mount a number of such programmes has its limits. In addition, it can be risky to distort the institution's programme portfolio in order to generate more cash in the short run.

(4) Increase prices:

It has already been mentioned that course, consulting and other fees have to follow the pace of inflation and cost of living. It may be necessary, too, to adjust the fees for underpriced services. However, unjustified price increases are not a normal method of generating income in management institutions.

(5) Plan additional programmes using external collaborators:

This may be helpful if good part-time staff is available for fees relatively lower than the cost of using permanent staff for identical tasks. Limits to this approach were explained earlier.

(6) Seek higher grants or subsidies:

This way is open only in certain cases. Normally, higher grants and subsidies would be planned in the budget on the basis of preliminary negotiations and only if the institution believes that its request will not be rejected by its constituents or parent body.

Reducing expenditure

The possibilities of reducing expenditure without terminating the contracts of some professional or support staff are fairly limited in view of the fact that staff costs normally represent about 70 to 75% of expenditure. If demand is dropping considerably, the institution may have no other choice than to reduce the volume of activities and staff to arrive at a balanced budget. In other cases savings can be sought in sober administration, by reducing expenditure on activities that do not generate income as mentioned under (2) above and by reconsidering certain expenditure items that constitute an abnormal financial burden. For example some research and training institutions are accommodated in buildings which are not functional and whose cost of amortisation and maintenance is absolutely out of proportion to their volume of activity and budget.

Budgetary deficit

When all possibilities to increase income and reduce expenditure are exhausted, the institution may still have a deficit in its budget. Management institutions able to generate a large budgetary surplus and not knowing how to use it are rare birds. Most institutions have either to make great efforts to break even or they operate at a loss. It might be bad advice if we wrote that an institution must never operate at a loss. This must be judged in each particular case, comparing the institution's work programme to the budget, and considering the chances of raising more money from the government, university, business or individual alumni in order to cover the deficit. The quality of the work programme is a major asset. If the institution can demonstrate that its programme meets priority needs and is well thought through, its chances of raising further funds are better. Quite a few institution heads are aware of this rule and a moderate budgetary deficit does not prevent them from sleeping at nights.

Financial flows

In addition to its total budget, a management institution needs to have a more detailed (as a rule monthly) break-down of its cash flows to be sure that it will not suffer from cash shortages in one period of the year

while having surpluses in another. It is useful to determine precisely the pattern of financial flows in each
particular case since various types of institution acquire
finance and incur expenditure in different ways and at
different periods of the year.

The differences are not so much on the expenditure
side. Because of the high share of staff cost and other
recurrent operating costs, which are spread more or less
regularly over the whole year, the expenditure side
exhibits a fair regularity in any management institution.
In particular, staff has to be paid every month; the
atmosphere in institutions which occasionally have been
unable to meet this elementary commitment is sufficiently
well known in several countries.

Major changes in the regularity of financial flows
are more often found on the income side. One of three
typical patterns is seen in most institutions.

First, there are institutions whose income is forthcoming more or less regularly over the whole year. This
is characteristic of institutions providing a number of
shorter fee-earning management courses or consulting services; as a rule more or less the same number of programmes and assignments start and finish every month.

Second, at the other end of the spectrum one finds
institutions whose direct income from services is relatively small, say, less than 15% of the budget. The bulk
of finance is provided by a parent body, e.g. a university
or a chamber of commerce, or directly by a government department. The main factor determining the cash flows
will be not only the formally established practice of
transferring finance to the institution's bank account,
but, in many cases, the real capability of the sponsor
to respect his commitments in time. This problem is
well known to many institutions, especially in developing
countries, including some regional institutions depending
predominantly on contributions from member governments.
But, even if financial commitments are met as scheduled,
the institution may experience cash shortages at certain
periods of the year; to avoid this, a working capital
fund may have to be used or permission obtained to borrow
money for expenditure that cannot be delayed.

Third, many institutions can be positioned somewhere
between the two extremes. Cash generated by fee-earning
activities will constitute their more or less regular income, while grants and subsidies may be received less
regularly. Such institutions will try to plan and make
their expenditure accordingly.

6.5 Programme monitoring

Programme monitoring is a review of current operations and performance, organised on a periodical, recurrent basis. Its basic method is comparing the real course and results of operations with what has been programmed, and analysing variance. As a rule, institutions select certain indicators and aspects of operations for periodical control and review, and avoid collecting and controlling data on the basis of which no meaningful action can be taken.

Coherence between programme planning and budgeting on the one hand, and record-keeping and accounting on the other hand, cannot be overemphasised. The institution's system of operational management should be conceived as one whole, keeping in mind the controllability of data, their real use for operational decisions and the cost of recording them.

The nature of activities and resource needs determines the frequency of reports and reviews to be used in monitoring. In management institutions, monthly reviews tend to be given priority but, as will be shown below, some selected data may be reviewed weekly. Essential information is normally reviewed by the head of the institution and the whole management committee, while some other indicators may be followed by individual programme co-ordinators or by administrative officials.

Monitoring operations

In the monitoring of operations, institutions focus on indicators showing whether the work programme is being implemented as scheduled and on warnings permitting management to intervene in time.

In the area of teaching and training, all institutions without exception pay great attention to course applications. In some cases a detailed record of applications to all scheduled programmes is up-dated weekly and circulated to the programme co-ordinators. Disturbing cases are reviewed by management, which may also decide to enhance programme promotion. In institutions where participants have to pass through examinations or selection procedures the ratio of applicants to places available is reviewed and compared with the ratio achieved in previous years, and by similar institutions.

The implementation of scheduled programmes is reviewed monthly; points of special interest include programmes which were started without enough participants, the number of participants who dropped out, programmes that could not start on schedule for any reason and the status of preparation of important new programmes.

In consulting, the management will be interested in following, usually on a monthly basis, key indicators such as:

- forward workload;

- actual versus budgeted utilisation of total staff time;

- number of surveys made compared with number of assignments negotiated.[1]

In addition, the status of individual assignments or projects will be reviewed case by case; they will be visited by a supervising consultant or the head of the consulting unit, or project managers will report on progress to their chief.

In research, the on-going programme is less suitable for control on the basis of data and ratios. Institutions would normally organise periodical, as a rule, quarterly, review meetings to examine progress and problems. However, contractual action research is often monitored in much the same way as consulting assignments.

Monitoring quality

The quality of the institution's services is largely determined by the quality of its staff and short-term quality monitoring cannot achieve any spectacular changes. Nevertheless, it draws everybody's attention to the importance of quality standards and reveals cases of substandard quality, which may be caused by various reasons requiring management action. For example an experienced faculty member who normally performs well may prepare himself inadequately for some sessions because his teaching load is too high or because he has underrated the level of the participants.

In management training, course evaluation sheets filled in by participants at the end of the programme are very popular. At some centres each participant is asked to rate the following aspects of a programme:

---

[1] See also M. Kubr (ed.): Management consulting: A guide to the profession (Geneva, International Labour Office, 1976). Chapter 25 is particularly relevant to programme planning and monitoring in institutions involved in consulting.

- over-all **quality**;

- composition of the group of participants;

- workload;

- duration;

- amount of group work;

- programme administration (including several more detailed questions, such as technical management, logistics, physical facilities, and quality of meals);

- content and methodology of presentation made by each faculty member.

Programme co-ordinators and faculty members who get low rating in several successive instances will have to examine the reasons jointly with the faculty chairman; and should low ratings continue, this would normally be taken into consideration in their periodic performance appraisal. In some institutions it is a sufficient reason for asking the faculty member to resign.

Other tools for short-term monitoring of quality are rarely used. They include, for example, a preliminary review of training materials prepared for a new programme; video-recording of sessions, followed by analysis of both content and method; and discussions with participants several months after the completion of the programme.

In consulting, work quality is controlled mainly by visiting the consultants working at client organisations, discussing their assignment plans and proposed conclusions and, in any case, examining important reports and proposals before their submission to clients. Feedbacks from client organisations is sought as well.

In research, the scope for short-term quality monitoring is more limited than in training and consulting. However, improvements may in some cases be achieved by reviewing the methodology and work organisation that has been adopted, the initial materials collected and preliminary findings.

Monitoring costs and financial flows

Stark reality has compelled most management institutions to instal systematic and conscientious reviews of their financial position.

Important cost items are normally regularly compared with what was originally budgeted. For example, to prepare a new programme considerably more professional time may be needed than was originally budgeted. The reason for overexpenditure should be identified and corrections made, if possible. This, however, is not possible in many institutions, as they have no record of time devoted to particular programmes.

A monthly review of cash flows is normal practice in most management institutions. It is based on the disaggregation of annual financial statements into monthly periods as discussed above. Monthly and cumulative expenditures are shown against budgets. In doing this, some institutions go into considerable detail and periodically examine all important items of cash inflow and outflow. Every institution will then have certain specific items that may be causing trouble. For example institutions in some developing countries experience chronic difficulties in collecting consulting fees from local enterprises and have to return to this question on the occasion of each monthly review.

PART II

CASE STUDY: THE CENTRE D'ETUDES INDUSTRIELLES (CEI), GENEVA

Max Daetwyler

7

7.1 Company school phase: 1946 to 1956

The CEI was founded in 1946 by Alcan, Montreal, a
company that had been formed in 1929 as an offshoot of
Alcoa - the Aluminium Company of America - for business
operations primarily outside the United States.   By
definition Alcan was to become a truly international
enterprise.

According to some verbal accounts, the president of
Alcan at that time, E.K. Davis, aware of the future international dimension of his company, had already thought
about starting an international management centre as far
back as the late 1930s, but the outbreak of the Second
World War prevented him from carrying out his plans.
However, immediately after the war he decided to go ahead.

Legend has it that Alcan was at that time interested
in a large aluminium project in China.   A group of
Chinese engineers were in Canada in connection with this
project.   There, Dr. Paul M. Haenni, director of the
Alcan Research Laboratories, invited them to his home
where mind-stretching, culture-related discussions took
place.   When Davis heard of this, he felt that this was
just the type of preparation that should also be offered
to future Alcan managers.   Haenni, 46 years old at that
time, Swiss, a chemical engineer by background, a complete
novice in the field of management education, was finally
entrusted with this task.   At that time, Alcan already
had a branch office in Geneva, and since Haenni was Swiss,
it was not surprising that Geneva was chosen as the location of the new school.

The objective was to prepare future Alcan managers
for international operations and to attract capable university graduates to the company.   To attain this objective, the newly created management school organised an

annual 11-month **programme**. The students were either
young Alcan employees, or, to a considerable extent,
graduates fresh out of universities, i.e. without practical experience, who were granted an Alcan scholarship
and were expected to join the company after their year in
Geneva.

It would have been easy for the first director to
adopt existing educational models. After all, the
Harvard case study approach to business education was
already well established at that time. Instead, he drew
on many sources of inspiration, placing the emphasis on
broadening competence and building personality. Out of
the 11 months, at least 3 were spent in the field in
various countries of Europe, partly in small groups.
During these field studies, the participants, besides
studying management subjects in the companies and organisations they visited, were also expected to pay close
attention to the economic, political, social and cultural
environment in which the companies were operating. In
line with these objectives, visiting lecturers had an
important place in the programme.

The legal form of the CEI during these years was
that of an Alcan branch office. The annual budget
amounted to some 700,000 Swiss francs, financed entirely
by Alcan. The director surrounded himself with several
permanent staff members, some coming from Alcan, others
not. Personal attributes were considered more important
than formal academic qualifications.

Some 170 students graduated from this programme
between 1946 and 1956. Today, some of them can be found
in senior management positions in Alcan, including the
presidency, but many others left, especially those who
had no practical experience before joining the programme.

Although all those concerned agreed in retrospect
that the foundation of the school was a pioneering feat,
it is equally certain that some persons in Alcan had
doubts about the effectiveness of the approach. As a
result, fewer graduates fresh from university were
accepted, and ever since the early 1950s, the average age
of the students, around 25 initially, began to rise.
Also, there were questions about the match of the programme to the objectives. Was it really possible to
broaden the personalities of the participants and prepare
them in the best possible way for the future career in the
company, if only one company was involved in the school?
So, for the first time in 1954, some participants from
other companies were admitted to the programme.

7.2 Transformation/going public phase: 1956 to 1966

The year 1956 was to become an important date in the history of the CEI. First of all, a formal decision was taken to offer the programme to non-Alcan participants, whether sponsored by other companies or applying independently. Next, the legal form of the CEI was changed: instead of remaining an Alcan branch office, it was converted into an independent foundation created under Swiss law.

An agreement was reached with the University of Geneva whereby graduates of the programme became eligible for a Diploma in Industrial Administration, awarded jointly by the University and the CEI. Under the agreement there was to be a general exchange of culture between the CEI and the University and, to strengthen this relationship, the rector of the University became the only non-Alcan member of the CEI's governing body. The CEI thus became formally affiliated with the University of Geneva whilst retaining its complete administrative and financial independence.

What factors and pressures led to this development is difficult for present staff members to know for certain. The desire to "go public" was certainly there, but this was also the time when INSEAD was founded in Fontainebleau, and when Nestlé, whose headquarters are located in Vevey, at the other end of Lake Geneva, were contemplating the creation of their own institute. Records show that contacts between the CEI management and Nestlé existed at the time, and the possibility of joining forces was studied. The conclusion must have been negative. IMEDE in Lausanne was started as a venture entirely independent of the CEI; there were thus to be two schools in the Lake Geneva area, only 60 kilometres apart, following similar objectives.

Whereas IMEDE established close links with Harvard Business School, the CEI continued to tread an independent path. Its objectives were widened. They were still to broaden and internationalise young managers, but non-Alcan participants were now actively sought. The 11-month annual course, attended by 20 to 30 persons, remained the main activity. Teaching methods were further developed. In addition to the two kinds of field studies - first, two or three study trips to an industrial centre made by the whole group, and second, nearly 3 months of study trips in small groups at the end of the programme - some of the group projects achieved a high level of sophistication. There was, for example, a "new industrial investment project", requiring small groups of 5 or 6 students to prepare a detailed feasibility study (product and location being the group's choice), which they then had to present to the rest of the class. There was also an individual work requirement: a 25 to 35-page essay on a topic defined in agreement with the student at the beginning of the year; the study was presented to the rest of the class near the end of the course.

This was also the time when the principle of continuing education in management started being slowly accepted. In the middle and late 1950s the CEI made some pioneering attempts to offer short courses at the post-experience level to specific industry groups. For example, participants from the Swiss watch industry followed a course at the CEI, as did groups of middle managers of Alcan. These courses were discontinued after some time, but the CEI management then took an active part in the creation of a separate organisation called COREDE (Communauté romande pour l'économie d'entreprise) which, in modified form, still exists and has ever since offered short courses to the managers of industry in the French-speaking part of Switzerland.

Also, contacts with Philips' Gloeilampenfabrieken in the early 1960s ultimately led to the creation of a 4-week international executive programme, held for the first time in 1963. The participant group, made up of company-sponsored managers only, was the first at the CEI to come from a number of different companies. The annual 11-month programme was still attended mainly by Alcan participants and independent students; only a handful of other companies also sponsored students to the long programme. For this new 4-week programme, where participants had an average age of about 42, recruitment was much easier. It thus became a regular part of the CEI course offerings.

During this period the composition of the centre's board remained unchanged. It was chaired by the president of Alcan. Several high Alcan executives were members, and the rector of the University of Geneva continued to be the only outsider. There was a small core faculty, supplemented by a comparatively large number of visiting faculty members, including some of very high standing. Contacts with several countries in Eastern Europe were established at this time. They included the exchange of students and faculty members, and industry visits.

The total annual budget remained fairly stable and, in 1966 for example, amounted to some 800,000 Swiss francs, of which 80% was still provided by Alcan, the rest coming from tuition fees. Alcan thus continued to give strong support to the school although the aluminium industry passed through a very difficult period around 1957-1958.

Around 1964, another problem was openly discussed at the school: that of succession. The school had been directed since 1946 by Dr. Haenni, who had become one of the pioneers in management education and training in Europe and whose name was closely associated and identified with the institute. He was due to retire in 1965. Would the school survive this change or was it going to disappear without the leadership of its founder? The suspense lasted quite some time. In the absence of a decision, Haenni was asked to stay an additional year.

7.3 Strategy/concept/growth phase: 1966 to 1971

Early in 1966 a successor was finally chosen in the person of Jean-Yves Eichenberger, a Frenchman and - like his predecessor - holder of a senior management position with Alcan. It was perfectly normal that this change - after 20 years of the same management - should result in a number of new developments. One was a very heavy emphasis on recruiting for the long programme for which demand had fallen considerably. Another was that, as continuing education in management was being slowly accepted, the time had come to offer additional short programmes. To begin with, a 2-week marketing seminar and an 8-week advanced management programme were planned for early 1968; some other programmes were to be added later. The faculty was reinforced, but many questions were raised on the CEI's future. To finance these and other changes, the budget had to be increased considerably. The Alcan contribution, which during 1965-1966 had been 580,000 Swiss francs, jumped to 1,090,000 in 1966-1967. Alcan underwrote these amounts without demurring as it was thought that the additional money would make it possible to decrease Alcan support considerably later.

About 2 years later Eichenberger accepted a top management position in French industry and resigned from the CEI. He was succeeded by Bohdan Hawrylyshyn, a Canadian of Ukrainian origin and an engineer by background. Hawrylyshyn had originally worked for Alcan in Canada and attended the CEI annual course in 1957-1958. Upon completing the course, he returned to Canada, but joined the CEI in 1960 as director of studies.

A strategy for the CEI

In the spring of 1968 the CEI held the first session of its 8-week international advanced management programme. One of the participants, the future president of Volvo,

Pehr Gyllenhamar, asked the CEI staff at the end of the
programme the pertinent question: "You are teaching us
strategic planning, but could you tell us what your own
strategy is?"

This triggered off intensive internal discussions
and the result was a document, dated December 1968, which
contained precise statements of the CEI's mission, objectives and means of achieving them, policies and other
fundamental aspects of the institution. The following is
an extract from the document:

I. MISSION

To contribute to improved management, particularly
that of international enterprise. The CEI should do
things in which its character and the structure of its
resources permit it to excel.

II. OBJECTIVES

Long term:

To grow and achieve pre-eminence in its field. It
should retain its separate identity, but should co-operate
with other educational institutions, if its status and the
quality of its work can be enhanced thereby.

Medium term (five years):

(1) Financial resources

About 60% of the necessary funds should be generated
through course fees, consulting and other income. 40%
should come from funded capital and/or business organisations, foundations, public sources. Within 5 years,
Alcan's contribution should be of the same magnitude as
that of other supporting institutions.

(2) Human resources

The critical resource is faculty. Its multinational
composition should be maintained. In 5 years though,
only about half of its members should be those with major
experience in industry, but with adequate academic qualifications; the remainder should have a more academic
background of teaching, research and publishing.

The permanent faculty should be supplemented by some
part-time faculty members all making major contributions:
one or more visiting professors of international reputation on a full-time basis for a year or so, mainly for
teaching; a visiting scholar financed through special
grants, mainly to do research work and guest speakers.

III. MEANS OF ACHIEVING THE OBJECTIVES

The long-term objectives will be achieved by:

(1) generating, through research, the knowledge about significant problems in management of international enterprises and by publishing results;

(2) offering a series of programmes for various levels of management;

(3) helping the firms to implement new knowledge through selective consulting.

. . . .

The word "strategy" is not mentioned, but the importance of this document was truly strategic. During these years constant review and discussion of these and other issues at the institute led to a number of concepts which all made a substantial contribution to the further development of its activities. Among them were the following:

The effectiveness of the enterprise

In order to help clients to manage better, it was essential to know what factors contribute to the effectiveness of the organisation. At the CEI they were summarised under four headings:

- the environment, which has to be assessed and understood;

- the strategy, including the values existing in an enterprise, the policies, the objectives, as well as the major action programmes;

- the structure;

- the performance of people.

It was felt that the CEI had to address itself seriously to these four areas. This meant that in contrast to the situation in other similar institutions, the environment received considerable attention, as had been a tradition at the institute right from the start.

Whom to teach and what?

The programme policy described in the 1968 strategy document gradually led to the development of the CEI pyramid concept, as illustrated in figure 16. It shows general management programmes, cutting across functions, designed for different levels of management, as well as a

203

Figure 16   The CEI programme pyramid

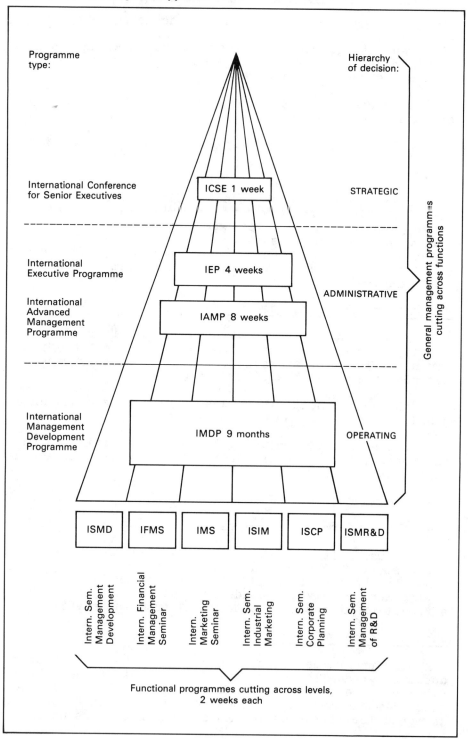

series of 2-week seminars dealing with different functions. This concept facilitated the decisions on what types of programmes to introduce and what activities not to enter.

How to teach?

Ever since its foundation the CEI had not used a single teaching method, but a whole package - lectures, case studies, field work, group projects, individual assignments - some of which it had developed itself. During the 1960s, the thinking on methodology became more systematic. It was summarised in a paper[1] which became a milestone in CEI's development. The idea of mixing a variety of teaching and training methods in order to influence knowledge, skills and attitudes in the course of the learning process has since that time been consistently applied to all programmes. In addition, the Ford Foundation provided a substantial grant to the CEI for research into the effectiveness of training methods. This was a major input in the institute's development at a crucial time.

The business associate programme

The CEI had been founded by one sponsoring company, Alcan. Since the intention was to serve a wider public, it was essential to create close relationships with other companies as well. This led to the CEI business associate programme. Selected international firms were invited to join the programme which was simply a co-operative approach to the solution of management education problems. For an annual fee of 20,000 Swiss francs, the companies are entitled to participate in a number of events at the CEI. From 5 companies who joined in the early 1970s, the programme grew to include 60 leading international firms.

The research model

Experience showed that to achieve a significant research activity was difficult. The CEI adopted the following approach in this area. Faculty members and research assistants work on long-term projects. Scholars and executives in residence, often from CEI business associate firms, join for shorter periods. Each works to-

---

[1] See B. Hawrylyshyn: "Preparing managers for international operations", in Business Quarterly, autumn 1967, pp. 28-35; or B. Hawrylyshyn: "Management education - a conceptual framework", in B. Taylor and G.L. Lippitt: Management development and training handbook (London, McGraw Hill, 1975, pp. 169-181.

towards outputs of particular relevance to his or her
interests. For example, a project of particular importance was in the field of environmental management, under
the sponsorship of the United Nations Environmental Programme.

Other developments

In parallel to all these developments, the composition of the CEI foundation's board underwent a fundamental
change, since non-Alcan members were now invited to join.
In 1971 non-Alcan members of the board constituted the
majority for the first time. The event was hardly
noticed or discussed at the CEI, although it was of the
highest significance.

Another noteworthy event in the early 1970s was a
major management symposium held in Davos on the occasion
of the CEI's 25th anniversary. With over 400 persons in
attendance, the event was a resounding success. This
then led to the question of whether such a symposium ought
to become a regular CEI event, an issue actively discussed by the faculty. This finally led to the foundation of a separate organisation, the European Management
Forum, and the Davos symposium has become an event offered
each year to senior managers from Europe and other regions.

The entire faculty was involved in the discussion of
these and other issues, and it was found useful at this
stage to create a formal management committee to which
certain decisions were delegated. It included the
director, as well as 4 associate directors, one each in
charge of education, research, institutional development
and administration. The committee still operates in
modified form. Meetings involving the whole faculty
continue to take place, but at less frequent intervals
and with a different agenda.

7.4 Institutional development:
     1972 and after

By the early 1970s the CEI had a clear view of its
mission. It had developed certain values and policies,
as well as a whole series of concepts. It had worked
out a set of long-term objectives, including independence
from its founding company and the building up of a group
of associate companies. All these ideas were firmly
anchored in the culture of the whole institution. There
was also the clear realisation that all this could only
be accomplished if the different actions and programmes
offered received excellent ratings for their effectiveness. Evaluation of all its activities therefore took
an important place in the institution's life. Every
single contribution by a faculty member was and continues

206

to be reviewed and evaluated by the participants, who are regarded as clients.

Achieving the objectives, especially the financial ones, was complicated throughout the 1970s by the fact that the CEI was operating from a home base whose currency, the Swiss franc, continued to appreciate year after year in relation to other currencies. For example, whereas at the beginning of the 1970s the exchange rate was 4.30 Swiss francs to the US dollar, it had dropped to around 1.50 francs by the end of the decade. This made the CEI's services very expensive when measured in other currencies. Without formally intending to do so, the institute thus became a price leader. This was difficult, but may have been healthy as well, since all the more emphasis had to be placed on the quality of whatever services it offered.

Strategic reviews

Two dates during the seventies marked key events. First the academic year 1975-1976, when a "strategy task force" was formed, chaired by the CEI faculty member teaching corporate strategy, Dr. Fred Neubauer. It looked at the CEI's position from all angles and summarised its work in a 50-page report. Among the recommendations made at that time was the reinforcement and the formal development of activities outside Geneva. Some such activities had already taken place, but they now received more emphasis, which led the CEI to organise programmes in North America, Latin America, the Middle East and Asia. More emphasis was also placed on internal company programme. Another recommendation of this task force was the introduction of a formal MBA degree for the successful graduates of the annual long programme. The first MBA degrees were awarded in May 1979.

A second comprehensive review of the CEI's position was triggered off by the realisation that 1978 was situated just half-way between 1956, the year the CEI had become an independent legal entity, and the year 2000. It was carried out under the heading "The CEI in the year 2000" as already described in chapter 2.

At the time of writing (1981) the CEI thus shows a number of characteristics of which the most important could be described as follows.

Independence

The supreme formal authority of the CEI, the foundation's board, is no longer dominated by one group of people. The centre of gravity in taking decisions lies at the institute and this is likely to remain so, unless

there is a need, at some future date, for a financial
rescue operation. The direction and faculty will obviously do everything to avoid this. The financial contribution of the founding company, Alcan, used to represent
some 80% of the budget in 1966. It now amounts to no
more than 2%.

A set of fairly clear, shared concepts

What constitutes the effectiveness of an organisation, what to teach, to whom and how, and other such
questions, are issues that have been and continue to be
widely debated among the faculty. The faculty shares
the objectives pursued by the institute. A question
raised at the CEI is to what extent some of these concepts can be applied not only to industrial or other cor
porations, but to governments or whole countries as well.[1]

International character

It is present in all aspects of the CEI's life. In
the foundation's board all major areas of the world are
represented. The faculty is international and includes
members from developing regions as well. The group of
60 CEI business associates includes firms from all parts
of the world. Course participants come from all over
the world and some programmes are held outside Europe.
Finally, practically all teaching and research has an
international dimension.

Tough challenges

The CEI is selling education at cost price. It does
not receive and has never asked for government subsidies.
Education is expensive. In our society, one is not used
to being confronted with the true cost of education.
Even at the CEI, there is, internally, a system of compensation. Short programmes for high-level participants
pay for the longer programmes, where it would be difficult to charge true cost. Obviously the pressure to
perform, under such circumstances, is severe, even if it
is healthy, and leads to challenging situations in different areas. One problem the CEI has yet to solve is
the expansion of its physical facilities, which have
become inadequate.

7.5 A few final observations based on comparison

When viewed from a distance, it is instructive to
see how the CEI reached its position today. An industrial

---

[1] See B. Hawrylyshyn: Road maps to the future:
Towards more effective societies (Oxford, Pergamon Press,
1980).

company, Alcan, felt the need for such an institution long ago. Inside Alcan, it was essentially one man, E.K. Davis, who had this vision. Over the years Alcan invested over 25 million Swiss francs in the venture. It then withdrew and, after giving the school a generous farewell present in the form of the land and building, set the school completely free. Ever since the early 1970s it has no longer been able to impose its views, even if it wanted to.

It is instructive to compare this approach to that of Nestlé, another major international firm, some 4 times the size of Alcan, which founded the IMEDE. Publicly available background documents show the following differences in strategic choices:

(1) To lead the institution, Alcan appointed persons from within the company. All three directors of the CEI so far were appointed at a time when Alcan still held control. All had started their career with Alcan. However, once appointed they were given much freedom. At IMEDE, Nestlé appointed to the post of director experts from outside, probably those considered the best available professionals for the task: professors with a Harvard Business School or another North American background.

(2) The CEI directors therefore did not enjoy a prestigious academic origin. They had to start from scratch. This was more difficult, but had the advantage that right from the start nothing was taken for granted: there was an active, sincere effort to search for one's own ways and original approaches. This was a real and tough endeavour, but one that led to an atmosphere of openness and innovation. At IMEDE, the highly qualified leaders probably had the tendency to transfer existing educational models which they had used earlier in their careers. Until recently, in all its publications the IMEDE cites the almost exclusive use of the case method, developed at Harvard, as one of its main strengths. This difference is further illustrated by the fact that the IMEDE entertained an institutional relationship with the Harvard Business School, without any doubt a great asset and advantage, especially in the launching period. At the CEI, no such institutional link with a prestigious American business school has ever existed.

(3) At the CEI the centre of gravity in decision taking was, and still is, at the institute. The board is international and the institute's director is a member. No single group has a controlling majority, as explained earlier. The governing body at the IMEDE includes a majority of Swiss nationals and is headed by the chairman

of the founding **company, the only foreigner** by nationality.   The director of IMEDE is not a member.

(4) The pressure to perform and become self-sufficient
was probably more severe at the CEI than at the IMEDE.
This may explain some major differences in programme
offerings.   There is a tendency at the CEI to offer more
shorter programmes at higher fees.   Until recently at
the IMEDE the number of programmes held every year was
lower, their total duration longer, and the corresponding
fee income per participant of necessity less.   Obviously,
both approaches have advantages and disadvantages which
could be discussed at length.

(5) Both management schools constitute classical examples of how leading international firms have taken initiatives outside their traditional fields of activity by
setting up major educational institutions which have become open to the general management public.   The models
and strategies may have been different, but they have one
thing in common: a strong determination to contribute to
the advancement of management education and to the dissemination of effective management practices world-wide.

CASE STUDY: THE IRISH MANAGEMENT INSTITUTE (IMI), DUBLIN

8

Ivor Kenny

8.1 The IMI in context

The Irish Management Institute is an independent, non-profit-making institution. It is controlled by a council and executive committee elected solely from its members, both corporate (public and private sector enterprises) and personal (individual managers). Its main activity is post-experience management development. It was founded in 1952 "by businessmen for businessmen", and by 1981 its total expenditure had reached about 3 million Irish pounds,[1] of which somewhat less than 30% is grants from the Irish Government and from the European Social Fund of the EEC. It has a total staff of 100, including a full-time faculty of 30. There is a large associate (part-time) faculty. The Institute is located in a prize-winning centre standing on 13 acres outside Dublin, the capital city of the Republic of Ireland.

The IMI is the only centre of its kind in Ireland. Ireland is a small country that could hardly afford another centre with the requisite critical mass of staff and facilities. The Republic of Ireland is composed of 26 of the 32 counties of the island of Ireland; the other 6, Northern Ireland, are under direct British rule. The population of the Republic is about 3.4 million of whom 1.2 million constitute the labour force. By EEC standards a high proportion of that labour force (20%) is still employed in agriculture. The Republic of Ireland is, however, industrialising at a rapid rate and with considerable success, the emphasis being on high technology and high added value.

Successive Irish Governments, which have been very stable, have favoured free enterprise, even though the

---

[1] For a rough US dollar equivalent, multiply by 2.

State now disposes of more than 50% of GNP. The Government's biggest concern is structural unemployment, which is of the order of 10% of the labour force. This 10%, sometimes more, seldom less, has proved remarkably intractable.

Ireland's industrialisation has been marked by some turbulence. Strikes, particularly in public utilities, tend to be uniquely long and bitter. The infrastructure - roads, telecommunications - has not kept pace with the needs of industry. However, the educational infrastructure - universities, colleges of technology - is relatively mature, and the workforce is young, educated and increasingly articulate. The country has experienced high inflation since the oil crisis. There is now the possibility of Irish oil, a possibility looked on with mixed feelings. Properly handled it could bring benefits; badly handled, with an eye only to the short term, it could damage the structure of Irish industry and seriously affect employment.

By European standards, Ireland is not rich, being the twenty-fifth richest country in the world. It was the first country to win its freedom from the British empire, and with their long history of exploitation, the Irish value their independence highly. The Irish diaspora in the United States, Australia and Britain considerably outnumbers the population of Ireland itself.

8.2 The development of the IMI

Within this changing community certain phases can be identified in the development and consequent characteristics of the IMI. The Institute is now perceived as among the leading management development centres in Europe. The truth probably is that in some areas (action learning, knowledge transfer, small business) it is somewhat ahead, while in others (research in particular) it is behind, and that in the bulk of its activity it is as good as most of what is offered in Europe.

The phases through which it came to its present status are as follows:

1952 to 1956

This was largely a promotional phase. The emphasis was on membership recruitment, on sharing experience, on creating an awareness of the fact that management could be studied and taught. There were occasions for senior managers "to tell war stories". There were interesting two-day seminars by foreign, mainly American, experts, mostly from the now defunct European Productivity Agency.

212

1956 to 1960

IMI committees of businessmen and academics produced reports on how management education and post-experience management development should be organised in Ireland. These were to lead to a considerable expansion of business education in the universities and in the technological and vocational colleges. The Institute ran its first series of 2- or 3-week general management programmes. The country, meanwhile, was emerging from a protectionist era into an era of international free trade.

1960 to 1964

Having become head of the Institute's embryo Management Development Unit, the author was sent - as so many Europeans then were - on a tour of American business schools. He used the opportunity to test with far more experienced people a few burgeoning ideas. They were: to research the needs of Irish management; to develop a nucleus of indigenous staff (we could not for ever live off interesting foreign experts); and to seek a degree of state aid. These three objectives were attained.

A study of management in Irish industry[1] was the first of its scope conducted in any country. It had two purposes, one scientific, the other political. The scientific one was to give a solid, statistically valid, basis for priorities in management education and development. The political one was to prove to business, and more particularly to government, that increased resources were necessary. This second purpose was to lead the Institute at times to make rather heroic claims for the role of management development in economic and social development. Investment in bricks, mortar and machinery was more attractive to government than investment in management manpower. (The claims have with the years become more realistic; the need to make them forcefully has not diminished.)

The first IMI "specialists" were recruited. Significantly, they came not from academia but from senior practising managers, with at least a good primary degree, an ability to conceptualise and to communicate, and a high sense of the mission of the Institute. This policy has continued, though recently with increased emphasis on higher degrees. It was during this period also that the question was asked: were the newly recruited IMI specialists to follow up the participants in their firms in order

---

[1] Cf. B. Tomlin: The management of Irish industry (Dublin, Irish Management Institute, 1966).

to help development?   Some attempts to do so were made,
but the Institute quickly discovered how demanding on
man-hours this was and it soon backed off.

A nucleus of specialists had now been formed.   With
hardly any local competition, there was an explosion in
functional and general training courses.   The graphs all
pointed upwards.

Government aid was secured.   The Prime Minister
warned that an institution could subtly change its character once it got government money.   But he said also that
he did not want the ship spoiled for a ha'porth of tar.

1964 to 1968

There was still an emphasis on bringing experts from
abroad.   But now the IMI specialists designed the programmes and themselves made major contributions.   There
was a more informed selection of visiting lecturers.   The
specialists ensured that the principles presented by the
visitors were illustrated in Irish terms.   Activity and
staff numbers were growing.   New premises were acquired
and became inadequate.

1968 to 1972

The longer general management programmes were not
selling well.   Time away from the job seemed to be a de-
terrent.   This led to the now-familiar modular approach.
Its success in general management programmes led to its
adoption in the functional areas.

Further research surveys showed a need for trained
managers.   There was a call for special programmes for
smaller businesses and a Small Industries Unit was established.   Its approach incorporated some of the need
achievement work of McClelland.

The Institute began to pay more attention to
research, particularly in in-company development programmes: job enrichment, the assessment of organisation
climate and the management of change.   A number of publications of some distinction emerged.   An In-Company
Unit was established to offer help on corporate planning
and organisation development.

1972 to 1976

In the earlier part of this period the Institute
presented programmes under the headings of: in-company;
management functions; small business and industrial sectors; and human resources.   A special Research Unit was

having another look at the stock of Irish managers and their level of expertise.[1]

In terms of quantity, this was the peak of the Institute's activity. It was also a boom time for Irish business. The Institute got from its corporate members the largest sum ever raised voluntarily in Ireland. With that sum, together with the proceeds from the sale of its former premises and a handsome gift from the Government, it build premises of a high international standard. They are equipped with computer facilities, television studios, library and ancillary facilities, and dining hall. They are not yet residential.

Courses were now getting longer and there was an increasing emphasis on evaluation. Action learning, which was being developed by Reg Revans, aroused the Institute's interest. It was decided to offer to senior managers a 2-year development programme based on the principles of action learning. To help make a programme of such length and intensity attractive and to ensure that it conformed with rigorous standards the University of Dublin agreed to collaborate and to award a new degree: Master of Science in Management. In recent years this collaboration has led to a further joint degree in organisation behaviour. A degree in finance is planned.

This link with a university was an interesting one. It was based on genuine collaboration around a real task: a joint degree. Each institution recognised the other's strengths. Each maintained its integrity and separateness.

The ceremonies marking the opening, on 25 September 1974, of the new premises marked also an apogee. A few months later the Institute was faced with a unique combination of unfavourable circumstances given impetus by the oil crisis: high inflation, deep recession, static (therefore declining) government and European Social Fund grants.

By 1974 the Institute's staff had grown to 135. Following a crisis review, it was decided that all activities that were "unprofitable" would be phased out. Nine senior staff were declared redundant. The view of the business community was favourable. The IMI was living in the real world. It had to take the same unpopular decisions that business faced. The response of the Institute's staff was different. Although their commitment to the Institute was considerable, their commitment

---

[1] See L. Gorman, R. Handy, T. Moynihan and R. Murphy: Managers in Ireland (Dublin, Irish Management Institute, 1974).

to the way it was managed was, to put it delicately, negative.   There followed a year of intensive internal negotiation, during which, to the outside world, the Institute's heart did not miss a beat.   What emerged was a
staff organisation changed radically in structure and in
norms.   The former hierarchy, with executive directors in
charge of units, was dropped.   It was replaced by a
matrix structure for the faculty.   The matrix was headed
by a faculty chairman selected for a 3-year term by the
director-general from a panel of 3 elected candidates.
There were new, partly elected, management and policy committees, accountable to the director-general, who chaired
them - in fact working with him as a team.   There was a
new staff group as a formal forum for consultation.   The
Institute's council and executive committee structures
remained unchanged.   The organisation norms were openness, equity, collaboration and individual autonomy.

     The "revolution", as it was rather grandly called,
served to show that the Institute had not been too skilful
at practising what it preached.   The quick slide into
economic recession could perhaps have been better anticipated.   What could certainly have been anticipated, and
was not, was the staff's dissatisfaction with a style of
management they had outgrown.   Hindsight, however, can be
self-serving.   One way or the other, the revolution
released creativity.   With their new sense of "ownership"
of the Institute, the productivity of the staff increased.

1976 to 1981

     Courses were now getting steadily longer.   The Ins-
titute moved, a little uncertainly, into diploma programmes.   On the one hand, it was felt that a relatively
long and intensive period of study deserved formal recognition.   On the other, there was a strong feeling that
the Institute should not become a half-baked university,
where one could "buy diplomas".   Following several
experiments, some successful, some less so, rigorous criteria were laid down and external examiners introduced.

     A development was the growth in international work.
The Institute's non-colonialist past, with English as its
language, made it attractive to developing African countries.   However, the work was not confined to them.   A consultancy was conducted for the Government of Canada.
Staff worked in Europe, the Middle East, south-east Asia,
Australia, the Caribbean and Latin America.   A series of
international programmes is now held each year in Dublin.
The first international programme on the management of
management centres was mounted by the IMI in 1978 using
the Institute as a case study.

The Institute's earlier work for small business was
virtually abandoned during the recession. Helping small
business is expensive. When things got brighter, however, the Institute initiated the Business Development
Programme. The small owner-manager does not want, and
will not participate in, long, though intellectually stimulating courses. He needs continuous help, highly relevant, over a long period, but making the best use of his
limited time. And he will not pay high fees. Two
Institute specialists single-mindedly set out to raise
adequate funding from big business. They developed an
18-month programme focusing on the entrepreneur the combined weight of the many Irish help agencies, including
the commercial banks. The programme, which is being continually developed, has attracted international attention.

8.3 The present and the future: some lessons learned

At the time of writing, Ireland, in common with most
European countries, is in the grip of a serious recession:
unemployment is high, inflation has touched almost 20%,
government borrowing and taxation have reached a point
where cut-backs were inevitable. The Institute has
coped well, but uncertainty about the future led to a
major review of strategy. This took a year to complete,
partly because of the necessity for extensive consultation at every stage, partly because it was carried out by
a policy committee whose members had other work to do.

The review confirmed the importance of an abiding
IMI characteristic: its ownership and control being in
the hands of those it serves. The Institute is, in a
unique way, permanently accountable to those it serves.
With the perspective of more than a quarter of a century,
and with increasing opportunities for international comparisons, this characteristic emerges as one of the most
important factors in the Institute's ability to influence
the quality of management in Ireland.

It is a delicate relationship. The Institute seeks
continually to foster it through membership activities
alongside management development courses. It is not possible to cover these activities in this short study,
except to mention that there are regional committees of
the IMI throughout Ireland, which organise exchanges of
experience. There is a monthly journal, chief executive
meetings, an executive health unit, and an annual national
management conference - the major business event of the
year. The Institute comments for managers on business
issues and publishes books on the business environment.
It maintains a high national profile.

Its relationship with those it serves could have
been upset by government subvention. It could have been
perceived as a parastatal body, an arm of government
policy, with overtones of coercive powers. That it was
not is due to the spirit in which subvention is paid by
the sponsoring ministry, the Department of Labour. Once
the case has been made and accepted, the Institute is
allowed to get on with the job. The Institute, for its
part, has always done what it said it would do and, critically, has always sought to earn at least 2 pounds for
every pound of grants. This relationship of mutual respect with the Department of Labour has been a major contribution to the Institute's ability to develop its relationship of mutual confidence with managers. Management
development is, among other things, about competence,
about learning, about creativity, about confidence in the
face of risk and uncertainty, about awareness of the
effect on other people of one's actions. These are qualities that can be encouraged and influenced. They cannot be imposed or legislated for.

The recent policy review served to underline a fact
that can easily get buried beneath survival, comfort or
risk-free objectives: that is that the legitimacy of a
management centre, its raison d'être, comes not essentially from its political quick-footedness, which is
important, but from its continuing ability to anticipate
needs that no one else meets, or meets as well, or meets
in the same way. The path the IMI has chosen to identify and meet those needs (and one which may not apply
equally to certain centres in other countries) is that of
independence, i.e. not being absorbed into the state system. While independence is the more difficult route
(particularly in an Irish environment increasingly dense
with competitors, many of whom are totally state-funded)
it keeps the Institute flexible and responsive. It
keeps it identified with those it serves. It frees it
from bureaucratic controls and it gives the staff greater
individual freedom.

Independence has costs. Decisions on expenditure
can be over-influenced by what can be afforded at the
time, at the expense of what needs to be done to ensure
the future. The short-term survival objective inevitably supplants the developmental (and long-term survival)
one. If the financial constraints are too tight, a
centre cannot both survive and develop. As the foregoing narrative has shown, the IMI has developed over the
years, but it has not developed enough, a fact that to
some extent was concealed by its very ability to survive.

There is no soft option for an independent centre.
The underlying philosophy of independence predicates a
creative tension between what the centre delivers and

218

what it gets paid. It will always be to a centre's
advantage to optimise earned income. Further, development (or investment) means money spent now in order to
earn increased income in future. The fact that business
pays a realistic price for a centre's services is one
good indicator that the centre is meeting business' needs.
What has to be got right is the balance.

The IMI has learned that there is also another balance to be maintained. For the staff, personal freedom
is the single aspect of the organisation's climate most
highly valued. It is strongly linked with the Institute's
independence. The spirit which animates an organisation
is as important as its effectiveness in identifying and
meeting needs or as its political skill in giving itself
space to do so. It is, however, of unusual importance
in a management centre. Its job is missionary. It is
about influencing. It deals with many intangibles not
susceptible to the cruder measures of the market place.

Whatever objectives a centre sets itself, no matter
how well based, will suffer death in the drawer if they
are not informed with a spirit of confidence, optimism
and tenacity. There is a nice balance to be maintained
here between necessary order - in budgeting, in allocation
of resources, in reporting systems - and not having someone breathing down one's neck. The responsibility for
maintaining that balance lies squarely with a centre's
management. It was put clearly by an IMI faculty member:
"We want freedom. We also want a strong hand on the
tiller".

The IMI has provided for Irish managers a bridge
between theory and practice. Without practice theory is
suspect. Without theory current practice is simply reinforced and there is minimal growth. To develop
farther, to innovate and to grow, the Institute now needs
substantial investment in research and development in
sharply focused strategic thrusts. It has identified
those thrusts. The next thing is to secure, by an array
of means, the investment. That will be one more step on
an interesting and endless path.

CASE STUDY: THE INDIAN INSTITUTE OF MANAGEMENT (IIMA), AHMEDABAD

9

Samuel Paul

The Indian Institute of Management, Ahmedabad (IIMA), was established in 1962 by the Government of India in collaboration with the State Government of Gujarat, the Ford Foundation and Indian industry. IIMA was one of the two semi-autonomous national institutes set up by the Government of India to meet the growing demand in the country for managerial personnel. The two institutes were set up outside the university framework as it was felt that, in order to innovate in the new field of management education, they would require a large measure of autonomy. Though this proposal was opposed by the major universities in India, which had by then established their own programmes for management education, the Indian Government decided that on balance the new institutes would perform better as autonomous centres rather than as part of the existing Indian universities. Like the Indian Institutes of Technology, which had also been set up on similar lines, IIMA was financed and supervised by the Ministry of Education of the Government of India through a board of governors which included the representatives of the Federal Government, the State Government of Gujarat and industry.

One of the earliest decisions of the Government of India concerning IIMA was in regard to the choice of a foreign collaborator for the new project. Though some Indian universities had their own management (business administration) departments and the Administrative Staff College of India was already in existence, the Government invited the Harvard Business School (HBS) to provide technical assistance to the new institution. The proposed assistance scheme was financed by a grant from the Ford Foundation, which had advised the Government earlier on the establishment of a national management institute.

9.1 Role of the collaborator

The role of IIMA's foreign collaborator, the Harvard Business School, was fourfold.

Choice of the educational model

The collaborator was to assist IIMA in choosing and adapting a model of management education appropriate to Indian conditions. Clearly, in this endeavour, HBS was very influenced by its own philosophy, past experience and assessment of what Indian managers needed. HBS professors visited India and prepared reports on the nature and scope of the roles they should play in relation to the development of IIMA. The model they recommended emphasised experience-based teaching with a heavy reliance on the case method. The Indian leaders involved in planning IIMA had prior associations with HBS and had little difficulty in accepting this advice.

Advisory services

The choice of the model implied a series of sequential decisions and specific actions in which the collaborator assisted IIMA. HBS had a team of consultants led by a senior person based in Ahmedabad and a project leader at HBS who visited and kept in touch with IIMA periodically. By virtue of their role as collaborators, they were consulted on major decisions though the formal decision-making rested with their Indian counterparts. In most academic matters, HBS consultants initiated a number of ideas and interacted closely with the Indian faculty both formally and informally. Thus their role in the planning and implementation processes was significant in spite of occasional problems and frictions, and extended over a period of five years.

Faculty development

A major role of the collaborator in the initial phase was in the selection and development of the faculty of the new institute. Several of the IIMA faculty were identified from among young Indians who were either in industry at home or in graduate schools abroad. Before they began to teach at IIMA, all or most of them in the early years were sent for further training at HBS for a period of one year. In some cases a few were sent for MBA or doctoral programmes, which meant that they stayed abroad for two or three years to complete their studies. The training given to the new faculty was not limited to academic courses. At HBS they were also exposed to the problems of curriculum planning, selection and admission of students, placement, case development and a variety of

222

other academic and administrative matters. The programme of training abroad was gradually phased out by
the end of the first decade. Though the understanding
was that the involvement of HBS faculty members in teaching at IIMA would be minimal, short-term assistance in
teaching was provided in the initial phase when many
Indian teaching staff were sent abroad for training.

Case development and
linkage building

HBS consultants based in Ahmedabad were active in
field work and case writing. This role flowed from the
educational model, which placed considerable emphasis on
problem solving and practice-oriented teaching. The case
writing programme helped to generate new teaching materials adapted to the needs of the Indian environment. This
programme also enabled the Indian staff to get acquainted
with the problems of management in Indian enterprises and
establish links with managers and entrepreneurs in a wide
range of industries and locations. Professional collaboration between the HBS consultants and Indian faculty
members in this area was particularly fruitful.

There were other areas also in which HBS collabo-
rated actively. The development of the library and the
planning of academic and physical facilities are some
examples. The selection of the director was not, however, a subject in which HBS had an active role. The
first part-time director of IIMA, Dr. Vikram Sarabhai,
who initiated the idea of locating the institute in
Ahmedabad, was already in position when HBS entered the
scene. The choice of his successor in 1965 was one on
which HBS advice was sought. The formal decision was,
of course, made by IIMA's board of governors with the
approval of the Government of India. On the whole, it
would be correct to conclude that the role of HBS was
largely confined to academic and technical matters and
that in administrative matters, its advice and assistance
were rarely sought. Though the formal collaboration
contract ended after the first five years, informal
exchanges and programmes of assistance continued between
the two institutions.

9.2 Strategic decisions

Industrialisation was a major theme in India's
development strategy in the 1950s. The second five-year
plan, which was initiated in 1956, allocated substantial
resources for industrial development. This pattern was
continued in subsequent five-year plans and led to the
establishment of a large number of enterprises in both
the private and public sectors. A major consequence of
this strategic shift was the growing demand in India for

managerial personnel at different levels. The number of Indians trained abroad in management and who returned to take up jobs was small. Awareness that professional training in management was desirable was also growing, some exposure having been provided by the Administrative Staff College and the university departments of management. The All India Council of Technical Education had also noted the importance of training managerial personnel, and as an apex body had considerable influence on governmental thinking on the subject.

The Indian Government's decision to set up IIMA was thus made in extremely favourable circumstances: there was growing interest in management education at the highest levels in government; there was genuine demand for trained managerial manpower; and the awareness of the industrial sector in this respect was also a positive factor. It is not surprising therefore that when IIMA was established, no formal demand forecasts of managerial manpower nor any systematic project analysis preceded the decision. The strategic decisions relating to IIMA fall into four categories, concerning relatively: IIMA's mission and goals, key institutional tasks, leadership and faculty, and linkage building.

Mission and goals of IIMA

The objectives of IIMA were stated in rather broad terms at the time of its foundation in 1962. IIMA was set up as a non-profit-making society under the Societies Registration Act so that it could operate autonomously under the Ministry of Education. Objectives were stated in broad terms so as to leave the new institute free to adapt and expand as the environment changed. But the mission of IIMA which could be discerned from the initial statement was that its primary purpose was to "improve management practices" in India and to augment the supply of managerial manpower. The original decision in setting up the institute did not specify the precise means by which this purpose was to be achieved nor limit its scope to management practices in industry, whether private or public.

Guidelines for establishing the priorities and phases of the IIMA's institutional tasks were worked out through the process of operational goal-setting by the board of governors and the Ministry of Education. Three key tasks were identified at the outset: teaching, research and consulting. The content of each and the impact each was expected to have on management practices were left for discussion between the foreign collaborator and IIMA leaders. In terms of priorities, IIMA's operating goals emphasised (1) the development of young people for careers in management, (2) the training of practising managers, and (3) advisory or consultancy services to organisations to improve their management. Research in the wider sense of the term was given priority only after educational programmes had taken off. There was, however, general agreement that teaching, research and consultancy were complementary and mutually reinforcing tasks and that eventually IIMA should work out a reasonable mix of the three activities. Initially, however, operating goals were stated in terms of the numbers and quality of graduates to be trained, the number of practising managers to be trained and the number of cases to be developed to support these two activities. Goals for consulting and research were not stated clearly and on the whole these two activities took on a residual role.

Key institutional tasks and programmes

Teaching was the key task identified as the "entry point" to achieve IIMA's mission. The immediate question that arose at this juncture concerned the magnitude and mix of teaching programmes to be introduced. It was finally decided to start off with a two-year "post-graduate programme" in management (PGP) for young people with a bachelor's degree in any subject, and to complement it with a short-term programme for practising managers, which came to be known as "the three-tier programme". Although questions were raised about the dangers of early diversification, the rationale for offering the three-tier programme was that it could help the PGP by creating client contacts for placement, and opportunities for the development of teaching materials, both of which were directly relevant to the new programme.

In subsequent years, additional executive development programmes were offered by IIMA, both in the general management and in specialised or functional fields. Similarly, a fellow programme in management (FPM) was started to augment the supply of teachers in management by offering the title "fellow", which was regarded as equivalent to a doctoral degree. Project research was also initiated in later years, though in the early phase "case research" was the major area of attention. The only exception was the creation of a small group to carry on research into the problems of agricultural and co-operative enterprises. Clearly, the focus of IIMA in the initial years was on the post-graduate programme and the three-tier programme and the strategy was to limit the diversification of tasks for fear that scarce resources, especially staff, would be spread too thinly.

Leadership and faculty

As already mentioned, the first director of IIMA was Dr. Sarabhai, an outstanding scientist-manager who unfortunately was able to perform his duties only on a part-time basis because of other commitments. Being a charismatic and effective leader, he was able to provide a sound foundation for IIMA in spite of this. A change in leadership took place in 1965, when the first full-time director was appointed to head the institute. The part-time and short-term nature of the first director's involvement was a handicap to IIMA in its initial phase of development.

The selection of faculty members was an activity in which the director, the board of governors and the foreign collaborator were involved. Though advertisements were used to attract candidates, informal channels were also employed to identify suitable persons and encourage them to join the institute. IIMA's basic strategy in this respect was to select relatively young people with a good academic record or work experience and develop them through further training, using the collaborator's facilities. In the new field of management, which required experimentation and adaptation, it was felt that reliance on older persons who were already set in the traditions of their discipline might be less appropriate. A common experience and some degree of indoctrination were provided to the young faculty members by their HBS training. The first 20-25 went through the HBS programme. Subsequently, training programmes and sources were diversified and the role of HBS declined. Deliberate efforts were made from the outset to recruit staff from the diverse disciplines and functional areas relevant to management and to evolve a mix of expertise in terms of both academic competence and field experience and knowledge. Blending such diverse groups was by no means easy and IIMA did have its own share of interpersonal frictions and tensions as a result.

Principal linkages

IIMA's leaders and collaborators devoted considerable attention to the creation of linkages critical to the development of the new institutes. The first director of IIMA was active in forging strong links with the Indian Government, the State Government of Gujarat and industrial leaders, all of whom were important in terms of financial and political support for the institute. These three groups were represented on the board of governors, provided the leadership for mobilising the resources needed by IIMA, and facilitated its early development.

226

As a prerequisite for organising the different training programmes and case development, IIMA also developed functional links with a variety of organisations which had a great deal to offer to it. For field work (case development) and consultancy, close contacts were established with many industrial enterprises. To facilitate the placement of fresh graduates from IIMA, links were forged with senior managers in many enterprises. Contacts were established also with academic institutions abroad where potential Indian staff members could be located or trained. In this sense, HBS also played the role of a functionally associated institution for IIMA.

It would have been of value for the IIMA to maintain co-operative relations with Indian universities and other academic bodies which had a common interest in management development. Unfortunately, because of the initial hostility displayed by the major universities, IIMA was unable to build up these links. Over the years, however, the situation improved considerably as IIMA began to offer programmes for university teachers and share cases and other teaching materials with colleagues in other institutions. It did not collaborate with its sister institute in Calcutta and the Administrative Staff College, largely because of the sense of competition that prevailed among them. However, there was a common forum, the All India Board of Studies in Management, in which all these institutions were represented and which provided occasional opportunities to share common problems and explore areas for mutual collaboration. This was an official body set up by the Government of India; although it too was marked by hostility and mutual suspicion when India started establishing its national management institutes, the situation improved somewhat in later years.

9.3 Organisational design

IIMA started with a small faculty nucleus which enabled some measure of informality to prevail in the institutional environment. Apart from the director, there was no other functionary in IIMA who had formal powers. Even when co-ordinators and committees were appointed to plan and manage different programmes, collegiality rather than formal authority was the basis of decision-making and action. Occasionally problems arose because of a lack of clarification of the channels of communication and distribution of power. The situation was further complicated by the involvement of the foreign collaborator who had considerable prestige and influence, but no formal power in the institutional structure. The role of the faculty in the formulation of policies and academic decisions was left to evolve and this again caused some friction between the director and the faculty. The strategy of the director seems to have been to leave things deliberately vague and not to structure the organisation too rigidly right at the outset when the setting, people and programmes were all new and creative initiatives were most desirable.

By appointing chairmen for its different programmes, IIMA adopted an organisational structure that was built around its major task groups. The focus was on planning and operating programmes of training and research and not on the different disciplines which provided inputs to the programmes. Eventually, academic and functional groups called "areas" were also created in order to provide an intellectual or academic base to the faculty members coming from different disciplines. Every faculty member belonged to a programme as well as an area. IIMA thus moved towards a full-fledged matrix form of organisation with dual controls operated by programme chairmen and area chairmen, both of whom were supervised by the director.

Many of the academic norms which were evolved in IIMA came out of the joint deliberations of the faculty, the director and HBS consultants in the early years. In academic decision-making, the faculty's role progressively expanded over time and the director confined himself to setting broad directions, allocating resources, resolving conflicts and monitoring performance. Staff evaluation and promotion were initially decided by the director alone. This approach was subsequently modified to one involving a faculty committee which advised the director in these matters.

An innovative aspect of IIMA was the decentralised planning of academic programmes, which was encouraged almost from the beginning. Faculty members, irrespective of rank, participated in different committees and took turns in holding academic administrative positions. The wider sharing of these responsibilities and the experiences it provided seem to have contributed to a greater sense of commitment, maturity and vigour to the staff. The director has also encouraged the faculty to review activities periodically and to think about the future directions of the institute, an exercise which has forced them to look at their environment and potential choices critically and propose realistic goals and action plans for the years ahead.

9.4 An assessment

IIMA has been in existence only for about two decades. Its experience and problems are perhaps not sufficiently broad and diverse to let us draw definitive conclusions on **strategic management.** A few tentative insights may, however, be offered.

There are five factors that appear to have contributed importantly to IIMA's success:

(1) The quality of the faculty and leadership at IIMA is a significant factor to which those who planned the institute paid considerable attention. This tradition has been kept up in spite of growth.

(2) The degree of autonomy that IIMA enjoyed was deliberately sought and achieved. The decision to earn a substantial part of its revenues instead of relying only on governmental funding was a conscious choice which gave IIMA a good deal of independence and flexibility.

(3) The special and consistent efforts made to create links with client groups, sources of financial and political support and other institutions deserve to be noted. Without these links, IIMA could not have moved ahead even with strong academic resources.

(4) IIMA was fortunate to have a foreign collaborator of international standing who played supportive and adaptive roles in key areas in which the new institute needed special assistance. Staff development and case development through field work in India are prime examples of this contribution. The fact that collaboration could be phased out without creating a dependency syndrome again reflects the positive role played by the collaborator.

(5) Though not as evident as the foregoing factors, the participative management processes developed at IIMA have also contributed considerably to its performance and stability. These are difficult and delicate processes to operate, and yet are capable of creating a greater sense of commitment and enthusiasm among the key actors involved in the institute.

While these positive features are impressive, it is important to point out some of the weaknesses in IIMA's strategic planning:

(1) The frictions and tensions which developed between the IIMA leadership and the foreign collaborator show that better planning of the roles of each would have been of considerable assistance. Lack of clarity of roles and too narrow a definition of technical or academic assistance may have limited the full contribution that the collaborator might have made.

(2) The historical setting in which IIMA was born and
the determination to preserve autonomy seem to have led
to rather dysfunctional relations with universities.
The potential influence of IIMA was limited in the early
years simply because of the manner in which the universities were dealt with in the entire process.   Clearly,
this is a problem in linkage building which, with hindsight, appears to deserve greater attention.

(3) As an institution grows in size and complexity, the
nature of faculty participation and decentralised
decision-making needs to be reviewed carefully.   A special problem with the way in which the IIMA's staff
evolved has to do with the administrative load that many
of its members seem to carry.   Beyond a point, this can
be counterproductive and may also be at the expense of
their academic contribution.   While their active involvement in academic administrative matters was essential in the initial stages, the system can become cumbersome and self-defeating if a more efficient division of
labour is not worked out and scarce staff talent con-
served.

(4) The early growth of IIMA was made possible by its
sharp focus on certain key tasks and programmes.   There
is a real danger that as diversification is encouraged,
goal achievement gets blunted and control of performance
becomes more difficult.   Internal conflicts tend to
multiply as an institution moves into highly diverse
activities simultaneously.   Striking a balance in this
difficult area of choosing goals is precisely the task
of strategic planning.   If choices are not made more
carefully, this is a problem which could pose a potential
threat to IIMA's viability and its organisational
strength in the years to come.

CASE STUDY: THE INSTITUTO DE ESTUDIOS SUPERIORES DE ADMINISTRACION (IESA), CARACAS

10

Henry Gómez

10.1 A management institute approaching maturity

IESA, Venezuela's only privately-supported graduate study centre for management education, has established itself as a leading Latin American institution capable of contributing to the country's and the region's management development needs by means of its MBA programme, a wide range of post-experience management development programmes and research into various problems of national concern. In 1981 IESA can be viewed as an institution that has acquired considerable experience and that is approaching maturity.

This chapter reviews IESA's experience and examines a series of strategic issues that affect both the Institute's current posture and its long-term ability to make a marked contribution to management development in the Latin American region. While a great deal could be written about achievements, there is no doubt about it that the reader will draw more benefit from a frank discussion of problems that had to be faced by IESA's management, including problems that it has not been possible to resolve up to the present and that will face the Institute even in the future. To some extent the issues confronting IESA arise from the fact that it aims to achieve the standards of professional excellence attained by the best institutions in the industrialised world, without the benefit of the underlying societal conditions that have helped make such standards possible.

How IESA was conceived and planned

IESA was the first management school in Latin America and one of the first anywhere to design its original MBA

Henry Gómez wrote this chapter in collaboration with Moisés Naim.

programme curriculum to address both public and business administration.[1] An ambitious faculty development programme, initiated well in advance of the start of classes, was used to recruit talented candidates for doctoral studies in management or in related disciplines. At the time, no Venezuelan was known to hold a doctoral degree in management and, elsewhere in Latin America, the PhD was generally regarded as a costly and extravagant requisite for a management faculty. Nonetheless, only three years after the start of classes in 1968, which at first were led largely by a core of visiting professors recruited by an advisory committee including the deans of five renowned US business schools, a cadre of 12 Venezuelan doctoral graduates trained in the United States was on hand to work for IESA on a full-time basis.

Adequate financial support was raised under the leadership of Carlos Lander, IESA's founding board chairman, who also assumed the post of the Institute's president in 1977, after retiring as a director of Creole Petroleum, Exxon's Venezuelan subsidiary. The amounts raised were largely drawn from the international oil companies operating in Venezuela at the time, supplemented by contributions from local firms and a grant from the Ford Foundation. Funds from local sources helped build IESA's spacious and handsome physical facilities; the Ford Foundation's funds were used for planning purposes as well as to support the doctoral fellowship programme, the visiting lecturers and the advisory committee.

The charts reproduced in figure 17 show the growth of IESA's outputs in MBA studies, post-experience management development programmes and management research funded from external sources.

Relevance to Venezuelan needs

IESA's relevance to the country's needs may be illustrated in a number of ways. For example all of IESA's MBA graduates have obtained positions of responsibility in industry and government and several of those who graduated with the first class in 1970 already serve as top managers of nationally known firms. In post-experience executive education, IESA has for years proven to be the principal external centre used by the nation's petroleum industry, which is the largest industrial complex in the whole of Latin America and is regarded as

---

[1] For a review of IESA's early period of development, see H. Gómez and J.A. Bustillo: "IESA: shaping a viable strategy", in D.C. Korten (ed.): Population and social development management: a challenge for management schools (Caracas, IESA, 1979), pp. 82-92.

Figure 17   Trends in IESA's development 1968–1980

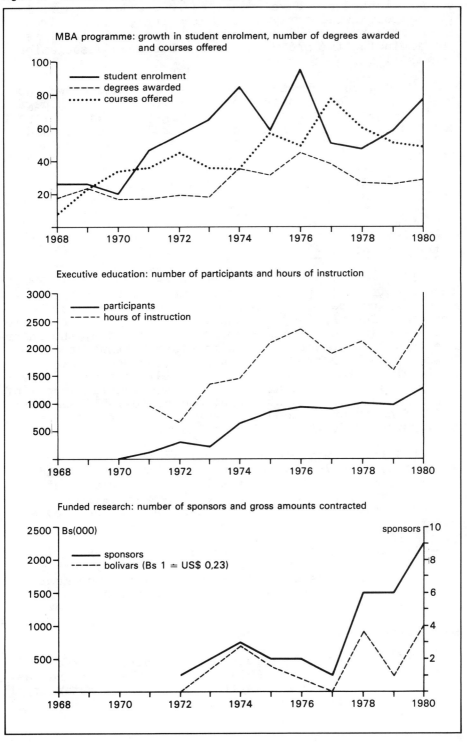

MBA programme: growth in student enrolment, number of degrees awarded and courses offered

—— student enrolment
----- degrees awarded
········ courses offered

Executive education: number of participants and hours of instruction

—— participants
----- hours of instruction

Funded research: number of sponsors and gross amounts contracted

Bs(000)
—— sponsors
----- bolivars (Bs 1 ≒ US$ 0,23)

sponsors

Venezuela's best managed sector. Open as well as in-company management development courses attract participants from a wide array of organisations, ranging from state enterprises and public agencies to private firms, and including the medium and small business association and the leading trade unions.

Funded and contract research at IESA has grown substantially. Most research projects focus on the management development needs of national agencies and on important social issues. Significantly, public agencies and other local organisations have in recent years replaced international donors as chief sources of support to research efforts. They have included the St. Lucia Group, an organisation representing a unique cross-section of leading personalities from Venezuelan business, politics, labour and the army, for which IESA has prepared several conceptual documents.

International dimension

IESA annually attracts about one-fourth of its MBA students from all parts of Latin America, screening hundreds of applicants from a score of countries, under a programme focusing on the management of regional economic integration. Fellowship support is provided by the Inter-American Development Bank and by other hemisphere agencies, as well as by the Venezuelan Government's Gran Mariscal de Ayacucho Programme. In 1978 a faculty exchange programme was initiated with the Wharton School of the University of Pennsylvania; and since 1981 IESA has had a faculty and student exchange agreement with the University of North Carolina at Chapel Hill.

IESA's executive education offerings have also reached outside Venezuela. Short courses on risk and insurance management, for example, regularly attract managers from Colombia and other countries in Latin America; in addition, IESA has organised a number of such courses outside Venezuela.

As regards internationally funded research, IESA has for years generated projects with support from the Ford Foundation and some other foreign agencies. The most recent grant, from the Rockefeller Foundation, was received in support of IESA's contribution to the work of the Management Institutes Working Group on Social Development already described in chapter 3.

IESA is an active member of the Consejo Latino-americano de Escuelas de Aministración (CLADEA); and has carried out the functions of the executive secretariat of this Council since 1981.

10.2 Factors influencing IESA's performance

Notwithstanding IESA's record of achievement, in certain respects its performance has fallen short of expectations. Even a superficial examination of the data presented in figure 17 reveals signs of what might be described as "under-performance".

At least four areas where deficiencies may be cited are clearly relevant to our discussion: student recruitment, alumni relations, faculty development and administrative support services. As in any other institution, the situation in each of these areas has been affected by two sets of factors: by the external environment in which IESA operates, and by IESA's ability to influence and manage its own development as an institution. These sets of factors are not static and should, therefore, be related to particular stages of IESA's development. At the risk of great oversimplification, we have opted for a simple two-stage approach, which nonetheless seems appropriate for our purpose: a first stage of evolution centering on the period between IESA's start of classes in 1968 up to 1981; and, from 1981 onwards, a second and distinct stage with clearly differentiable characteristics.

The first stage was chiefly marked by the pursuit of such objectives as institution building, survival and generating acceptance and recognition. Understandably, the burden of addressing such compelling objectives influenced a myriad of internal variables, ranging from organisational structure through resource allocation to IESA's curriculum. Having achieved success means that, as the first stage neared a close, these objectives lost some of their former top priority.

New objectives to be pursued as IESA enters its second stage of development will perhaps include, among others, more concentration on problems of national relevance (for example, in the form of closer participation in national debates on policy issues where the Institute may possess a comparative advantage), substantial growth in student enrolment, active recruitment of additional faculty members, a new type of relationships between the faculty and the Institute, and a more aggressive fundraising programme. The pursuit of such a set of objectives will undoubtedly penetrate a wide range of internal processes.

Student recruitment

Clearly, measuring IESA's performance only in terms of the number of MBA degrees awarded would be myopic. Nonetheless, the fact that the average number of graduates in a given year scarcely reaches 25 might be interpreted as evidence of under-performance. However, this figure has been influenced by the critical environmental factors including in particular:

- a limited potential market for graduate studies in Venezuela;

- a non-competitive labour market for managerial positions;

- a high opportunity cost of pursuing graduate studies in management;

- a cultural bias in favour of foreign graduate education, coupled with a government subsidy for graduate studies pursued abroad;

- declining academic quality of university graduates and

- the absence of local tradition for actively recruiting the best candidates for educational opportunities.

Perhaps the most important single constraint is the size, structure and other features of the market from which IESA draws its students. Venezuela's population is predominantly young, uneducated and poor. Even though as many as seven out of ten secondary school graduates enter college, the fact is that only one out of three children aged 7 to 13 finish primary school; and a scant one out of ten young people of secondary school age actually complete their studies. Among university graduates, a significant share is represented by women, many of whom are not career-oriented or, for other reasons, are unlikely to seek a graduate degree in management.

Additionally, Venezuelans tend to pay a high opportunity cost when pursuing graduate studies, given the considerable local demand for trained manpower. In Venezuela, high earnings often require only a university diploma and some natural talent. Moreover, for the talented Venezuelan college graduate, enrolling in an MBA programme may be perceived as extremely expensive in terms of the income and promotion opportunities foregone during the two-year period required to earn the degree. This, of course, does not mean that IESA's graduates are not sought after by Venezuelan organisations. But given the excess of demand over supply, there is room for everyone in the executive suite - with or without the MBA.

A third constraint stems from Venezuela's massive government scholarship programme, which funds literally thousands of students abroad. Why should a talented applicant for graduate study turn to IESA, when he or she could qualify for a generous scholarship to live and study abroad, and learn another language?

An environmental constraint which tends to be overlooked is the quality of the country's educational system. During the past 20 years, Venezuela has made impressive strides in broadening educational opportunities for its population. But mass education has not been achieved without eroding academic standards throughout the school system. The consequences of IESA's consistent attempts to maintain standards of academic excellence in such an environment are strong and clear. Probably the most concrete expression of this reality is the relatively low number of applicants, of whom only about 33% qualify for admission. IESA's standards are well known in Venezuela and undoubtedly deter many potential candidates from applying.

Turning to internal factors, no single unit or person within IESA has been explicitly charged with undertaking a systematic effort to recruit students. Although occasional visits are made to undergraduate institutions, featuring presentations to students in their final year of studies, student recruitment is largely undertaken by means of newspaper advertising. Underlying this approach is the assumption - no doubt partially valid - that the need for management education is so great in Venezuela, that potential applicants simply need to be reminded that the IESA admissions process is under way.

As IESA enters a new stage of development, more systematic efforts to increase enrolment in the MBA programme must necessarily be considered. Not doing so would mean that IESA would focus primarily on post-experience management development programmes and defeat the long-standing purpose of building a professional faculty meeting both high academic standards and the requirements of rapidly developing Venezuelan management practice.

Attention to alumni relations

As with student recruitment, IESA has focused little or no attention on cultivating alumni relations. Again, this may be attributed to both external and internal constraints.

Venezuela's higher education system differs from that of countries where school loyalties and attachments are significant and provide a sense of lifetime affiliation to a specific and particular community. Perhaps the fact that local universities make no effort to compete either in recruiting students or in placing their alumni in the labour market, also accounts for the relative unimportance the country's culture attaches to which Venezuelan university one graduates from. These universities are largely supported by public funds, thus providing little or no economic incentive to develop strong alumni relations.

Internal constraints include the comparatively small number of graduates from long MBA programmes (about 300) many of whom reside in other countries, beyond reach of alumni-centered activities. Then too, as a young organisation seeking community acceptance, IESA necessarily has had to look for financial support during its first stage of development from established enterprises and individuals.

As IESA enters a new stage of development, the same reasons which compel greater attention to student recruitment should impel the Institute to devote increased attention to alumni relations as a new and strategic priority. Not only is the number of alumni starting to become significant. More importantly, IESA's early graduates are attaining influential positions in business and government. Mobilising them may prove to be a resource of the utmost importance.

Faculty development

As noted above, at the turn of the 1960s IESA undertook an unusually ambitious faculty development programme. Early in the 1970s several additional faculty members were recruited, but candidates for doctoral studies and future faculty service were not aggressively recruited even when fellowship support funds from public sources became available. As a result, the size of the faculty has grown more slowly than the volume of IESA's programmes.

Some external forces make recruitment to IESA's faculty difficult. As in many other countries, the Institute cannot offer the same salaries as industry. In addition, in Venezuela a career with a professional management education and training institution tends to hold less appeal than in North America and Europe. In fact this may be due to the discipline-orientation as opposed to problem-orientation of many faculty members, a common disease already discussed in chapters 1 and 4. They tend to seek personal professional exchanges and involvement in research outside the country and even outside Latin America. Most of the original group of IESA's doctoral graduates pursued studies in conventional management fields, such as finance, marketing and organisation; but the balance, together with virtually all of the faculty recruited independently of the fellowship programme, were trained in disciplines such as economics, sociology,

political **science and operations research.** Some of them
have become local authorities in their own field of
specialisation and represent an asset to IESA, linking it
to the community. Others on the faculty, perhaps more
determined to pursue a career in accordance with IESA's
goals or imbued with a sense of mission, have tended to
shift from a discipline to a problem orientation.

Internal constraints on faculty development are
similarly complex. Once faculty salaries started lagging
behind the rate of Venezuelan inflation in the 1970s,
faculty members were indirectly encouraged to allocate a
rising share of their time to private consulting. This
could be interpreted as an adroit means of matching constraints with faculty needs. In several key instances,
however, consulting became an initial step in a gradual
process that eventually led to separation from IESA.[1]

In the coming years a new scheme for faculty compensation and service will become necessary. IESA cannot be
expected to compete on a one-to-one basis with industry,
but vigorous efforts should be made to narrow the extent
of the current remuneration gap and keep pace with inflation. Funded research will probably have to play a
greater role in assuring higher incomes to faculty members
as well as more attractive non-financial work incentives.
In turn, staff should be expected to carry a teaching,
research and administrative load that is commensurate
with their talent and rank. Lastly, the reasons why a
faculty member comes, stays or leaves IESA should be
examined. No doubt the answers to these questions will
relate to both internal and external factors, as well as
the complex interaction between them.

Administrative support services

IESA's administrative support services have tra-
ditionally proven deficient. Budget control, management
information systems in general and accounting and financial information in particular, as well as the recruitment, training, evaluation, compensation and promotion
of administrative personnel, have all been areas in which
the Institute's performance has been weak.

Good and sustained administrative support depends on
the availability of middle managers as much as on the
design of efficient administrative methods and procedures.
In Venezuela, educational and training establishments
have to compete with industry for competent middle management and administrative support personnel and the cost of
this personnel is relatively high when compared to hiring
an additional faculty member.

---

[1] See also section 1.3.

To address the administrative support needs of IESA's next stage of development, it could well become necessary to call on the faculty to help design appropriate control mechanisms and participate directly in training administrative personnel. Neither task will be easy, given the external demands already being made on the faculty for more productive - and lucrative - uses of their time.

The above assessment of IESA's shortcomings augurs well for the school's future. New policies and approaches for dealing with student recruitment, alumni relations, faculty development and administrative support services should stand to benefit from all that has been learned. Only a few years after IESA was launched, it had become evident that the challenge it faced was far more daunting than its founders had expected. As IESA enters a new stage of development, its leadership will hopefully be equipped with the know-how drawn from past experience.

10.3 Challenges faced by IESA's management

The problems discussed in the previous sections can be resolved, but will require considerable efforts on the part of IESA's management. However, at the time of writing, there are some further issues about which many faculty members and others who are close to the institution are seriously concerned. Aware of the fact that IESA has rendered useful services to its environment and to the whole region, they nevertheless worry whether the Institute can progress beyond its current capabilities to meet the challenges of the future. They view IESA as an essentially vulnerable institution, one that could be seriously harmed by a sudden loss of key faculty members, a change in the economic climate resulting in a reduced income from post-experience executive programmes, or a wrong policy decision that might tarnish IESA's reputation. Some of these concerns deserve to be examined in greater detail.

How much emphasis should be given to executive programmes?

The importance of post-experience management development programmes to a management institution operating in a developing country has been explained in chapter 1. At IESA, the extent to which faculty time should be allocated to executive programmes became an issue as soon as the first doctoral fellows completed their overseas training and began to earn an IESA salary in 1970. The faculty had no experience in executive programmes and preparing the first courses to be offered under the MBA programme was itself a formidable assignment. Nonetheless, a short course drawing on materials used in the MBA programme was presented to one of Venezuela's state-owned enterprises.

Not surprisingly, the course failed to satisfy the expectations of participants, whose interests centred on tools immediately applicable to their job assignments. As a result, in succeeding years the executive programmes offered by IESA depended largely on contracting packaged courses or individual faculty members from North American universities. Certain IESA staff members, rewarded with additional compensation and recognition for their contribution, gradually acquired the skills needed to organise and lead such courses and the number of locally designed courses increased progressively.

By the mid-1970s, executive education was far and away IESA's principal source of income. Meanwhile, Venezuela's rate of inflation, triggered largely by the increase in oil prices in the fall of 1973, rose from the level recorded in previous years. Hence the prevailing economic climate influenced both the school and many staff members, who were anxious to earn additional income, to increase the number of courses offered. In 1975, for example, two members of the faculty recorded an astonishing 400 hours each in executive programme offerings.

As IESA continued to rely heavily on short courses to finance operations in succeeding years, the executive programmes became a bitter source of contention within the faculty and between the faculty and the administration. Partly as a result of the emotions generated by this issue, certain staff members left IESA and others refused flatly to teach executive programmes. In 1979, teaching executive programmes became a "voluntary" faculty prerogative; but the strength of this prerogative has never truly been tested. Since executive programme offerings in 1981 were substantially greater than in 1979 and the number of full-time faculty had declined, outright refusal to teach in such programmes would almost certainly bring some pressure on the faculty member concerned.

The question of how much time a faculty member should properly devote to executive education has yet to be resolved. Given the high share of IESA operating income that such programmes contribute, however, it is unlikely that the emphasis on executive programmes will be reduced, at least for some time.

How to integrate faculty members' interests with those of the institution?

This issue has two aspects: how to keep the talented faculty member from allocating too much of his time to lucrative private consulting opportunities; and how to dissuade him from leaving the school altogether, in order to accept better rewarded positions in government or industry, or establish his own consulting firm.

It can be argued, of course, that competent management faculty, by definition, are prone to allocate a substantial share of their time to consulting activities and to direct personal involvement in the management of business firms. In developed countries, many universities and other institutions have gradually evolved a series of restrictive guidelines governing the extent to which a faculty member can attend to outside avtivities; but in a developing country, the fact that no local replacement for the talented faculty member is likely to be available may render such restrictions unenforceable.

At least one additional factor also influences the faculty member's disposition to blend his professional activities with those pursued by his school: how much or how little he has to say about the management of his own institution. Many of the developing country management institutes, including IESA, were purposely created outside the university system precisely in order to allow them to innovate freely and break away from the academic, administrative and political constraints under which the established universities generally operated. Accordingly, the civic and business leaders who became promoters and constituents of a new institute understandably expect to maintain some form of control over its programmes. At the outset the faculty may reluctantly concede that such leaders - who may not be familiar with the nuances of professional values - can properly exert such control, perhaps depending on whether the faculty considers its interests to be adequately represented. In time, however, a mature faculty which has earned its share of community recognition, can become a powerful balance to the economic and social groups to which the institution owes its existence. If the institution's management tried to restrict faculty influence over key decisions related to institutional strategy and policy, this can become a source of frustration that encourages the faculty to look elsewhere for professional satisfaction.

How to curb undue academic proliferation?

A choice of strategic importance concerning the number of specialisations in which a management school in a developing country decides to offer MBA or similar programmes and recruit students. External pressures to add fields of specialisation arouses expectations that economic pressure which stems from servicing an under-sized student body can be substantially relieved. This is clearly the case when a proposed specialty is to be fully funded by an external sponsor, as was IESA's educational administration programme. Additionally, by offering a specialised degree in, say, bank management, an institute can help assure its survival by making itself critically important to a particular economic sector. On the other hand, as decisions are made to add specialised courses, questions should be raised concerning the impact of such decision on future costs. For example, is a sufficient number of specialised faculty members locally available for staffing advanced courses in the proposed specialty? Since the market for any one specialty is likely to be small, does the new course really contribute to reduced costs?

At IESA, a powerful incentive to broaden the general management degree was the perceived need to legitimise the institute in the eyes of the public sector. Regardless of the benefits ultimately attained by avoiding affiliation to a university, the fact is that IESA operated for a number of years with no official accreditation. In addition, IESA's early development had been financed essentially from international and private enterprise sources. Hence in the eyes of certain critics in political, bureaucratic and academic circles, during this period, IESA represented "an instrument of foreign penetration", an enclave of alien interests seeking to introduce foreign teaching methods for training local managers and public administrators, thus promoting the country's dependence on the United States and other industrial powers. Fortunately, this view has virtually disappeared and IESA is now looked upon as a legitimate institution that responds to a felt national need.

IESA's first departure from general management into specialised offerings was an MBA programme in the management of regional economic integration in 1974. The following years witnessed courses in educational administration (1975-77); financial management (since 1976); risk and insurance management (started in 1980); and a proposed (but not yet approved) MBA in communications (mass media) management. IESA has undeniably benefited from each of these offerings. The regional integration programme, for example, has generated international prestige, as well as student fellowship support from the Venezuelan Government and international agencies; and, together with the educational administration course, it may have helped IESA earn the official accreditation obtained in 1975. The financial management and the insurance and risk management programmes have added credibility and valuable links to important sources of financial support. Negotiations concerned with the proposed communications management programme have helped IESA explore new ties with the nation's mass media and with the sponsoring agency, the Ministry of Information.

On the other hand, academic proliferation has entailed a series of costs which have become more visible over time: the need for scheduling a large number of specialised courses with undersized enrolments, reliance on part-time specialists for staffing advanced courses in certain fields; and understandable disappointment when developments beyond IESA's control, such as a budgetary cutback that led to discontinuing public support for the educational administration programme, forced the school to abandon a recently launched offering.

How to generate new management technology?

Hitherto, management institutes in developing countries, including IESA, have been predominantly transferring management technologies from industrialised countries. For some years, however, it has become clear that such management concepts, methods and techniques are not necessarily appropriate to the socio-economic and cultural set-up of developing countries and that management institutes in these countries have to undertake a broader and considerably more ambitious task than merely transferring management knowledge generated by the industrialised world.

In Venezuela and other developing countries, there are many unexplored issues in both private and public enterprise management, to which western experience and theory provides no ready-made solutions. For example there is the question how to adapt incentive systems used in industrialised countries to local cultural patterns in order to motivate people to increase productivity and reduce labour turnover. Other key issues concern the management of other sectors and other areas of social activity than the modern industrial sector, on which all management institutes tended to focus at a time when industrial growth was seen as the passkey to total economic and social development.[1]

At IESA substantial progress has been made in generating faculty interest in social development management. Studies concerned with the management of health, housing and other public programmes focusing on the needs of Venezuela's poor or "marginal" population hold the promise for making a significant contribution to local management technology. Other studies concerned with a variety of issues, such as industry regulation in a developing country setting, also suggest forthcoming outputs of national and international interest. Nonetheless, the

---

[1] See also L.D. Stifel, J.E. Black and J.S. Coleman (eds.): Education and training for public sector management in developing countries (New York, Rockefeller Foundation, 1977), and chapter 13 in D.C. Korten and F. Alfonso (eds.): Bureaucracy and the poor: Closing the gap (Singapore, McGraw-Hill, 1981).

proportion of faculty time currently being assigned to such studies is far below the needs of even a moderately ambitious research agenda. This too, therefore, represents a challenging issue that IESA's management must address.

How to attract appropriate leadership?

The critical importance of talented and committed leadership to a management institution established as a new element in a developing environment has been emphasised in chapter 1. IESA has been fortunate that Carlos Lander, its founder, chairman of the board and current president, has combined outstanding prominence in the community with a deep respect for professional values. Lander's leadership has enabled IESA to overcome serious financial threats to its survival, which in turn permitted founding president Santiago Vera and the academic deans drawn from the faculty to concentrate on programme design and faculty development. Significantly, at no time has IESA been forced to cover its operating deficit by undertaking certain activities merely to please one or another economic or political sector that has contributed to the Institute's survival and development.

On the other hand, Carlos Lander has for at least two years actively sought, to no avail, a successor with qualifications similar to his own. In a bold move to assure IESA's future development, he has proposed that the Institute's executive board, heretofore comprised of prominent business and civic leaders, be drawn exclusively from the faculty. Only such a board, Lander feels, will fully tap the faculty's energies and be competent enough to reckon with the challenging issues to which this chapter draws attention: such questions as how much executive education the Institute should properly offer; how to blend such activity with the faculty's responsibility for academic development and research; how to motivate the faculty to build their professional development round that of the Institute; how to satisfy Venezuela's management development needs without incurring costly academic proliferation; how to generate new management technology suited to the country's and region's needs; and how to attract outside support without mortgaging the Institute's future to the interests of a particular economic or political group.

At the time of writing, IESA's governing council is about to select the members of the new executive board and pass judgement on Lander's proposal to make the faculty responsible for the Institute's leadership. Only time will tell whether the proposal was approved and, if approved, whether the faculty's leadership was equal to the challenge at hand.

APPENDICES

Appendix 1
Guidelines for a strategic audit
of a management development institution

Introductory note

The outline given in this appendix provides an over-all view of the problem areas to be covered and indicates the sort of questions to be asked in analysing and defin-ing the strategy of a management development institution.[1] It is a generalised outline and should be used as a basis for preparing a more specific and detailed outline for a particular institution, with due regard to its environ-mental and institutional set-up.

The questions have intentionally been kept broad; they are headings indicating topics or problem areas to be examined rather than questions lending themselves to precise answers. In quite a few cases the questions over-lap or return from another angle to a topic reviewed in a previous section. This is impossible to avoid due to the complexity of management institutions, their pro-grammes and links, and the ways in which the various factors influence each other. There is no harm in some repetition provided unnecessary repetitions and redun-dancies are avoided.

An attempt has been made to word the questions as neutrally as possible, i.e. to avoid loaded or biased questions that would preclude certain answers or would force an institution that wants to be seen as effective into a particular answer. The diversity of situations in which management institutions operate makes it very difficult to say in advance what approach should be valued positively and what negatively.

---

[1] Some institutions prefer to use terms more common in their environment: diagnostic survey, survey, review, strategic diagnosis, self-appraisal and the like.

In principle, **every question requires** to be handled as follows:

(1) Collect and record facts (data) related to the question;

(2) Analyse and appraise the situation (examine facts and different views, compare with other situations, analyse trends, determine potential for improvement, define desirable measures);

(3) Draw up strategy and action proposals.

The order of questions could also be argued. It is extremely difficult to say in advance what the course of the exercise should be - even what the point of entry and the first question asked will be. For example the fact that constituents are not happy with the institution's performance may be a starting point and the first question to be discussed, the institution's basic philosophy, goal, etc., will then be brought up after reviewing its performance and image. If a new institution is being planned, some environmental analysis and considerations related to the client base and its needs will normally precede the definition of the institution's role and profile. Eventually, even though the starting points and the order in which questions are raised may be different, the audit will have to embrace all areas needed for a comprehensive diagnosis of the institution and its development prospects.

Some further suggestions can be made for the attention of the "auditors":

- prepare a work-plan, time-table and outline of the audit, but keep them flexible and do not hesitate to revise them if necessary;

- provide sufficient time, not only because the exercise is technically difficult, but also for psychological reasons; on the other hand, the audit should have a definite starting and completion date;

- define participation and responsibility for inputs, but keep the exercise open to new inputs and initiatives, in particular for involving those who at the beginning were reluctant to contribute;

- make every effort to develop a positive attitude to the audit in all departments of the institution; there should be no fear, apathy or hostility although various staff members may be involved and affected to a different degree;

250

- do not overdo analysis to the detriment of synthesis: the purpose of the exercise is not to present a nice report full of figures, but to shape the institution's future!

Audit outline

1. Our role and profile

1.1 What "business" are we in? What sort of institution are we?

1.2 What are our basic philosophy, values and beliefs concerning management and its improvement in society? What is our conception of the roles of management institutions?

1.3 What is our ultimate, principal purpose (mission)? When, on what basis and by whom was it defined? Has it ever been revised?

1.4 What basic strategic choices have we made? When and why?

1.5 What are our specific objectives? Are they coherent and do they provide clear orientation for our activities?

1.6 What is the portfolio of our main activities (client services)? How are they related to our mandate, philosophy, ultimate purpose and objectives? What are the relations between our main activity areas?

1.7 What is the degree of our autonomy and our legal status? Does our organisational location and legal status help us to meet our objectives?

1.8 What is our image? Do we know what it really is? Is it what we would like it to be? Are we understood and accepted by the environment?

2. Our environment

2.1 What constitutes our micro- and macroenvironment?

2.2 What environmental factors and trends are most determinant for our work and what do they require from us?

2.3 What are the specific characteristics, development trends and needs of our business and managerial environment?

2.4 How do we follow and analyse new trends, developments, needs and challenges and their implications for our strategy and policy? How do we screen the environment for programme innovation?

3. Our client base

3.1 What market do we serve and who are our clients (target groups)?

3.2 What sectors and sorts of organisations do we serve? What categories of managers do we serve?

3.3 On what basis and how do we identify potential clients?

3.4 How do we recruit and select participants?

3.5 What do we know about the background, needs and priorities of our clients? How do we identify what they need and want?

3.6 On what basis and how do we decide what intervention means and programme types are relevant to different clients?

3.7 What is our share and position in the national (local, international, etc.) market? Who else serves the same market?

4. Our links

4.1 What is our policy concerning links with the environment?

4.2 What relations do we have with our constituents and other principal stakeholders?

4.3 What links do we have with the government, the business community, the employers', workers' and other important social organisations and groups?

4.4 What links do we have with our alumni?

4.5 How are we integrated in the local community?

4.6 What are our links with university and other institutions in basic disciplines and with professional associations?

4.7 What are our links and how do we co-operate with other management institutions in our country and abroad?

4.8 Do we operate as part of an organised system embracing several institutions? What framework does the system provide for our operation? Are we helping to shape the system?

4.9 How do we use international technical co-operation (bilateral, multilateral)? What is our policy and experience?

4.10 Do we inform our environment effectively about our objectives and services? What are our public relations and promotional activities? What are our links with the mass-media?

4.11 Are we involved in links that make us highly vulnerable? Do we maintain unproductive links?

5. Our resources and capabilities

People

5.1 What is the size, structure and competence of our professional staff? How is the staff structure and competence related to our objectives, activity areas and intervention means?

5.2 Do we use external collaborators (part-time) staff effectively?

5.3 What is the size and competence of our support and administrative staff?

5.4 What is our recruitment policy and its implementation?

5.5 What is our career and staff development policy and its implementation?

5.6 How do we appraise individual and group performance and how are the results of staff appraisal used?

5.7 What motivates our staff?

5.8 What is our remuneration policy and how does it influence staff performance, recruitment, turnover and development?

5.9 Are we attractive as an institution in which to work?

Professional know-how

5.10 What types and levels of educational training and development programmes are we able to deliver? What is the quality and relevance of our programmes? Do we keep them in step with changing needs?

5.11 What is our library of training curricula and materials?

5.12 What is our ability to develop new types of training and development programmes? In what areas?

5.13 What is our case-writing ability and experience?

5.14 Are we up to date in training methodology and in using modern educational technology?

5.15 What is our organisation development and in-plant training capability?

5.16   What is our consulting and practical problem-
       solving capability and experience? What sort and
       complexity of assignments can we undertake?

5.17   Do we have clearly-structured consulting procedures,
       operating manuals and a library of assignment re-
       ports?

5.18   Can we deal with policy questions and major design
       or redesign of management systems at sectoral or
       national level?

5.19   What type of management research are we able to
       undertake? How strong are we in research methodol-
       ogy?

5.20   How are the results of our management research
       disseminated and used?

5.21   How are we able to co-ordinate and combine our
       educational, training, consulting, research and
       other activities in serving the client system and
       developing our own professional capabilities?

5.22   What is our publication record? What contribution
       to management practice and theory are we able to
       make through publications?

5.23   What are the objectives and organisation of our
       library, documentation and information services?
       What is our information base and what service can
       it provide to our staff and our clients? How are
       our services used?

Facilities and equipment

5.24   Are our facilities adequate in terms of space,
       location, functional design and standing?

5.25   Are our residential facilities (accommodation,
       catering) adequate to our programme types, client
       base and work facilities?

5.26   Do we have a programme for developing our facili-
       ties and for financing this development?

Finance

5.27   What is the portfolio of our financial resources?
       Is it clearly defined, balanced and stabilised?
       Are we able to control it?

5.28   What is our financial situation? Are we short of
       finance? Are we financially vulnerable? Do we
       have to run some activities for financial reasons
       only?

5.29   What is our pricing policy and its impact on our
       financial resources?

5.30 Do we get paid in time for our services?

6. Our management system

Organisational structure

6.1 What alternative of internal organisational structure have we chosen and why? Does it reflect our strategic priorities? How does it affect the utilisation of our resources?

6.2 How effective are our collective decision-making, advisory and co-ordinating bodies?

6.3 How effective are the key individual functions in our structure (director, faculty chairman, programme co-ordinators, department heads, etc.)?

6.4 Is the organisation of administrative and support services satisfactory? Do these services provide adequate support to professional services?

Management style

6.5 What are the main characteristics of the management, leadership and communication style applied in our institution?

6.6 How do we organise consultation and participation?

6.7 What impact has this style on the motivation and behaviour of professional staff?

6.8 What impact has our style on our performance and image?

Planning

6.9 Do we have a system of planning that can be defined as strategic? Is this system of our own design or does it follow national or sectoral guidelines?

6.10 What has been the real impact of strategic planning on our development and performance?

6.11 How effective is our operational programme and resource planning?

Performance monitoring and evaluation

6.12 How do we monitor and control our operations?

6.13 Who evaluates our performance?

6.14 What is considered as our output and achievement?

6.15 At what levels are our various outputs identified, measured and evaluated (e.g., participant, client or expert opinion; learning; behavioural change;

change in management practice; improved organisational performance)?

6.16 Are our outputs compared with inputs? What does such comparison show?

6.17 Is our performance compared with that of similar institutions (at home and abroad)? What can be deduced from such comparison?

6.18 What conclusions are drawn from performance control and evaluation? How are they used to improve strategic and operational management of our institution?

7. Summary

7.1 Which of our activities have been most (and least) successful? Why?

7.2 What are our main achievements?

7.3 What future challenges and opportunities are most important to us?

7.4 What are our critical strengths and weaknesses?

7.5 What principal conclusions for future strategy can be drawn from this audit?

Appendix 2
Basic data and ratios for
a management development institution

Introductory note

Both strategic management and current operational
control of a management institution use data that throws
light on the institution's resources, capabilities, activities and performance from several angles. These data
are the backbone of the institution's management information system. As there is a great variety of institutions,
it would not be advisable to establish one standard list
of such data to be recorded and used by every single
institution. To provide meaningful management information, data and ratios for planning, control and diagnostic purposes should be chosen with due regard to the profile, objectives and activity portfolio of the institution. The list of data and ratios given below should
help institutions in this effort, but would be of little
help if it were merely copied instead of being adapted
and further developed.

If an institution decides to reconsider the data it
has used hitherto, it is advisable to think in terms of
a co-ordinated and integrated system. In particular, it
is necessary to keep the various uses of the same data-
base in mind: for recording and evaluating performance,
reporting to the constituents, comparing with other institutions, defining strategy, programme planning, assessing
plan implementation, monitoring operations, etc. In addition, it should not be overlooked that an information
system has to provide data for decisions in various parts
and activity areas of the institution. However, while
different types of managerial decisions and activity
areas will, as a rule, require different data, the integrity and comprehensiveness of the system should be respected when determining what data are necessary for
various specific purposes. In particular, it is desirable to make sure that data can be aggregated, compared
and used by various sectors of the institution; double or

multiple recording of the same basic data, overlapping records and conflicting data are to be eliminated.

Careful consideration needs to be given to the number and degree of detail of data. The more numerous and detailed the data, the more time they will take to collect, record and analyse. But will they actually be used for managerial decisions? Global and aggregate data are totals of detailed data, but they often can be obtained and dealt with directly, without compiling separately more detailed data that are "nice to have" but will not be used for any decisions.

A clear definition of the meaning or content of this data is essential. For example, if an institution intends to collect separately data on its long and short programmes, the characteristics of these types of programme should be compared and each precisely defined.

Determining the periods of time is equally important. In most cases, annual data will be collected and institutions will choose between the academic, budgetary or calendar year. Data on a particular "product", e.g. a course, will be related to its duration (including preparatory work, etc.). Operational control will, as a rule, use quarterly, monthly or weekly data in addition to annual data, etc.

The number of periods for which data are collected should be sufficient for showing trends and major structural changes. Strategic planning and management will need data for 5, 10 or more years. However, if data recording and analysis becomes a routine management technique, information for several years will be readily available whenever required.

1.   Teaching and training

If the teaching and training activity embraces two or more different programme types (e.g. long programmes of undergraduate or graduate studies, post-experience training courses and tailor-made in-plant programmes for particular client organisations) data should be collected and analysed for each programme type separately. In addition, programme types should be compared with each other. If an institution wants to have a deeper insight into its operational efficiency, data for important individual programmes have to be examined. For example, this will help to identify programmes whose cost is out of proportion to their practical impact or to the income they generate. Comparing the numbers of applicants and participants by programmes shows which programmes are oversubscribed and which arouse little interest, etc.

Courses

- Number of courses run
  - Number of new courses introduced
- Course days taught[1]
  - Course days taught by external teachers
- Average days per course
- Ratio: Course days taught by external teachers/Total course days taught
- Participant days run
- Cost of one course day taught by internal staff[2]
- Cost of one course day taught by external teacher[2]
- Ratio: Cost of course day taught by external teacher/Same by internal staff
- Cost of running courses
- Income from courses
- Ratio: Cost of running courses/Income from courses
- Ratio: Outstanding course fees/Total billing for courses

Participants[3]

- Total number of participants
- Average participants per course
- Ratio: Applicants/Participants
- Ratio: Participants who complete/Participants who start course

---

[1] Some institutions prefer to calculate in course (programme) weeks.

[2] See chapter 6, section 6.3, for the method of calculating these figures.

[3] An alternative and often more accurate indicator of sectoral, etc., focus of training and other activities is the volume of services provided to a given client group.

By course type:

- In long courses (graduate study, etc.)
- In short (open) courses
- In in-plant tailor-made courses

By level in management:

- No management experience
- Lower and supervisory management
- Middle-management
- Senior and top management

By sector (in post-experience programmes):

- From private sector
- From public sector

By size of enterprise (organisation):

- From small enterprises
- From medium enterprises
- From larger organisations

By branch of activity, e.g.:

- Manufacturing and mining
- Transport and public utilities
- Construction
- Agriculture
- Commerce and distribution
- Finance and insurance
- Public administration
- Other (specify if important)

By age, nationality, level of education, ethnic origin, etc.

2. <u>Consulting</u>[1]

- Total number of assignments
  - Number of completed assignments
  - Number of new (started) assignments

- Consultant days delivered (total)
  - Chargeable consultant days
  - Other consultant days

- Average size of assignment in consultant days

- Total income from consulting (billing)

- Income per chargeable consulting day

- Cost of chargeable consulting day[2]

- <u>Ratio</u>: Cost/Income from consulting

- Maximum daily fee charged

- Minimum daily fee charged

- <u>Ratio</u>: Outstanding consulting fees/Total billing for consulting

Consultant days by client sectors:

- For public or private sector, etc.

New assignments agreed but not started (backlog):

- Number

- Volume in consultant days (total and chargeable)

3. <u>Research and publications</u>

- Number of research projects
  - Number of completed projects
  - Number of new (started) projects

---

[1] Some further controls used by management consultants can be found in Kubr M. (ed.): <u>Management consulting: A guide to the profession</u> (Geneva, International Labour Office, 1976), pp. 264-286.

[2] See chapter 6, section 6.3.

- Researcher days delivered
  - Researcher days internal (non chargeable)
  - Researcher days external (chargeable)

- Researcher days by sector, topic area, etc.

- Average size of research project in researcher days

- Books published (titles and number of pages, copies sold)

- Articles published (number)
  - Articles published in "best" journals

  Case studies and simulation exercises produced (number)

- Income from research and publications
  - Income from research grants
  - Income from contractual research
  - Income from publications

- Cost of one researcher day[1]

- Ratio: Cost/Income for chargeable research

New research projects agreed but not started (backlog):

- Number

- Volume in researcher days

4. Library and documentation

- Volumes in library (total number)
  - New acquisitions

- Loans (total)
  - Internal user loans
  - External user loans

- Periodicals (total number of subscriptions)

- Information requests handled (total)
  - Internal
  - External

---

[1] See chapter 6, section 6.3.

5. <u>Human resources</u>

- Number of employees
    - Number of professional staff
    - Number of administrative and support staff
    - Number of residence and catering staff

- <u>Ratio</u>: Number of professional staff/Number of
    employees

<u>Professional staff</u>

- Professional staff turnover

By technical profile, e.g.:

- General management and business economics

- Finance and accounting

- Production and technology

- Marketing, distribution, purchasing

- Personnel and behavioural science

- Operations research and management science

By activity area:

- Teaching and training

- Consulting

- Research

- Information and library

- Other

By grade:

- Professors (senior consultants, project leaders,etc.)

- Associate professors, lecturers, etc.

- Assistants, junior consultants, etc.

By teaching and consulting experience:

- Over 10 years

- 5-10 years

- less than 5 years

By education:

- University

- Masters degree

- Doctorate

- On fellowship for higher-degree studies

By practical management experience:

- Over 10 years

- 5-10 years

- 2-5 years

- Less than 2 years

By age:

- Over 50

- 40-50

- 30-40

- Less than 30

Remuneration of professional staff

- Average salary of senior staff member

- Ratio: Average salary of senior staff member/Average salary of comparable senior position in business or government

- Average salary of middle-level staff

- Average salary of junior staff

- Ratio: Additional income opportunity[1]/Average salary

- Remuneration of external teachers (daily or hourly rate)

---

[1] Income from private consulting, board membership, etc. done during authorised times.

Time utilisation of professional staff

The time-budget can be expressed in days or hours using the total annual number of working days as a starting point. If staff is fully specialised by activity areas (teaching, consulting, etc.) time budgets are to be calculated for each group of staff separately. Both total budgets and average budgets per one staff member should be calculated. If the institution uses standards of faculty workload as discussed in section 6.2, it can compare them to the actual workload.

- Total time budget[1]

- Direct - classroom (student contact) hours or days[2]

- Preparatory time for teaching

- Other teaching-related tasks

- Consulting

- Research

- Managerial and administrative duties

- Study and self-development

- Absence from work (all reasons)
  Specify:
  - Annual leave
  - Sick leave
  - Unauthorised absence
  - Authorised absence for private consulting
  - Other

- Total fee-earning (chargeable) time

- Ratio: Total fee-earning time/Total time budget

- Ratio: Preparatory time for teaching/Direct classroom teaching time

---

[1] Time budget (course days run, etc.) of external teachers should be calculated separately. The structuring of the time budget should be consistent with the standards of faculty workload.

[2] To be defined in accordance with the institution's teaching methods.

- Ratio: Students/Teachers[1]

6. Facilities

- Teaching space (m^2)

- Conference rooms over 50 seats (number)

- Classrooms (20-50 seats)

- Seminar rooms (10-20 seats)

- Ratio: Teaching space occupancy in %[2]

- Office space (m^2 and number of rooms)

- Office space per professional staff member

- Office space per administrative staff member

- Library and other space (m^2)

- Performance indicators and cost of computer installations

Residence:

- Number of beds

- Ratio: Room occupancy in %

Catering:

- Number of meals that can be served

- Ratio: Utilisation of catering capacity in %

7. Finance

- Annual budget (income)

- Financial resource portfolio (totals and % of annual income)
    - Government budgetary allocation
    - Private bodies budgetary allocation

---

[1] Recommended to establishments providing long-term full-time management education programmes.

[2] The institution has to determine what maximum possible occupancy is in its particular case.

- Membership and affiliation fees
- Donations
- Income from teaching and training
- Income from consulting
- Income from research and publications
- Other income (specify if important)

- Annual expenses

    - Cost of professional staff
    - Other expenses
    - Cost of administrative and support staff
    - Material and other general expenses[1]

- <u>Ratio</u>: Other expenses/Cost of professional staff[2]

- Annual surplus (profit) or shortage (loss) of finance.[3]

<u>Concluding remarks</u>

(1) The reader has probably noticed that the list of indicators given in this appendix focuses on the institution itself and on selected characteristics of its client base. It does not include data illustrating other environmental aspects and factors and the impact made by the institution in carrying out its various activities (e.g. changes in client organisations achieved as a result of particular consulting interventions). The range of such data can be very broad. As already mentioned in chapters 1 and 2, it is useful to try to define and collect such data and use them in planning and evaluation. However, it is necessary to be cautious in interpreting data whose relationship to the given institution's resources and activities is difficult to establish and which are subject to other influences. For example a reduced

---

[1] Further breakdown of these expenses is normally established by existing budgetary and accounting procedures.

[2] Various alternatives of this ratio are used for establishing the overhead rate.

[3] Cost and income figures for residence and catering facilities should be shown separately, if possible. Therefore, the amount charged for board and lodging in residential programmes has to be deducted from the course fees collected by the institution.

volume of work in progress, hence of working capital needed, can be traced to specific consulting and training interventions in production scheduling and stock control. However, global improvements of economic and social performance achieved by a client organisation or even by a whole sector will be the result of numerous forces, influences and actions taken by various organisations. It will be virtually impossible to quantify the contribution of a given institution even if this contribution is assumed to be very considerable.

(2) An institution can select key data from the groups described above and establish a summary table of management controls to be followed and analysed regularly by its management, e.g. in monthly or weekly meetings of the management committee.

To all chapters

Anthony R.A., Herzlinger R.E.: Management control in non-
    profit organisations (Homewood, Illinois, Irwin, 1980);
    600 pp.

L'Arroseur arrosé: Report of the committee of the EFMD on
    management of management centres (Brussels, European
    Foundation for Management Development, 1978); 59 pp.

College administration: A handbook (London, National
    Association of Teachers in Further and Higher Educa-
    tion); 890 pp.

Connors T.D. (ed.): The non-profit organisation handbook
    (New York, NY, McGraw-Hill, 1980); various paging.

Foy N.: The missing links: British management education
    in the eighties (Oxford, Oxford Centre for Manage-
    ment Studies, 1978); 183 pp.

Hyman S.: The management of associations (Beckenham, Kent,
    CBD Research, 1979); 160 pp.

Inayatullah (ed.): Management training for development:
    The Asian experience (Kuala Lumpur, Asian Centre for
    Development Administration, 1975); 300 pp.

Korten D.C., Alfonso F.B. (eds.): Bureaucracy and the
    poor: Closing the gap (Singapore, McGraw-Hill, 1981);
    258 pp.

Korten D.C. (ed.): Population and social development
    management: A challenge for management schools
    (Caracas, Instituto de Estudios Superiores de
    Administración, 1979); 179 pp.

Kubr M. (ed.): <u>Management consulting: A guide to the profession</u> (second (revised) edition), (Geneva, International Labour Office, 1986, 626 pp.

Kubr M., Vernon K. (eds.): <u>Management, administration and productivity: International directory of institutions and information sources</u> (second (revised) edition), (Geneva, International Labour Office, 1981), 305 pp.

<u>Organising schools and institutes of administration</u> (Washington, DC, Agency for International Development, 1969); 241 pp.

Ménissez Y.: <u>L'enseignement de la gestion en France</u> (Management education in France), (Paris, La Documentation Française, 1979); 216 pp.

Rausch E. (ed.): <u>Management in institutions of higher learning</u> (Lexington, Massachusetts, Lexington Books, 1981), 318 pp.

<u>Report of the committee of review into the Kenya Institute of Administration 1978-79</u> (Nairobi, Government Printer, 1979); 80 pp.

Simon H.A.: The business school: A problem in organisational design, in <u>Journal of Management Studies</u>, No. 4, 1967; 16 pp.

<u>Social and cultural factors in management development</u> (Geneva, International Labour Office, 1966), 178 pp.

Stifel L.D., Black J.E., Coleman J.S. (eds.): <u>Education and training for public sector management in developing countries</u> (New York, NY, Rockefeller Foundation, 1977), 147 pp.

Taylor B., Lippitt G. (eds.): <u>Management development and training handbook</u> (London, McGraw-Hill, 1975); 650 pp.

Wills G.: <u>Continuing studies for managers: Some illumination of educational innovation in a university business school</u> (Bradford, MCB Publications, 1981), 282 pp.

Zaltman G.: <u>Management principles for non-profit agencies</u> (New York, NY, AMACOM, 1979), 584 pp.

Zisswiller R.: <u>Gestion des établissements d'enseignement</u> (Managing educational establishments), (Paris, Sirey, 1979), 166 pp.

To chapter 1

Andrews K.R.: <u>The concept of corporate strategy</u> (Homewood, Illinois, Irwin, 1980); 180 pp.

Andrews K.R.: Toward professionalism in business management, in <u>Harvard Business Review</u>, Mar.-Apr. 1969; 12 pp.

Ansoff H.I: <u>Corporate strategy</u> (New York, NY, McGraw-Hill, 1965).

Benton L. (ed.): <u>Management for the future</u> (New York, NY, McGraw-Hill, 1978); 355 pp.

<u>Development strategies for the 1980s: Report of the Asian Productivity Congress 1980</u> (Tokyo, Asian Productivity Organisation, 1981); 184 pp.

Eaton J.W. (ed.): <u>Institution building and development: From concepts to application</u> (Beverly Hills, CA, Sage Publications, 1972); 271 pp.

<u>Education and training needs of European managers</u> (Brussels, European Foundation for Management Development, 1977); 25 pp.

Esman M.J.: Building institutions for management development, in <u>Interregional seminar on the use of modern management techniques in the public administration of developing countries</u> (Washington, 27 Oct.- 6 Nov.1970); <u>Vol. II: Technical papers</u> (New York, NY, United Nations, 1971); 12 pp.

Garratt B., Stopford J. (eds.): <u>Breaking down barriers: Practice and priorities for international management education</u> (Farnborough, Hampshire, Gower for the Association of Teachers of Management, 1980); 333 pp.

Hansen H.L.: Business schools and management education, in <u>Pakistan Management Review</u>, Second quarter 1980; 11 pp.

Hawrylyshyn B.: <u>Road maps to the future: Towards more effective societies</u> (Oxford, Pergamon Press, 1980); 193 pp.

Hill T.M., Haynes W.W., Baumgartel H., Paul S.: <u>Institution building in India: A study of international collaboration in management education</u> (Boston, Massachusetts, Harvard University, 1973); 381 pp.

Hofstede G.: Culture and organisations, in <u>International Studies of Management and Organisation</u>, Winter 1980-81, 27 pp.

Hogarth R.M.: Assessing management education: A summary
    of the CEDEP project (Bradford, MCB Publications,
    1978), 32 pp.

Industry 2000: New perspectives (Vienna, United Nations
    Industrial Development Organisation, 1979), 242 pp.

Kanawaty G.: Turning the management occupation into a
    profession, in International Labour Review, May-June
    1977, 13 pp.

Koontz H.: The management theory jungle revisited, in
    Academy of Management Review, No. 2, 1980, 13 pp.

Levitt T.: Marketing myopia, in Harvard Business Review,
    July-Aug. 1960, 12 pp.

Management and the world of tomorrow: The proceedings of
    the 18th CIOS World Management Congress (Farnborough,
    Hampshire, Gower, 1981), 437 pp.

Management education: A world view of experience and
    needs (report of a Committee of the International
    Academy of Management) (London, printed and
    distributed by the British Institute of Management,
    1981), 70 pp.

Management education in Europe: Towards a new deal
    (internal and external training) (Köln, Hanstein for
    the European Foundation for Management Development,
    1977), 134 pp.

Management education in the European Community (report
    prepared by the European Foundation for Management
    Development) (Brussels, Commission of the European
    Communities, 1978); 68 pp.

Managers for the XXI century: Their education and
    development (international conference, Paris, 15-18
    June 1980) (Brussels, European Foundation for
    Management Development, and Washington, American
    Assembly of Collegiate Schools of Business, 1981),
    116 pp.

Neck P., Nelson R. (eds.): Small enterprise development:
    Policies and programmes (Second (revised) edition),
    (Geneva, International Labour Office, 1987), 227 pp.

Newman W.H. (ed.): Managers for the year 2000 (Englewood
    Cliffs, New Jersey, Prentice-Hall, 1978); 133 pp.

Paul S.: Strategic management of development programmes
    (Geneva, International Labour Office, 1983), 137 pp.

272

Proctor R.: An educational philosophy for an in-house management education centre, in Management Education and Development, (UK), No. 11, 1980; 12 pp.

Professionalisation of management in developing countries (papers on strategies, processes and programmes of management education institutions in Africa and Asia) (Ahmedabad, Indian Institute of Management, 1978); 192 pp.

Revans R.W.: Action learning and the nature of knowledge, in Education and Training (UK), Nov.-Dec. 1977, 5 pp.

Revans R.W.: Action learning: New techniques for management (London, Blond and Briggs, 1980): 319 pp.

Siffin W.J.: Institution building: Feasibility and techniques (Bloomington, Indiana, Indiana University, technical paper, 1976): 25 pp.

Strategy for institutions (Boston, Massachusetts, Boston Consulting Group, 1970).

Toffler A.: The third wave (London, Pan Books-Collins, 1981); 544 pp.

Training systems and curriculum development for public enterprise management (recommendations for national policies and programmes by an expert group, Reduit, Mauritius, 23-28 Apr. 1979) (London, Commonwealth Secretariat, 1979); 203 pp.

Wills G.: Today's revolution in management education (Bradford, MCB Publications, 1978); 19 pp.

Zaki R.: Management training, consulting and research: Are they separate? (Arusha, East African Community Management Institute, technical paper 1976); 8 pp.

To chapter 2

Abramson R., Halset W.: Planning for improved enterprise performance: A guide for managers and consultants (Geneva, International Labour Office, 1979); 178 pp.

Higgins J.S.: Strategic and operational planning systems: Principles and practice (Englewood Cliffs, New Jersey, Prentice-Hall, 1980); 257 pp.

Highman A., de Limur Ch.: The Highman-de Limur Hypotheses (Chicago, Illinois, Nelson-Hall, 1980); 183 pp.

Hunzinger J.Q.: The malaise of strategic planning, in Management Review, March 1980; 6 pp.

Kreiken J.: **Formulating** and implementing a more systematic approach to strategic management, in Management
Review, July 1980; 7 pp.

National Institute of Business Management Corporate Plan
1980-1984 (Colombo, NIBM, 1979); 56 pp.

Proyecto ESADE 80's (Barcelona, Escuela Superior de
Administracion de Empresas, technical paper, 1979).

Steiner G.: Strategic planning: What every manager must
know (New York, NY, The Free Press-MacMillan, 1979).

To chapter 3

Eaton J.W. (ed.): Institution building and development:
From concepts to application (Beverly Hills, CA, Sage
Publications, 1972); 271 pp.

Education and training needs of European managers
(Brussels, European Foundation for Management Development, 1977); 25 pp.

Esman M.J.: Building institutions for management development, in Interregional seminar on the use of modern
management techniques in the public administration of
developing countries (Washington, 27 Oct.- 6 Nov.1970);
Vol. II: Technical papers (New York, NY, United
Nations, 1971); 12 pp.

Hogarth R.M.: Assessing management education: A summary
of the CEDEP project (Bradford, MCB Publications,
1978); 32 pp.

Kubr M.: Trends in co-ordination and planning of management education, in Management International Review,
No. 1, 1974; 15 pp.

Levitt T.: Marketing intangible products and product
intangibles, in Harvard Business Review, May-June
1981, 9 pp.

Mahon J.J.: The marketing of professional accounting
services (New York, NY, Wiley, 1978): 189 pp.

Opportunities and priorities for co-operation: Report of
the Global Meeting on Co-operation among Management
Development Institutions, Geneva, 9-12 Dec. 1980
(Geneva, International Labour Office, 1981); 37 pp.

Paul S.: Strategic management of development programmes
(Geneva, International Labour Office, in print).

Thorpe R.M.: The external environments of organisations, in Management Bibliographies and Reviews, Vol. I (Bradford, MCB Books, 1975); 12 pp.

Wills, G.: Today's revolution in management education (Bradford, MCB Publications, 1978); 19 pp.

To chapter 4

Career planning and development (Geneva, International Labour Office, 1976); 140 pp.

An introductory course in teaching and training methods for management development (Geneva, International Labour Office, 1972); 350 pp.

Report of the committee on the development of teachers and researchers in management (Brussels, European Foundation for Management Development, mimeographed, 1977); 32 pp.

Revans R.W.: Action learning and the nature of knowledge, in Education and Training (UK), Nov.-Dec. 1977; 5 pp.

Revans R.W.: Action learning: New techniques for management (London, Blond and Briggs, 1980); 319 pp.

Reynolds J.: Case method in management development: Guide to effective use (Geneva, International Labour Office, 1980); 264 pp.

To chapter 5

Bogard M.R.: The manager's style book (Englewood Cliffs, New Jersey, Prentice-Hall, 1979); 179 pp.

Davidson J.: Effective time management (New York, NY, Human Sciences Press, 1978); 98 pp.

Famularo J.J.: Organisation planning manual (New York, NY, AMACOM, 1979); 372 pp.

Galbraith J.: Designing complex organisations (Reading, Massachusetts, Addison-Wesley, 1973); 150 pp.

Greiner L.E., Schein V.E.: The paradox of managing a project-oriented matrix: Establishing coherence within chaos, in Sloan Management Review, Winter 1981; 6 pp.

Handy Ch.: The organsations of consent, in Piper D.W., Glatter R. (eds.): The changing university (Windsor, NFER Publishing Co, 1975).

Hofstede G.: Culture and organisations, in International Studies of Management and Organisation, Winter 1980-81; 27 pp.

Knight K. (ed.): Matrix management: A cross-functional approach to organisation (Westmead, Farnborough, Gower, 1977); 233 pp.

Maccoby M.: Leadership needs of the 1980s, in Human Futures (India), Winter 1980; 8 pp.

Margerison Ch., Lewis R.: Mapping managerial styles (Bradford, MCB Publications, 1981): 24 pp.

Mintzberg H.: The structuring of organisations: A synthesis of the research (Englewood Cliffs. New Jersey, Prentice-Hall, 1979); 512 pp.

Peters T.J.: Beyond the matrix organisation, in Business Horizons, Oct. 1979; 19 pp.

Skinner W., Sasser W.E.: Managers with impact: Versatile and inconsistent, in Harvard Business Review, Nov.- Dec. 1977; 9 pp.

Tannenbaum R., Schmidt W.H.: How to choose a leadership pattern, in Harvard Business Review, May-June 1973; 12 pp.

To chapter 6

Altman M.A., Weil R.I.: Managing your accounting and consulting practice (New York, NY, Matthew Bender, 1980); various paging.

Jones R.L., Trentin H.G.: Management controls for professional firms (New York, NY, American Management Association, 1968).

Knox F.M.: Managing paperwork: A key to productivity (Farnborough, Hampshire, Gower, 1980); 249 pp.

Powell R.M.: Accounting procedures for institutions (Notre Dame, Indiana, University of Notre Dame Press, 1978); 440 pp.

Powell R.M.: Budgetary control procedures for institutions (Notre Dame, Indiana, University of Notre Dame Press, 1980); 333 pp.

Powell R.M.: Management procedures for institutions (Notre Dame, Indiana, University of Notre Dame Press, 1979); 401 pp.

Pratt J., Travers T., Burgess T.: Costs and control in further education (Windsor, NFER Publishing Co.); 242 pp.

A recommended costing system for the CPC (Nicosia, Cyprus Productivity Centre, research report, 1980)